UNDERSTANDING SOCIETY

Through Spiritual-Scientific Knowledge

Social Threefolding, Christ, Lucifer and Ahriman

UNDERSTANDING SOCIETY

Through Spiritual-Scientific Knowledge

Social Threefolding, Christ, Lucifer and Ahriman

Fifteen lectures given in Dornach between 3 October and 15 November 1919

TRANSLATED BY MATTHEW BARTON

INTRODUCTION BY MATTHEW BARTON

RUDOLF STEINER

RUDOLF STEINER PRESS

CW 191

The publishers gratefully acknowledge the generous funding of this publication by the estate of Dr Eva Frommer MD (1927–2004) and the Anthroposophical Society in Great Britain

Rudolf Steiner Press
Hillside House, The Square
Forest Row, RH18 5ES

www.rudolfsteinerpress.com

Published by Rudolf Steiner Press 2017

Originally published in German under the title *Soziales Verständnis aus geisteswissenschaftlicher Erkenntnis* (volume 191 in the *Rudolf Steiner Gesamtausgabe* or Collected Works) by Rudolf Steiner Verlag, Dornach. Based on shorthand notes that were not reviewed or revised by the speaker. This authorized translation is based on the latest available (third) German edition (1989), edited by Robert Friedenthal

Published by permission of the Rudolf Steiner Nachlassverwaltung, Dornach

A catalogue record for this book is available from the British Library

ISBN 978 1 85584 542 8

Cover by Mary Giddens
Typeset by DP Photosetting, Neath, West Glamorgan
Printed and bound by 4edge Limited, UK

CONTENTS

of dead human bodies as necessary rejuvenation of the earth. Materialism as a path to freedom. Modern theology.

pages 30–45

Lecture 4

10 OCTOBER 1919

The forces of decline in our civilization: lack of a cosmogony; instead of freedom, fatalism or natural imperative; instead of altruistic feelings, egoism. Disposition of different peoples to partial truths: the Asiatic to a fraternal outlook, the European to freedom, the Westerner to cosmogony. Ideas sundered from reality. Conservative and liberal party positions in their connection with agriculture and industry.

pages 46–61

Lecture 5

11 OCTOBER 1919

Regional and national predispositions. The intellectualism of Europeans inhibits development of religious and economic impulses. The gulf between knowledge and faith. Lujo Brentano's superficiality of thinking. The economic stream from Europe towards America. Most recently, in Europe, faltering of the religious stream from the East and of the economic stream from the West. The streams can only be configured anew by means of threefolding.

pages 62–71

Lecture 6

12 OCTOBER 1919

Superficiality of the materialistic view of history, originating with the economic shift amongst the population at the time of the Reformation. In Egypto-Chaldean times, initiates ruled out of spiritual impulses, while priests ruled in the Graeco-Roman period. Since the Reformation, 'Homo economicus' has become dominant. Changes to the human configuration of soul: a real connection with worlds of spirit until the eighth century BC, awareness of the divine origin of human intelligence until the fifteenth century. Since then, belief in the dependency of intelligence on the body. Spiritualization of the intellect. James I of England as successor to the old priest kings, Cromwell as representative of modern economic man. Rapid

turn makes us briefly fall asleep. This back and forth reverberation is the archetypal element of social interplay between people. The old forms of affinity based on blood and race must be overcome. Three stages since the Reformation: the dominance of economic man, of the banker and of capital. But now social understanding must arise, creating understanding of karma in a following incarnation—that is, understanding for each person's individual destiny.

Lecture 10

23 OCTOBER 1919

Life incomprehensible without enlarging our awareness to encompass pre-birth life and life after death. To secure power, the Church has withheld from human beings an insight into pre-birth life. All individual qualities are the echo of pre-birth existence; the social realm is where the germ for life after death is engendered. If you deny pre-existence you also deny individual gifts. The education arising from this leads to standardization. Social democracy issued from Catholicism. We must overcome our entanglement in languages. From ancient Egyptian hieroglyphics to modern stenography. The building at Dornach as a world hieroglyph.

Lecture 11

1 NOVEMBER 1919

The third post-Atlantean epoch and the present era. Ancient pagan culture was one of wisdom. At that time the human being felt himself to be a part of the cosmos, and did not need intrinsically moral impulses. The initiates read from the stars what human beings should do. This pagan wisdom was inspired by the wisdom of Lucifer, who incarnated in the third pre-Christian millennium. This was followed by the Christ incarnation at the dawn of a new age. Well before the end of the third millennium after Christ, an incarnation of Ahriman will occur in the West. Ahriman is already preparing this incarnation: he is doing so by promoting the view that the cosmos should be regarded as a machine, the sense that economic security is sufficient for public life, the principle of nationalism, partisan perspectives, and one-sided understanding of the Gospels. The collaboration of Lucifer with Ahriman.

Lecture 12

2 NOVEMBER 1919

The life of spirit must be separated not only from the life of rights but also from economic life. Ahriman is interested in conflating the life of spirit and culture with the state and economic life. Romain Rolland. Humanity must advance from words to a perception of spirit. Space and time convey only the outer aspect of things. Science as ahrimanic mirage. Within us, Lucifer acquires special power if a person only mystically deepens what he was endowed with by birth. We must try to establish equilibrium between luciferic and ahrimanic power: the ahrimanic must be permeated by the luciferic, the luciferic within us by the ahrimanic element. The longing of Cardinal Newman for a 'new revelation'.

Lecture 13

9 NOVEMBER 1919

The human being as a being of will and intellect. Will forces and natural forces. Immorality led to the Atlantean catastrophe. The will has a disintegrative capacity and is connected with our planet's destructive forces. The workings of black magic are based on this. The forces that build up the world lie in the pole of the human being's intelligence acting in sleep life. Humanity has responsibility for what the earth undergoes in cosmic ages. With world consciousness human responsibility expands to world responsibility. True art is a reflection of supersensible truth. Goethe's *Faust*. The rise of landscape painting as a symptom of the materialistic outlook. Modern civilization regards everything outwardly apparent as reality. The human being is not a reality without the earth, nor the earth without the human being.

Lecture 14

14 NOVEMBER 1919

Primordial wisdom diversified and specified, and faded away. Without a new influx people across the globe would become entirely differentiated in terms of their specific regions: in the West only economics, in the East, spiritual truths, while central Europe would cultivate the intellectual realm. The East would become an object of economic exploitation by the West. The three aspects of earthly cultural life: the Orient as home of ethics, the West of the utilitarian principle, and at the

INTRODUCTION

In the poem by William Butler Yeats, 'The Second Coming', composed in 1919 shortly after the First World War and the Russian Revolution, the poet laments the 'blood-dimmed tide' of war and famously writes:

> Turning and turning in the widening gyre
> The falcon cannot hear the falconer;
> Things fall apart; the centre cannot hold . . .

This and other things in the poem chime remarkably with some aspects of the lectures in this volume, also given in 1919. The old forms of authority and hierarchy were ending at the time in social upheaval and convulsion, and the measures and models proposed to remedy chaos were, as Steiner keeps reiterating here, attempts to impose human constructs on a living reality and thus not only in vain but a violation of that reality. This imposition, as Steiner makes clear, always follows from the individual human *mind*, from thoughts and concepts, programmes and tracts, which, however idealistic, do not arise from the ever-changing immediacy of a truly social context: one in which actual people relate to each other, intuiting from this interaction what each necessary next step together might be.

In general, says Steiner in lecture 14, prefiguring the words of Eliot in *The Four Quartets*, people cannot bear very much reality. Taking refuge in the intellect, they wrap themselves in a comfortable cocoon of ideas about how things should be shaped. Science, founded on the remedies of peer review and the correction of hypothesis through actual observation, is less prone to the intellectual or mechanistic malaise; but what Steiner laments particularly is the uncorrected application of the scientific method to all other realms of life, including social thinking and education. An education that prioritizes the child's understanding over the development of all other capacities, embracing the scientific paradigm as unquestioned, universal standard, will, he thinks, inevitably become shallow and superficial. Education for life, if it is to have real meaning, creates warmth, love and enthusiasm in the child's soul, out of which deeper understanding can later be born.

That Steiner emphasizes education in these lectures on society suggests he was concerned about the effect of a primarily intellectual upbringing on later generations and their ability to act morally and creatively within society. At the other pole from the intellect, which is past-related in Steiner's view of the human being, lies the will, a faculty that carries us into the future, is born in warmth, and is by definition much less easily accessible to our conscious perceptions. It is through the will that we relate in moral intuition to others in society, that we actually 'engage with life', changing and shaping it for the future. Thus social interaction between two or more people, as the core and essence of all society, involves an unconscious element: in a continual alternation, we only perceive others by momentarily 'dreaming into and falling asleep' in them, then waking up to ourselves again. To be alive to the reality of this process is to allow others' reality to inform us, is to honour the gifts that each one brings and to incorporate them into a living weft of mutuality, an awareness of reciprocal dependence that enlarges us, as opposed to the construct of an 'agenda' or 'programme' for social reform pursued or imposed (inevitably in a top-down manner) without this awareness.

'The best lack all conviction', writes Yeats, 'while the worst / are full of passionate intensity'. In lecture 6 Steiner likewise stresses how our political leaders, with all their rhetoric, have the least insight, while deeper natures find it most difficult to get anywhere with or in society as it currently is. But it is also worth remembering that there are grassroots and civil society movements today who know that real hope and change is created in community together, very often outside the power-mongering of the political machine.

Between Yeats in 1919 and Eliot in 1935, the artist René Magritte painted his famous image of a pipe, with the subversive caption below it: 'This is not a pipe'. The sensory or intellectual image is not the full reality, and recognizing this can jolt us awake for a moment to the provisional nature of all appearance and to the comfortable fixity of our perceptions and mental definitions. So where, in this flux, do we find a way forward? Inevitably Steiner takes us back repeatedly here to the human being's actual nature, seeking to read from this the social forms that most fully accord with it; not offering these as a model to be imposed but as ongoing, evolving perception of the realities we inhabit. He returns here to human faculties, related respectively to the past, future and present in the broadest sense: of the free individual spirit and its gifts, intellectual and otherwise; of our will and moral actions, through which we create future social realities together; and of the bridging realm between them, our scope for true feeling and perception in the moment. While the distinct 'spheres' of society founded on these three aspects of reality—those of cultural and spiritual life, freedom of thought and *liberty*, of economic *fraternity*, and of political rights and *equality* before the law—might seem like just another programme, it is central to Steiner's appraisal that these are not abstract ideas but contain the seeds of true development which, like any reality, might assume very varied and diverse forms in actual and always different conditions.

All this requires an enormous amount of inner activity and awareness on our part. Alert to the dangers awaiting us at every turn, Steiner warns us against nationalism, utilitarianism and any other 'ism'. Like Dickens before him in his humorous and ironic depiction of the bureaucratic 'Circumlocution Office', he pours gentle scorn on the exponentially increasing 'data' (lecture 11) in which we can have such misguided faith, in the numerical or quantitative mass of proofs and evidence that clog our shallower minds. He warns, somewhat prophetically, against our failure to think or create for ourselves because of all that is 'given' to us on a plate, without any need for us to process it ourselves (think devices).

In his poem, Yeats writes of the 'rough beast ... slouching

towards Bethlehem to be born'. The spirit of cold divisiveness and isolationism, of unsympathetic feeling and enmity, of action either immobilized or excessively violent, is clearly incarnating amongst us. But Steiner offers us remedies, and in an insight of real genius, instead of dogmatically castigating the coldness of science or the self-referential voluptuousness of our subjective feelings, he proposes a beautiful reversal: to regard ourselves and our subjectivities with scientific objectivity, and to observe the outer world and its phenomena with all the subjective warmth of our keenest interest. For me, this has all the persuasive depth, simplicity and difficulty of a true way forward.

Matthew Barton

Lecture 1

DORNACH, 3 OCTOBER 1919

MANY very diverse points of view have recently been expressed, here in Switzerland too, about the relationship that exists between the anthroposophically oriented spiritual science we have been cultivating in our circles for years—and has led to the construction of this very building, the Goetheanum—and on the other hand our efforts, ultimately, to engage with contemporary social movements, our striving to realize something in society and the world. Our need to complement anthroposophic endeavours with these social endeavours has met with the most varied responses, both dismissive and welcoming. Such reactions cannot of course be the determining factor in the way we pursue our aims, and yet we do also need to look at various realities that have emerged in this context.

Anthroposophists often say that our movement ought not to have burdened itself with what is implicit in the movement for a threefold social organism. And on the other hand, some of those whose interest has been awoken for this social movement find it troubling that this idea began with an anthroposophic outlook which they may often feel to be obscurely mystical and lacking in clarity. Thus social threefolders are often criticized by anthroposophists, and anthroposophists by social threefolders. The area of commonality between them is sometimes a bone of contention for both sides.

As I say, this cannot lead us astray; but it is important to be fully aware of this state of affairs and keep remembering the inner connection between both outlooks, which we have often had cause to highlight in our reflections here.

But there is another thing that has increasingly become apparent—something which may have still greater bearing on our task. You see, ultimately, if sociologists censure any commonality with anthroposophists, there's nothing we can do about it, just as little as when anthroposophists assert it would have been better not to saddle ourselves with ideas about society. There's nothing much to be done about that either, except pursue our path unerringly since we have recognized it to be right. But more urgent for our consideration, perhaps, is that there are more and more people saying that an anthroposophic foundation is needed for them to understand the idea of threefolding. The threefold social organism would be much better understood, they say, from an anthroposophic perspective. And this anthroposophic foundation is increasingly being called for precisely in proletarian circles. This is something that may surprise people, although it isn't really all that surprising.

The way our friends pursued anthroposophic endeavours in the past—also determined by differences of class—made it difficult to introduce anthroposophy into proletarian circles. But now it is unavoidable that anyone who engages with threefolding also hears something about anthroposophy, becomes at least outwardly acquainted with it. And in fact it is very remarkable that this is creating a lively need for anthroposophy.

In Stuttgart, for instance, after disseminating the idea of social threefolding for a period, without referring to anthroposophy as such, we found it necessary to give lecture series on purely anthroposophic subjects. There were well-founded reasons why this became necessary; and these series are continuing still.

We should take particular note of this here, and today, by way of introduction, it is really only this that I want to impress on you. Here in Switzerland, we are in a very particular position as regards both these orientations—the social impulse and the impulse, which for us at least is connected with it, of anthroposophy. The question of social endeavours born out of anthroposophic thinking is actually very different for central Europe from the way it appears to us here in Switzerland. In central Europe it is a matter of life or death, the life or death of national culture and tradition. There may be many today who do not realize the gravity of the situation—but the life or death of national culture is at stake. When they hear something like this, people think far too superficially. If you say 'the death of national culture' they think it completely exaggerated—you can't kill off 80 million people in a short time, they say, so how can we be facing the demise of national culture?

But this is to entirely misunderstand what is at stake. Naturally 80 or 90 million people are not going to be killed off all of a sudden. But the death of culture means something quite different. We need only recall that when Jerusalem was destroyed it wasn't just a matter of the death of individual Jews living there, but of the death of a culture—which can happen in a quite different way from how it did there. It really is true to say that this is a life or death question, and that life will only prevail if we begin to create a threefold social order. If this were not so one could easily regard social threefolding in some other light. But here we are truly facing an either/or situation in the near future: either developing understanding of threefolding or the death of culture. People may hear this and think it immodest or even absurd. And yet it is so. There are good reasons why circumstances compel us to resort to threefolding. We may have more time or less, but there are compelling reasons—in eastern Europe, likewise, this region that has been indescribably downtrodden by its karma.

Things are different here. Here there still is, and potentially will be, a chance to resort to something like threefolding out of free will. Here, you see, as in the West, it is not a matter of life or death so much as the continuation of events in either a more spiritual or an unspiritual manner. In Switzerland and in the West we can pursue life materialistically for long periods, without any spiritual impulse. Or alternatively, out of our own free will, we can come to see in an eminently spiritual movement such as threefolding something essential for providing a new impulse. We do not need to think in terms of life or death.

Well, it makes a great difference whether we undertake something out of free will or by compulsion, in an unfree way. In fact, it would signify something entirely different for the world's whole evolution if people in a place like Switzerland were to form the free resolve to embrace the threefolding movement. It is extremely difficult nowadays, even for me, to formulate and express these things objectively. I believe that it would be a great blessing if someone in the West, especially someone in a neutral country, were to find the courage to say this in unadorned fashion. It would signify something quite different in the public domain. In particular the following should be considered: whatever came from the few countries that have remained neutral would have the greatest significance, also in an inner sense. If the threefolding impulse could proceed from a country that has stayed neutral in the recent conflicts, this would be a deed of very great significance in world history.

To comprehend this is already an anthroposophic matter. You see, we can only say what integration of such an impulse into all human evolution would mean if we draw on anthroposophy. And it does matter if this impulse is simply formulated in abstract form or emerges from particular realities: whether it proceeds from the fact of free discernment or emerges from necessities, as it can only do in central Europe since at present nothing can arise there except through bitterest calamity.

So specifically here in Switzerland, it seems to me, we should view the idea of the social organism and its threefolding with enthusiasm. But then a question becomes pressing: how do we surmount a particular dilemma? Some among you here have been participating in our anthroposophic movement for rather a long time, and have been able to observe how quickly or slowly—and it is usually slowly—the intentions of this anthroposophic movement penetrate human souls. This takes its time. And if it were necessary for people to become anthroposophists first in order to think in the right way about society, it might well be far, far too late. For this reason we must think of putting the idea of threefolding as such out into the world even if it then appears to have less sure foundations—because we can't afford to wait until anthroposophically oriented thinking has become a matter of course. But then this threefolding idea will need a certain kind of support. Since it won't get this from a real spread of anthroposophy—which takes its time—it must be supported by the presence and engagement of members of the anthroposophic movement; in other words, members of the anthroposophic movement should try to elicit trust through their social conduct and activities.

This is at least a question that cannot be resolved theoretically but only practically, through life itself, since it is a question of our manner and demeanour. We must try to represent social thinking in a way that elicits trust from others, even if is not possible to create an anthroposophic foundation quickly enough.

You will ask how this can be done—how can you develop the right tact as you work to promote the social movement? Again, this cannot be answered categorically. But there is something that will help if given enough consideration. Every individual here amongst us should try increasingly to familiarize himself with the nature of the social movement in a real and living way. That this was lacking was evident in our circles when attempts were first made to launch a kind of social movement. Amongst the most well-meaning of our members, amongst the most benevolent adherents of our anthroposophically oriented spiritual-scientific movement, were really quite a few who had slept through the modern social movement that arose in the second half of the nineteenth century and through into our own times. I don't mean they were all unaware that a social movement existed. But it's not enough to know this theoretically, or to read about such things in the papers. Instead one needs to really be familiar with the utterances and aspirations of this movement. Not that long ago I met people in our midst who, as the threefolding movement began, did not know that unions existed, or what they are. We have become too used to passing people by and not concerning ourselves with what they are actually doing, their actual lives. We must learn to really concern ourselves with human souls, to show real interest in them. And here there is a great hindrance which, without wishing to offend anyone, I would term 'middle-class benevolence' towards the working class. This middle-class benevolence towards the workers, often as it were dripping with social impulses, is actually a serious obstacle to modern social effectiveness. We have seen what I mean here in the most varied spheres. Think of how 'the people' have been portrayed to us, in historical novels, popular novels, by authors who understood nothing about ordinary folk—Berthold Auerbach[1] and suchlike. We have been shown the nature of ordinary people in a kind of theoretical engagement with them. The middle classes consider themselves to be engaging with the social question when they watch, say, Gerhart Hauptmann's *The Weavers*.[2] Well, certainly this play does portray the misery of the masses—it shows them surviving by eating a dead dog. But it is an odd way to understand the nature of society if we watch a poor family eating a dog onstage and then return home to our usual, pleasant supper. I'm not saying we can bridge the class divisions in society by tomorrow morning, but we can at least get a real sense for what's happening instead of just passing people by and not knowing the circumstances they live in. It is very important that every individual today should be able to summon before his mind's eye a broad, world-historical panorama—one that only becomes apparent if we look back to former times that have left certain social residues still existing today, and look as well at new things that are erupting through the surface of life as though from primordial depths into modern society.

One question that repeatedly surfaces when people are talking about modern society is the question of organization. Our ways of life have become complex. Division of labour has increasingly come to the fore, so that an individual works within a narrow sphere of activity. We can only work and act as modern people through and within organizations. Organizations have always existed. But no account is taken of the fact that organizations in the old days were quite different from those that now must arise. Nowadays almost all our organizations perpetuate the old as well as already encompassing new elements, and are in continual upheaval. But so far an awareness is lacking that must allow something radically new to erupt from the depths of humanity's evolution to its surface.

Older forms of organization were really governed by human blood, by blood relations. Looking back to olden times we see tribal and extended familial groupings, things belonging together and organized by the blood principle rising from human depths. This meant that organization was something largely unconscious, not surfacing fully into awareness. People were *involved* in organizing themselves but this didn't become fully conscious. Higher spirits aided human beings in this organizing activity.

Today we face the need to accomplish consciously ourselves what once occurred unconsciously, that is, largely by virtue of higher powers than the human. We must work together in associations, in organizations to sustain society. The blood ties between people are gradually losing their meaning.

The observed and recognized aim and concern, the objective, must provide the basis for this associative activity. Unconscious or subconscious confederacy must give way to conscious and intentional association. At present we live in the midst of an interplay of these two streams, conscious and unconscious organization, and the convulsions in society today are very much connected with the confluence of these two currents. Just consider for a moment the efforts of socialist parties of all shades today. In them lives a certain impetus towards conscious organization, albeit as yet instinctive. People want to organize themselves. But on the other hand they have not yet found the objective that provides a foundation for this conscious organizing activity.

If you want to understand this, just look at the primal phenomenon of modern social striving. Let's assume someone stood up here—let's be clear and honest about this—and said, 'We must endeavour to work socially!' What would he mean by this? He would mean that this effort should be undertaken here in Switzerland. If you were to suggest that he should think differently, he would of course take offence. Or imagine someone standing up in France and saying the same thing—he would be speaking of social endeavours within French borders. It has also been stated, theoretically, that socialist programmes should use the old national borders as a framework for great socialist cooperatives or collectives. But the state is a residue from the old groupings based on blood relationship. In other words, socialist programmes today seek only to impose something new, put something different on top of the same old blood affinities.

It is asking a lot for people today to think clearly about such matters. People simply won't be able to do this without becoming anthroposophists. However strange this may sound, it is true to say that people won't be able to think clearly about these things. A call is sounding across the globe today: freedom for the people. In other words, the old blood relationships originating in long-gone times should somehow be reorganized. Freedom for the people! But this trumpet call resounding through the world completely overlooks the nature of conscious organization. This is how greatly things clash in our time. In fact, only truly universal, anthroposophic insight into human nature will lead us where we need to go.

But there's a long way to go to achieve this. Anthroposophic and particularly theosophic insights, as they were, have always been stumped by this question. Yes indeed, people said that we need brotherly understanding of human beings without distinction of race, colour and so forth. But has this become a reality in our era? No, it has become theoretical, abstract, not real. And at present it is least real of all.

And in consequence these anthroposophic and theosophic endeavours have been drawn into a general love for the abstract which we have so often discussed here—a general love of abstraction that lives in thinking and feeling capacities that sunder themselves from life. As modern people today we live a life we ought not to live, a double life: on the one hand life in outer work, our profession and various other things resembling or relating to it; and then a life of thinking and feeling. A workaday life and a Sunday life, if you like. When someone speaks of the spirit we don't really care to hear this intervening in our Monday-to-Saturday existence. Talk of the spirit, we think, belongs in the Sunday sermon, which we can enjoy in its separate and distinct place, when we don't have to remember the business of the week. Then, and only then, we can feel a certain pleasure when we hear about fraternity, neighbourly love and so on. This double life extends into science. And here we must see the historical causes of it clearly.

You see, our mundane academic disciplines no longer allow themselves to speak of the soul, let alone the spirit. It is thought perfectly self-evident that they should not. Academics today tell us that science must be free of belief, and in saying this they think that they serve unprejudiced science. They say that anything connected with soul or spirit will constrain and hamper scientific enquiry, since such matters are decided only by subjective faith—or that is what they believe. But what is this due to in reality? In fact, in our era, religious faiths and confessions have as it were monopolized the soul and spirit for themselves. And nowadays the view that anthroposophy should not be cultivated is regarded as quite self-evident, that science must be free of such taints and should have nothing to say about soul or spirit since that is a domain monopolized by the confessions. Academics proclaim that science must be 'objective' and therefore refrain from engaging with matters of the soul or spirit, since this will violate rules of scientific exactitude. It is very humorous really. Forgive me for speaking of humour in such a serious concern, but there is such a thing as serious humour. Sometimes the tragicomic is more important for the world's development than the purely tragic or merely comic. It is humorous to hear academics discourse in this way since it is actually due to the fact that they were forbidden for long periods to speak of spirit and soul. Those who today believe they should keep science untainted by faith for the sake of its exactitude are unaware this 'purity' results from a dogma that prohibited them from thinking about soul and spirit. What academics proclaim as the dictates of exact science is the deposit and residue of the old ecclesiastical ban. People are simply unaware of this, of the historical antecedents to what they announce and proclaim as a self-evident and—sometimes in their view—lofty truth. But we should wake up to this, not sleep through it, and without doing so we won't get anywhere. However fine our declarations about the social question, we will get nowhere if we give ourselves up to illusions about the greatest lie that exists—the scientific lie of the modern era. As yet we do not have a real feeling of this lie in science, but we must learn to feel it.

What I have just said is not intended emotionally but entirely theoretically, and can only be properly understood in its theoretical intentions. You see, I only feel obliged to speak of the 'scientific lie' because, as much as I unreservedly criticize modern science from this point of view, at the same time I defend it equally staunchly. Science became great by virtue of the very fact that people only focused on the physical, corporeal realm for a period, and no longer concerned themselves much with soul and spirit. But we should only regard this as a principle of utility, and as a pedagogical principle in humanity's evolution, and not as something of fundamental, intrinsic value.

Today it should be realized that the mundane sciences need once again to be imbued with real knowledge of the soul and spirit. This alone will give rise to vigorous engagement with social problems. In our time, it is necessary for people to start to perceive and discern things differently from the way recognized in our schools. There are matters of knowledge and discernment that are now becoming incumbent upon us in a way that, for a long period, they were not. The Copernican world-view[3] was entirely sufficient for a long time—it was useful for people to conceive of the cosmos in these neat terms: here the sun, around which the earth orbits in an ellipse; and around the earth the moon orbits in turn; and then between sun and earth we have Mercury, Venus, and Mars further off and so on. It was very neat to have this whole picture of the movements of the planets in ellipses round the sun. Humanity found this perfectly sufficient until now.

But what were the historical origins of this picture? I have often referred to this. Historically it arose when the great Copernicus wrote his book about the revolution of the planets, at the beginning of which we find three key principles. If all three are considered, that's fine. But they were not all given due weight: only the two first

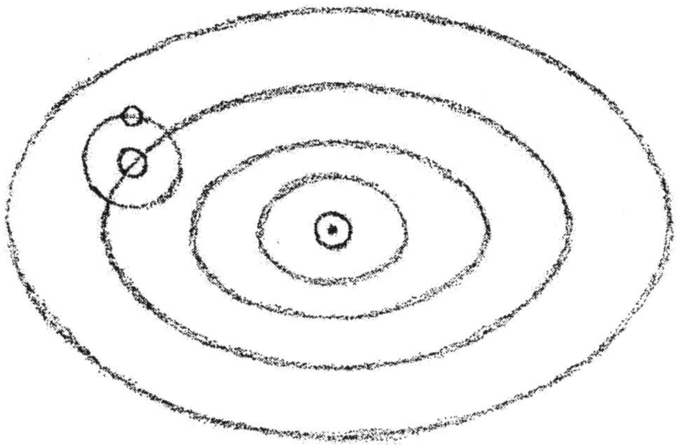

*Board drawing 1**

principles were taken up, while the third was overlooked. The first two give us the Copernican system as later elaborated by Kepler and Newton. But unfortunately this system is not correct. If, in the calculation of this system, a particular planet is supposed to occupy a particular position and you direct your telescope to where it ought to be, you find it is not there! The system says it should be, but it isn't. This is why people have been using 'Bessel's Reduction' or 'Bessel's Correction'[4] for a long time now, to correct the calculation. You direct the telescope not to the point you should according to the Copernican system but to the point established after you have corrected the calculation. What are these Bessel's Corrections exactly, what do they mean? They signify the need to always apply anew something one would apply only once and for all if proper account were taken of all three Copernican laws instead of ignoring the third. But if we do include this third law of Copernicus, then in turn the whole picture, with the planets revolving round the sun, no longer works so neatly at all, and we have to conceive a different cosmic system. In fact, people will not conceive this different picture of the cosmos until they have been properly prepared to think differently by anthroposophically oriented spiritual science. You see, how do people look at the world nowadays? They look at it as if they were sitting in

* See page 222 in relation to the board drawings.

a railway carriage but never looking out of the window or alighting from the train: just sitting inside and living with the other passengers. In fact you can travel for a while, then, when the train stops, get out and visit a town or city to see what is there, then perhaps board another train and travel further to another town, and do the same again. These are stages of experiences and you carry them with you.

But modern astronomers see the passage of the earth through the cosmos as if they were sitting in a railway carriage, never alighting, and experiencing nothing but the other passengers. You might ask how one can stop the world and get off? Is this possible? Well you can, actually, though it is different from getting out of a train. To alight from a train you depart through the carriage door and head off in some direction. To alight from the earth means to go inwards, into the soul. If you really penetrate into the soul you come to what lives within the soul and you have alighted from the earth. In relation to the earth you have undertaken the same procedure as alighting from a train and boarding it again. But the remarkable thing here is that, when alighting in this way—that is, going deeply within in contemplation, not in an illusory but a real, tangible way—you experience something different each time you do so; something really different each time. Mystical professions of finding God in the soul through inner contemplation are declamatory statements. Really experiencing something inwardly, it turns out, is different in different eras, an ever-renewed and different experience. Why so? Because we experience the cosmos when we do this, always a different place in the cosmos.

The ancients discovered their system of the heavens through such inward experience rather than through purely outward observation. The Copernican system, on the other hand, arose by a mode of experience that resembles sitting in a train carriage. The system of the cosmos in future will have to become inner experience once more, a journey through inward experiences, and this will give rise to a different picture. Above all we will learn to experience the world in a tangible way, rather than through the abstract cognition so prevalent today.

Something curious, and actually very pleasing happened to me in Berlin recently. Not long ago a squalid piece appeared in the German journal *Die Hilfe*,[5] entitled 'False Prophet'. Such articles are read and forgotten. But a few weeks back, when I was in Berlin, an American visited me and told me he had come to see me because he had read this article and reckoned that such a diatribe must mean there was something interesting afoot. This only by way of introduction to what actually pleased me, which was a question the man posed, a very apt question. He said he had quickly understood what was involved in threefolding of the social organism but he wanted to ask this: Do you think that this threefolding of the social organism is an eternal truth which, once discovered, will create social conditions that hold sway for ever more, or is it a truth that applies to a particular time, which will eventually give way to something else? I was very struck that one could still find people today who show such insight, who do not believe in millenarianism,[6] in some thousand-year Reich, in some absolute, single and never-to-be-questioned truth that applies uniformly, ubiquitously and for all time. Socialist thinkers believe that the socialist state must be realized tomorrow, and once it has been established it will never have to change.

I replied to him as follows. Naturally people have striven for a unified state in recent centuries; but now we have got to the point where we need to structure this state in a threefold way. After a further period something else will come, a synthesis; and in turn the opposite will inevitably appear.

You see, it is not always so comfortable to have to engage with actual specifics and real conditions—it is not as easy as working out an absolute system. But it is necessary to deal with specific conditions today, to be aware that what we must create is something that accords with the current situation in the world. This can already be understood today in terms of 'astronomy'—by seeing, for instance, that mystical experiences vary depending on whether they occur in one or another decade or century, and that we can observe the *actual* movements of the earth, experience them mystically within us. But today the 'great astronomical principle' must be seen and felt in relationship to society, to social realities. We need to develop the capacity to progress by going beyond a stage that bears only an outward parallel to stages of former times in that they too were not only transitional stages but impulses for evolution.

Think of the ancient Greeks. They inhabited a particular region extending as far as the Pillars of Heracles. Within those confines the earth was specific and tangible for them. Beyond that was only vagueness and generality. The Greeks had a regional consciousness. Then the modern era arrived, the discovery of America, the voyages to the East Indies and suchlike. Earthly consciousness arose. The regional consciousness of the Greeks became our modern global awareness. Just as everything further than the Pillars of Heracles was vague and undiscerned for the Greeks, so today everything that goes beyond earthly consciousness is indeterminate for us—merely mathematical fantasy, Galileian or Newtonian fantasy. Such fantasy must be replaced by realities. We have to transform earth consciousness into cosmic consciousness in the same way that the regional or national consciousness of the Greeks was transformed into global consciousness of the whole earth. That is where we are today, at this point, and we will make no social progress unless we find the way to elaborate the cosmic consciousness of the future from the earthly consciousness of today.

Unless we develop, through the teachings of anthroposophically oriented spiritual science, the great astronomical world picture of what lies beyond us in the cosmos, we will not comprehend the truth of the cosmos. And if we do not do so, we cannot become citizens of the cosmos. But we will not become social citizens, either, until we become conscious citizens of the cosmos.

Lecture 2

DORNACH, 4 OCTOBER 1919

In this second of three lectures, I want to elaborate a few anthroposophic truths in particular. We will then see how these anthroposophic truths strongly affect daily human life—we'll speak of that tomorrow. Today I'd like to point to some deeper aspects of human nature.

It is not commonly asked which powers in the human being make it possible to gain knowledge of supersensible worlds. People try to answer the question merely by saying that we can perceive the supersensible realm through certain powers within us, but often do not go on to enquire into the particular relationship between these faculties and human nature. But this means that very little attention is given to making perceptions of the supersensible worlds really fruitful for ordinary life. In our era, this knowledge, these perceptions, however, will become ever more necessary. But then they must be comprehended in their relationship to ordinary, everyday life.

As you know, the first capacity that leads us upwards into supersensible reality is the power of Imagination, the second that of Inspiration, and the third the power of Intuition. Now the question is this: are these faculties ones that only concern us in relation to knowledge of supersensible worlds, or do they play some other role in ordinary life as well? The latter is the case. We see human life—as you can discover in the little book *The Education of the Child in the Light of Spiritual Science*[7]—in terms of three stages: that between birth and the change of teeth, then from second dentition to puberty, and from puberty to roughly the age of 21. A view of human nature that is not merely superficial will see that our whole development in the first seven years is different in quality from the second seven-year period, and different again in the third seven-year period of adolescence. The emergence of our permanent teeth, as I have often said, is connected with the development of forces not only affecting, say, the jaws or neighbouring organs; these forces driving the emergence of the second teeth have their seat in our whole physical being. Between birth and the age of 6 or so, something occurs in this physical being that is concluded, culminates if you like, when the permanent teeth are driven forth from human nature.

These forces actively working upon our physical nature are—I'd like to say self-evidently—supersensible in nature. The sense realm is simply the material within which they work. These supersensible forces working in our whole organization in the first seven years are, you might say, laid off when their goal has been achieved, once the permanent teeth have appeared. After the age of 6 or 7, the forces go to sleep. They are hidden in human nature, they sleep there; and they can be drawn forth from it if one does the kind of exercises leading to the faculty of Intuition that I described in *Knowledge of the Higher Worlds.* The powers used in Intuition, in intuitive perception, are the same as those active until the age of 6 or 7 in the growth that finds its expression at second dentition. These slumbering forces, which until the seventh year work within human nature, are used in supersensible perception to develop Intuition.

The forces active until puberty, from the age of 7 to 14, before they too go to sleep and come to rest in the depths of human nature, are likewise raised upward to create the power of Inspiration. And the forces which once gave human beings their youthful ideals between the ages of 14 and 21—it would be claiming too much to say they still do so—and created organs for these youthful ideals in the physical body are the same powers that can be drawn forth from their sleeping condition and give rise to the faculty of Imagination.

You can see from this that the powers of Imagination, of Inspiration and of Intuition are not arbitrary powers whose origin is unknown but are the very same powers through which we grow from birth to the age of 21. Thus the powers living in Imagination, Inspiration and Intuition are very healthy ones—the same as we needed for healthy growth and which then, once each phase of growth has ended, fall asleep in the depths of our nature.

These, then, are the connections between supersensible powers of cognition and ordinary human nature. But we can say the same of ordinary human faculties that we employ in daily life, though they are less apparent there. One very important faculty in ordinary life, as we have frequently discussed, is the power of memory, which we use inwardly whenever we recall something we once experienced. But as you all know, this memory faculty has a curious quality: we both do and yet do not entirely control it. Many struggle to remember something but can't. This desire to remember accompanied by a failure to fully remember is due to the fact that the same power we use inwardly as faculty of memory also serves to transform the food we digest into substances that our body can use. If you eat a piece of bread and this bread is converted inside you into a substance that serves your life processes this appears to be a physical occurrence. Yet this physical process is governed by supersensible powers—and these are the same that you use when you remember things. The same kind of forces are used for memory on the one hand and for assimilation of nutrients on the other. And really you always have to swing back and forth a little between your soul and your body when you try to employ the faculty of memory. If your body is digesting all too well, you see, you may not be able to reclaim enough forces from it to clearly remember something. When you try to remember something, you always have to wage an inner battle—which occurs in the unconscious—between a soul process and a bodily one. If you consider the faculty of memory in these terms, this is the best way to recognize the foolishness, from a higher vantage point, of seeing some people as idealists and others as materialists. Digestion and assimilation of nutrients in the human body is without doubt a material process. The forces governing it are the same, though, as are active in a process of ideation: the powers at work in our memory faculty. We only have a true view of the world when we see it neither materialistically nor idealistically but instead are able to recognize the ideal nature of material phenomena, and equally to trace the entirely material processes underlying ideal ones. The spirituality of a world-view is not a matter of relegating 'lower materialism' to the 'dregs' of humanity and according idealism to the elect—amongst whom, of course, the person propounding this will count himself one—but to ensure that a spiritual outlook on the world is able to bring what it encompasses in the spirit down into material existence, grasping this material existence also, thus comprehending and not denigrating it. This is the great error of many religious persuasions: they despise material existence instead of comprehending it and seeking the spirit within it.

And so what we have to do is engage with things, not, as so common today, dwell in mystic phrases: really engage with things. Having shown an example of how we can do so, I want to turn to something of very great importance. People usually see material existence unfolding in the mundane world while supersensible existence, invisible to the senses, spreads either above or behind it. But seeing this physical and sense existence as separate from the supersensible realm will never enable us to understand the human being. The duality of sensory and supersensory makes it impossible to comprehend human nature. Instead the following is true. Around us spreads the sense world and the world in which we work, in which our social interactions also occur. We can represent this sense world schematically with this line here [see drawing, horizontal line]. You only gain a full picture of what actually happens in the world if you imagine that there are, above this line, supersensible forces [red arrows] which cannot be perceived by our ordinary senses, nor with the powers of reason bound up with them. We only perceive what lies in the region of this line.

But there are also forces at work *below* this line. We only fully comprehend the non-sensory, spiritual realm if we speak of super-

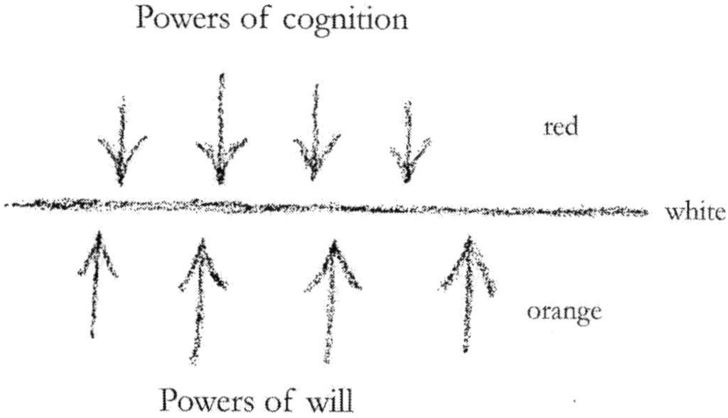

Board drawing 2

sensible and subsensible forces. We need to picture the subsensible forces down here (orange arrows).

Thus we have the sense world, the supersensible forces and the subsensible forces. Where does the human being himself belong, as he stands before you in bodily form? The bodily reality standing before you belongs entirely within this line; and into this human nature enter supersensible forces on the one hand and subsensible ones on the other. The human being is the result, the outcome, of the combination of supersensible and subsensible forces. So now, which forces in human nature are supersensible and which are subsensible? The supersensible ones are all those connected with cognition; everything we employ for cognition is supersensible. And these same powers also form our head.

What are the subsensible forces that also play into us, what kind of forces are these? They are will forces. All will forces in us, everything of the nature of human will, is subsensible.

This begs the question of where these subsensible forces, these will forces, come from. They are the same forces as those of the planet: for us here, therefore, of the earth. Into us the forces of the earth do indeed continually enter. And the forces of will, those of a will-type nature, are connected with these forces of the planet, these earth forces. Powers of a cognitive nature and quality come from the peripheral realm outside the earth and pour down upon us from there. Forces of a will nature and quality penetrate us from the planet: these forces of the earth live in us. At the moment we enter upon earth existence at birth the forces of the earth become active within us.

Then we must ask how the action of these forces is distributed within us. Here again there is a considerable difference between the first phase of life, the second, and the third. What works as will nature in us until the age of 6 or 7 works entirely out of the interior of the planet. It is very interesting to study through spiritual science how the forces of the earth's deepest interior are active in the child up to his seventh year. If you wish to discover how the forces of the earth's interior manifest, you should study everything that occurs in a child up to this age, for there you will find forces of the earth's interior at work. It is very misguided to delve into the earth itself in a search for the forces at work in its interior—all you will find are the earth's substances instead. The forces active within the earth are revealed, rather, in what they accomplish in a human being up to his seventh year. And then between 7 and 14, the forces of the atmosphere also become active in the child, this atmosphere surrounding and belonging to the earth. They are the primary element acting in everything the child develops between the ages of 7 and 14. Then comes the most important phase between 14 and 21, when, you can say, the subsensible passes over into the supersensible. A kind of balance is established then between the sub- and supersensible. The forces of the whole solar system, the solar system belonging to the earth, now exert an organizing effect upon the young person.

Thus in the first phase of life the earth's interior; in the second the atmosphere, in which the earth itself is mantled; and up to the age of 21 the forces streaming down from the cosmos in so far as this encompasses our own planetary system. Only from the age of 21 do we tear ourselves free, in a sense, from the influences of what has been brought about in us by the earth and the planetary system belonging to it.

Everything I have now described as acting upon the developing human being certainly also includes the influence on corporeal life.

The forces acting from the interior of the planet up to the child's seventh year give rise to corporeal processes. And corporeal processes are created by the interplay of the atmosphere, the atmospheric cycle, with a person's respiration between the ages of 7 and 14, and so on. These are certainly bodily processes, transformations of the bodily organs, connected with the child's growth and development. Thus we grow up from, and out of, what the earth configures in us, and this comes to an end at the age of 21.

But what happens then, after the age of 21? Until this age we have been nourished by the earth and its planetary system. We have fed upon what the earth has organized into us. But now, from the age of 21, we must draw from ourselves what we need to live. We must slowly draw up again the forces of the earth and the planetary system that we previously led downwards into our organism.

To ensure this always happened in the past, the forces of human blood were active. The human being was able to draw forth the earth's forces from himself without having learned to do so. He did this as an unconscious process; it lay within his blood. He had been configured and organized in a way that enabled him to do so. In our own time—though this of course encompasses a long period of centuries—a significant change is that human blood is losing the power to draw forth what has been configured into the organism in this way up to the age of 21.

The important thing happening in this present era is that the blood's forces are waning. These things cannot be confirmed by outward anatomy, outward physiology. But if you examined human bodies in the tenth and ninth centuries you would find that their blood was different in nature. The chemical reagents to prove this would not even exist. But through spiritual science we can know with certainty that human blood has grown weaker; and that this great change, this weakening, began in the mid-fifteenth century.

What does this mean? It means that since we are no longer able to bring about something unconsciously through our blood we must now consciously undertake it. We must educate ourselves to accomplish something consciously which used once to occur unconsciously simply by virtue of human blood. The power of the blood has faded and is increasingly fading. And if no remedy were found, what would happen in an era when people lost the benefit of their youth, and were no longer able to fruitfully draw on their youthful powers because what the blood once unconsciously accomplished could not be consciously undertaken?

Naturally we should not discuss these things in a theoretical way alone. Theoretically they may be interesting truths, but it is not enough to consider them theoretically. Today we must relate to them practically since they are connected with the actual realities of humanity's evolution. In practical terms we must become aware that the whole education system needs to change. We have to enable a person to develop the conscious power to re-experience at a later age, as if in vivid memory, what he assimilated in his youth.

At present people everywhere are doing the opposite. They are proud, for instance, to conduct what are called 'object lessons' in primary schools—that is to introduce everything to children in terms they can immediately and tangibly grasp. At all costs, they think, they should avoid presenting children with anything that exceeds their present comprehension. Instead the teacher, the parent, should talk down to the level of the child's comprehension. There are arithmetical calculators used to teach children all the mathematical processes by counting off little balls. Nothing is meant to exceed the child's level of understanding. But these object lessons become appallingly trivial and banal. Descending to the child's level of comprehension leads ultimately to teaching him only banal concepts. And those who do this completely overlook an important albeit subtle experience in human life.

Imagine that a child is taught so that he absorbs something not because it already entirely matches his level of comprehension but because the teacher's inspiring warmth communicates itself to the child; the child absorbs it because the teacher conveys it to him through his capacity to inspire, his enthusiasm. The child assimilates it through living in the warmth that emanates from the teacher. He absorbs something that goes beyond his understanding, doing so simply because of the teacher's infectious warmth and enthusiasm. The child does not yet understand what he has absorbed, but it settles in his mind and soul. And what a child has absorbed in this way when he was 10 is something the adult may remember when he is 30. He re-experiences it but now he is mature and can understand what he draws forth from the depths of his sensibility, which, when he was young, he absorbed only through the enthusiasm of the teacher. Now, as an adult, he can draw it forth from his mature mind. Look, these are the most fruitful moments of life—when we don't simply grasp what approaches us from without but when we re-experience something that we once absorbed with inadequate understanding, drawing it forth from within us and only then properly comprehending it with deepened insight. The more we can ensure, when teaching, that a child does not simply assimilate what he understands—which vanishes anyway with childhood, and will be no source of either joy or enthusiasm in later life—the more we nurture a person's future development. What is absorbed simply through the communicating warmth of the teacher gives us life forces when we later re-experience it.

In teaching today this needs special attention. In former times it was not so important since the blood itself raised things upward. Now, things must be brought to consciousness. It is not a matter of indifference whether we understand things such as those spiritual science today makes fruitful. If we properly understand them then somewhere or other in practical life we will find a way to use these things for the benefit of humanity. So for example we find a way to use the fact that our blood has grown weak, if we really comprehend it, by placing more value on the teacher's capacity for enthusiasm.

But in our time there is little awareness that such things are needed. Normative pedagogy still plays a major role—an education that works with all kinds of norms and standards. One learns educational methodology, how a child should be taught, methods used in teaching. At our present level of consciousness we ought to regard this really as if we were to refrain from eating until we have understood that the human being is composed of carbohydrates, proteins and so on, that they are converted thus and thus in the body. It is like thinking we should not eat before we have understood the physiological processes of digestion. I once told you, and you may have had the same experience, that on visiting someone on one occasion I saw he had a pair of scales next to his plate. He placed a piece of meat on the scales, and weighed it, since he was only allowed to eat a very specific amount of meat. Here physiology dictates appetite. But, thank God, we have not yet come to the point when everyone does this. It is important to recognize that knowledge of physiology is not required for eating: we can eat without having studied it, without knowing the physiology of the nutritional process. Most people know this, and yet they do not recognize that one should also teach, teach in a lively and living way, without having absorbed this normative pedagogy. For the most effective teacher, this normative pedagogy is exactly what an aesthetics of colour is for the painter. He may well have studied colour laws but this does not mean he can paint. He paints by virtue of something other than what he learns through colour aesthetics. One can teach by virtue of things quite different from the study of pedagogy. A normative pedagogy that dogmatically asserts particular methodologies in teacher training courses is not what is needed today. Instead those who are going to teach should be introduced to something that helps them become teachers in a way resembling how a person becomes a painter or botanist. That is, the teacher must be born from the human being rather than simply learning pedagogy.

Precisely because of this transformation in human nature, we must understand today that pedagogy needs to become a true art. In the era of transition people did not rightly know how to tackle education, and so they invented all kinds of abstract pedagogical methods. But the most important thing now is to give someone who teaches real insight into the human being. If you have real human insight and if you use this with the child, something remarkable happens. Imagine you are a teacher, and you have schoolchildren before you. As an adherent of normative pedagogy that works according to specific laws, you know how to teach, you have learned these norms and methods. Today you teach according to them, yesterday you taught according to them, and tomorrow and the next day you will teach according to them. But if you are a pedagogical artist, it is not so easy—you cannot teach yesterday, today, tomorrow and the next day according to the same norms and methods, but each time you must learn from the child himself how you must teach him. Each time you must follow what you need to do from the nature of the person before you. And the best thing of all for the teacher is to be able to teach as the child requires of him, in this way or that, and always to forget what pedagogy actually is—to have no inkling at all of pedagogical rules. When the child stands there before you, again you are completely electrified by this developing human being and by what you need to do with him.

Please note how one has to speak of these things today. Nowadays one cannot do so in a way that offers comforting principles of all kinds, but only by pointing to something that lives, that cannot be formulated in abstract principles—something that lives and by living engenders life. That is the important thing. And that is why spiritual science is needed for ordinary life since it is something that is not merely head-oriented but concerns the whole human being, and releases will impulses in us. This has to enter into many realms of life so that ultimately all human life and activity is informed and instigated by impulses of will.

I have elaborated on this here in respect of a particular area of life, of education, trying to show how we can make education fruitful up to the age of 21 and also in later life. In fact we do not educate people only up to 21 since education continues throughout life. But it is only healthy when people educate themselves through each other.

This was also something given naturally in the blood in former times. People did this unconsciously, educating one another in social interplay in which one person learned more from the other, the other less from the first. The blood mediated all this. But the blood has grown weak, has lost its powers. And this too requires more conscious replacement. People must come to the point of having relatively more from the other person than they have through themselves. In former times it was sufficient to leave oneself to life, as you might put it. The blood took care of everything. But now it is important that people really develop a sense for the being and nature of the other. This arises by itself if we orientate our thoughts towards spiritual science. Through the science of the spirit thoughts are stimulated in us that are different from those we otherwise entertain.

This can scarcely be in doubt, since it is apparent from the way spiritual science is dismissed by those who don't wish to absorb its ideas that the latter are different from the ideas that otherwise approach us. One has to develop a quite different way of thinking. This mode of thinking we develop by concerning ourselves with supersensible realities is one that at the same time works back upon our organism. A little while ago I said that the faculty of memory is the same power as that which converts food into nutrients we can use in our organism. You will hardly be surprised, then, to learn that other forces can be transformed within us similarly—that the power by virtue of which we gain insight into the supersensible realm leads us to a clearer discernment of human nature than we have without a healthy inclination for supersensible knowledge.

You have been studying my book *An Outline of Occult Science*. To do so you have to develop concepts which most people will dismiss as pure idiocy. Just a few days ago I received a letter from someone who had been reading *Occult Science* and told me that almost every chapter was utterly crazy. It's understandable, perfectly natural, that people think so. And yet those who do not take the trouble to assimilate concepts such as those of the planetary stages of Saturn, Sun, Moon, Jupiter, Venus and Vulcan, and who therefore do not elaborate ideas beyond the scope of the senses, do not acquire real knowledge of human nature either. They pass others by and notice, at most, that the other has a pointy or less pointy nose, or blue eyes, or brown; but not the soul quality manifesting within and organizing the whole body. The same faculty that enables us to have real interest in supersensible insights—though not necessarily to develop esoteric powers—is also what endows us with the kind of knowledge of human nature we need today.

You can establish the grandest social programmes and develop the finest social ideals, but if people refrain from developing knowledge of the human being, and so fail to encounter each other with inner perception, they will be unable to change social conditions. You cannot change society without making it possible for there to be social human beings. And social human beings will not exist if people pass one another by, and live only in themselves. Social human beings only arise when people meet each other in life and something passes from the one to the other. Only here can we begin to formulate what is today called the 'social question'. Most people today think that the social question involves establishing this or that institution, and that people will then live socially and communally. But that is not so. Go ahead and establish such institutions—the naturally social people will be good, social citizens within them; but antisocial ones will be antisocial whatever institution you establish and organize.

One facility which really will enable people to develop social impulses is insight or discernment. But as long as you educate people for specific ends—to be a postman or a lieutenant, or some other role for the state—you will not be educating them to perceive others. You see, this kind of education which produces postmen and lieutenants only enables someone to see the other as a potential postman or lieutenant too, whereas an education that makes a person fully human also enables him to perceive the human being in the other. It is not possible to perceive the human being in the other if we do not develop a faculty for supersensible perception. And the most important realm in which supersensible perception must work is the art of education. The greatest damage wrought in recent history is that the scientific and materialistic mode of thinking has also taken hold of education. One can experience some extremely peculiar things in this area.

In all fields of work there are very well-meaning people, people of good will, who want to reform and even revolutionize everything. But when you speak to them about these things, something curious becomes apparent. They stand fully and authentically behind reforms of one kind or another, but when you question them more closely they reveal an anxiety about anything changing that would endanger their profession—as a tailor, say, or railway official. If circumstances change, they worry their job and their way of life will not be secure. People see fully that things should change as long as these changes alter nothing. This outlook is extremely common today: everything should stay as it is when it changes! We ought not to overlook the fact that human yearning for change has a very abstract quality in society. People would like to see a great deal changing as long as it doesn't affect their own comfort.

This is particularly true where people should also enter inwardly into new conditions and circumstances. But this above all is the important thing—that people become able to find the transition to a new kind of thinking that requires us to change inwardly.

Well, all kinds of questions will arise from these reflections, questions of the most diverse kind which also directly and immediately concern how we live. In grappling with these questions we need to remember that we have created a certain deeper foundation for answering them by establishing that certain forces, initially appearing to be soul-spiritual in nature, also come to expression in the body. Too often today we lack the ability to introduce into material life what we picture in our mind. Unless we succeed in introducing things we picture in the spirit into material life, we will not be able to grasp the real core of the social question.

And therefore we must strive for a life of spirit, a cultural life, that develops real knowledge of the human being and thus also social impulses. Yes, a life of spirit that is forged out of quite other conditions and circumstances will not suffice. I mean that the cultural and spiritual life formed by the state or by economic conditions creates the postmen and lieutenants that it needs. But the spiritual life we need forms human beings. And this can only happen if this life of the spirit sunders itself from economic life and from the provisions of the state. For this reason our 'threefold social organism' had to emerge. We had to demonstrate in radical fashion that all kinds of dependency of spiritual and cultural life on economic life and the life of the state should end so that culture is established on its own intrinsic foundations. Then the life of spirit and culture can give to the economy and the state what the latter cannot give to spiritual life.

That's the important, essential thing! People will only regain their full humanity when we work out of an independent, autonomous life of spirit.

LECTURE 3

DORNACH, 5 OCTOBER 1919

DURING our days here together I have spoken of how a person can move forward from our present earthly consciousness to a cosmic consciousness in the same way that we once moved forward from ancient Greek and Roman culture to the Middle Ages, and to the end of the medieval period, by virtue of national consciousness changing to global consciousness. We don't consider these things in abstract terms but we try really to explore them so that they can become tangible aspects of our awareness.

In connection with this idea of enlarging our consciousness, I told you that in the first three phases of our life we live under the influence of forces which we can, really, call supersensible. From birth to our seventh year we are connected with the forces of the earth itself. The shaping, configuring forces acting in the human organism are largely ones anchored in planet earth itself, in its interior. Then, from our seventh to fourteenth year, the forces of the atmosphere exert an organizing, enlivening action on us. These surge through us and penetrate us via our breathing especially, enlivening the forms and configurations that were created in us in our first seven years. After this a time begins when, though it does not reach our awareness, we are exposed to the forces that work upon us from the planetary system, mediated by the earth.

In other words, the forces organizing and configuring us are not only ones we bear in our body or within its confines, but these forces issue and emanate from the earth itself and later from the whole solar system. Such considerations should gradually lead us to realize that we form a unity with the whole earth.

On previous occasions I often used a comparison to characterize this awareness from a different angle. I said that a human finger is only a human finger as long as it remains connected with the human body. If we amputate it, it withers. And just as the finger relates to the whole body, as I often said, we ourselves relate to the whole earth, and indeed to our whole solar system. We would wither and die like the amputated finger if sundered from the whole earth, and from our whole planetary system. In life it is important to progress gradually from awareness of the parts to the larger whole. When we consider our human nature we are really only partially accounted for as a physical organism and an etheric body too. We are only a *whole* organism in our connection with the earth and the larger planetary system. But if we become vividly aware of this, we realize that we belong more to the whole cosmos than merely to the earth since the earth draws its forces from the cosmos. Thus we pass from a sense of dependency on the earth to a larger sense of dependency on the cosmos.

But we can deepen these things further. As you know, the sun and moon are predominant for us amongst the heavenly bodies in the planetary system surrounding the earth. From the age of 14, thus the third phase of human life, we grow into a condition through which we become dependent upon the planetary system, including Mercury, Mars and so forth, but chiefly dependent on sun and moon. Our dependency on the sun and moon however can only be properly judged if we know more than outward observation tells us of their significance. Outward observation shows us the moon and its phases—full moon, new moon, first and last quarters as a crescent—as something intrinsically dark, which the sun illumines so that it turns a brightly lit aspect towards us. Yet this is not a full picture of the nature of the moon. We can only learn to discern what exists in the cosmos if we can always regard it as a sum of forces, an interplay of forces. And we have to ask what kind of forces are actually concentrated in the moon. Human will forces are chiefly concentrated there, or better, forces that have an affinity with everything that influences us from the subsensible realm. From the moon shine forces that are related to the subsensible aspect of human nature. It is fine for a physicist to tell us that the moon is made of a kind of slag, that the sun is something like a burning, glowing fireball with a corona, emitting its fire into the universe. This gives people a sense that if they were able to make their way slowly or quickly to the sun, they would fall into a kind of glowing furnace. I have often said that this is not so—that where the sun is there is a kind of vacuum, a void, and that light shines only from the sun's surface. In reality, where people believe there is something physical in fact there is nothing—for the being of the sun is very much supersensible just as the moon is subsensible. This supersensible and subsensible nature of the planetary system, concentrated in sun and moon, start to act on the human organism from around the age of 14. Firstly they work upon the human organization in so far as moon quality is more closely related to the female element, to everything feminine in the world, while sun quality is more related to male and masculine attributes. But they also act so that we have a solar quality in everything we elaborate through thinking and cognition, while every act of will, all will impulses, have a lunar quality. Sun and moon, you see, are not only outside us in the cosmos but also within us. And in our thinking we are sun beings, and moon beings in our will. Or, more precisely, from the age of 14, the supersensible sun forces work to develop the organs that mediate thinking in us, whereas the subsensible moon forces work to develop the organs in us that mediate will.

Thus, if we take such knowledge and transform it into living reality, we can tell ourselves this: In me lives not only what exists here on earth, but also what sun and moon constitute in me. I am a citizen of the cosmos. I would not be what I am as a human being if the cosmos did not act within me.

To know such things in the abstract is of no great value. But to feel inwardly that one is a being in whom sun and moon act gives us inner vitality. To feel that everything we can conceive supersensibly and will subsensibly comes from sun and moon enables us to recognize that, at every step we take on the earth, something more lives in us than burgeons and springs forth on the earth itself, than experiences pleasure and pain on the earth: as well as this, sun and moon live in me at every step I take. I am not only a citizen of the earth but a citizen of the universe. If this knowledge rises and builds like a living wave in us a certain power comes over our thinking that it does not otherwise have. In our present time, especially, people must learn to feel that the cosmos lives in them as they walk on earth—it must become strong feeling. As we gaze up at the sun we should know: I am likewise of your being, O sun! And looking up to the moon: I am likewise of your being, O moon!

Only if we carry this in us as a feeling do we become ripe to formulate social ideas. Otherwise thinking is burdened by a degree of earthly weight. Yes, one can formulate certain abstract ideas, but not inwardly and tangibly enliven them. The social realm is something the human being as such works and acts within whereas science comprehends only a realm from which the human being is absent. We can never understand social forces, social activity according to a scientific model but only with a thinking lifted upon feelings that tell us we are citizens of the cosmos. It is simply the case that this global consciousness of ourselves must emerge from our affinity with sun and moon. Only when we no longer feel that we are, let's say, implicated in the earth alone, but feel, rather, that we are only a passing dweller upon earth who introduces sun and moon forces into this earthly existence, does our thinking acquire both the strength and the lightness to enable us really to comprehend social ideas and social existence. You see, many an economist thinks that he can comprehend social concepts using the ordinary mode of thinking modelled on science. Read some books on economics: there you will find many concepts and many interpretations of them—the concept of goods and commodities, of labour (which I have mentioned in passing), and the concept of capital. But mostly none of these are much use; they do not cover what actually lives in society. If you want to try to formulate an idea of the circulation of goods in the economy, and you conceive this as you would the idea of a crystal, or a plant, or an animal, or even that of the physical human organism, nothing will come of it. You cannot comprehend the concept of goods and commodities according to the scientific model. If you wish, instead, to catch up with its living reality, as this exists in society, then really you need an Imagination, since goods have a quality that is indivisible from human beings. Every commodity is endowed with something of the human, whether it is a dress or a painting—in economic terms a painting is also only a commodity—or a school lesson. Yes, even a lesson is, in economic terms, only a commodity. The commodity concept is intrinsically connected with human output. Yet it is not ordinary, fully conscious life that informs the commodity but largely something arising from subconscious life. For this reason you need an Imagination in order to properly grasp the concept of goods, an Inspiration to grasp the concept of labour, and an Intuition to grasp the concept of capital. You see, the concept of capital is a very spiritual concept, albeit one turned on its head. That's why the Bible is quite right to call everything related to capitalism 'mammon'[8]—something connected with spirit but not exactly the very best spirit. Nevertheless, one penetrates the highest regions of spiritual discernment in seeking to grasp what capital actually does in economic life.

Here we encounter something very curious: to acquire correct economic concepts, we have to have an idea about supersensible perceptions. That is why all economic ideas emerging today are so amateurish—since people have no supersensible perceptions and therefore fail to grasp these ideas correctly.

Please do not misunderstand me. If you read my book *Towards Social Renewal,* you will say, 'But there is no Imagination there when you speak about goods and commodities; no Inspiration when you speak about labour, nor an Intuition when you speak of capital.' No, that's right, there isn't. One does not need to rise into higher worlds to perceive goods, labour and capital, although it is very interesting to do so and to see the reflected images there of commodities, work and capital. But there is no need to do so. Nevertheless one must be acquainted with the nature of Imagination, Inspiration and Intuition if one is to speak correctly of capital. That is the important thing. Someone unfamiliar with the faculties of Imagination, Inspiration and Intuition will be unable to speak correctly about goods, labour and capital. There is an intrinsic connection between spiritual science and modern sociology; and for people today there is no other means to comprehend the life of society than by rising from earth consciousness to cosmic consciousness and thereby acquiring the necessary lightness and strength of thinking. If we just crawl as it were upon the face of the earth and basically believe that we are nothing more than what we absorb and assimilate from plants, animals and minerals, and that these just compose themselves a little differently inside us, we will never recognize the truth of our nature. Only when I say that sun and moon act within me do I recognize myself as the human being I am. Consciousness of the universe must be achieved spiritually; by spiritual means we must recognize that we belong to a larger portion of the cosmos than the earth alone.

Now it is really important to get beyond ordinary everyday concepts to arrive at the kind of thinking I'm referring to. As you know, there are materialistic thinkers in the world—a very great number of them, and no doubt you are all firmly convinced that one ought not to be a materialist. Or at least you were persuaded to a certain degree that it would be good to cultivate a more spiritual form of thinking; at least you felt drawn to spiritual thinking as we cultivate it here in the anthroposophic movement. So we can leave ourselves aside here. But there are others who propound the spirit, numerous such people in the world who dismiss the idea that everything comes down to material processes and material realities. Those who think and feel spiritually stand in contrast to materialists. The former believe in the spirit, and therefore materialists often dismiss them as fantasists. They, for their part, believe that the materialists cannot see how right they are in holding to spiritual things. So here we have this distinction and divergence in the world between materialistic and spiritual thinking, with much dispute about who is right, materialistic or spiritual thinkers. From some of the things we have discussed it ought to be apparent that those who continue to dispute about such things have not yet grasped the nature and meaning of spiritual science. The only true appraisal is to say to a materialist that his point of view is correct as far as it goes, as is the point of view of the spiritual thinker likewise. You can photograph a tree from one angle and then a different one, and though each angle will present something different it is still the same tree. A spiritual view of the world is one angle, and a material view another. Materialist thinking seems to be quite different from spiritual thinking. In fact, we have the full picture neither in a materialistic nor a spiritual outlook, which are really only photographs from two different angles. The materialist is really just as right as the spiritual thinker, and these concepts, spiritual and material, only apply on the physical plane. The moment we go beyond it, these concepts are overcome. No further dispute, then, as to whether the world is material or spiritual in nature, since then one knows that these are just two aspects. But why do people dispute as to whether the human being is material or spiritual in nature, whether a person is only corporeal or only a soul? Why do some see in human nature only physical corporeality while others think there is soul and spirit present too? Because we are both! And here lies the secret of life. If you say that a thought is only a spiritual or mental entity, you are right, for the thought itself *is* only spiritual in nature. And yet the thought as soul-spiritual reality could never be in you without leaving a physical imprint—you can always demonstrate this physical imprint too. Thus every thought or idea also possesses something material. We might say that the universe has ensured in a most non-partisan manner that people can be both spiritual and materialist in outlook: seeing that we are soul-spiritual beings we can entertain a spiritual outlook. But we are also certainly a material impress of the soul and spirit; if we grasp this and overlook the other aspect, we can be materialists since we are in fact constituted of both, and the one is only the impress, a reflection of the other, and both resemble each other. A person can be more of a materialist because he focuses on his physical nature, or have a more spiritual outlook because he focuses more on his soul-spiritual being.

We do not evade this dichotomy as long as we stay with the ideas of ordinary, everyday life or those, too, of ordinary science. One can invent all kinds of theories. There are no end of theories about the body-soul relationship, about their 'parallelism' and so forth. But such things are ingeniously worked out without any actual roots in reality. You see, people have lost the ability—I have often stressed this—to think about these things in the right way; and this is because they were historically prohibited from doing so. In 869, at Constantinople, the Eighth General Council 'abolished' the spirit,[9] establishing the dogma that the human being does not consist, as was previously known in Gnostic scholarship, of body, soul and spirit but only of body and soul, though the soul was accorded a few spiritual properties. And therefore the medieval Scholastics were extremely wary of speaking of the 'trichotomy', of body, soul and spirit. This was forbidden. Our professors of philosophy today are not wary in the same way, not shy of entertaining anything, and yet they have not yet overcome the Roman Catholic prohibition—they too only speak of body and soul, a duality, and believe that they are engaging in open-minded, unprejudiced academic discourse, whereas in fact they are really only teaching the Roman Catholic dogma of the Eighth General Council of Constantinople. They believe that what they say follows from impartial enquiry, but they only say it because they are governed by historical imperatives.

It is our task today to return to a recognition of body, soul and spirit. Observing the outer world and our human organization in so

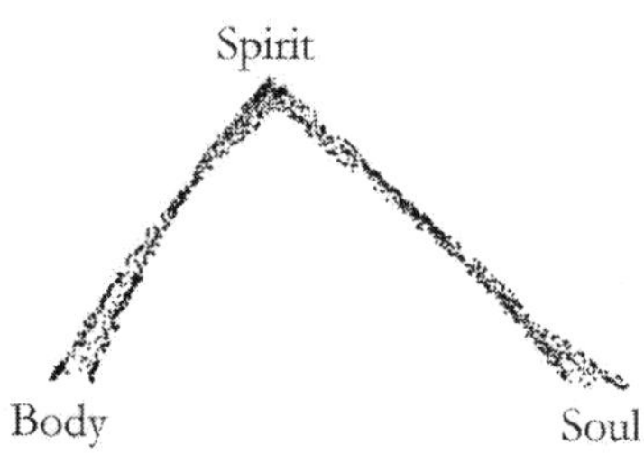

Board drawing 3

far as it is perceived in the same way as the outer world, we discern corporeality. If we then look inward we can either consider our thinking, will and feeling in an outward and superficial form of self-knowledge, or we may descend into them mystically: we experience a soul element—an outward corporeality and soul within. But the connection between them, perception of the interplay between spirit-soul and physical body, their continual interplay, is caused by the third aspect—for which we do not even have a proper word. We have to take one aspect of the word, and say 'spirit'. And so we can say there is body and soul, and the spirit creates the connection between them.

We have to return to a healthy idea of body, soul and spirit, otherwise body and soul will always tend to diverge and fall asunder. In the soul we can find nothing corporeal, in the body nothing of the soul, unless we recognize the spirit in them, at their centre.

Many years ago I used a comparison to try to clarify what I mean. Here, we can imagine, is a signet, with a name engraved in it—let's say a very uncommon one such as 'Smith'! And now I take sealing wax, perhaps on the back of a letter, and I can impress the name Smith into it.

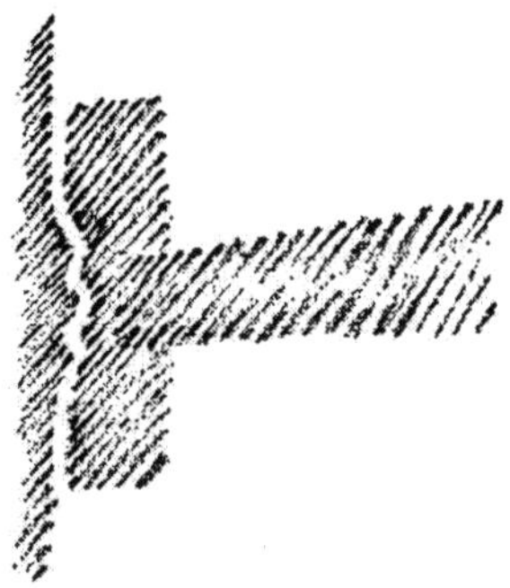

Board drawing 3

Well now, along come the Kantians and physiologists who will say that there is no connection between the signet itself, which might be made of bronze, and the sealing wax. True, the one is entirely bronze, the other entirely sealing wax. Nothing of the bronze will ever be transmitted to the sealing wax, nor vice versa. The two are definitely different in kind. The same is true of body and soul. The one imprints itself on the other, but nothing of either assumes the other's nature: each has its own substantiality, and nothing, nothing at all, passes from the one into the other. And yet, when you have pressed the signet into the sealing wax, you see the name 'Smith' there, the same as on the signet: they are one and the same. But this correspondence did not come about because something very subtle flowed or oozed from the signet into the sealing wax. No. Something occurred that is intrinsically neither sealing wax nor bronze but is a shared element in both. The fact that this is 'Smith' has no connection whatever with the bronze itself not its constituents, but with a real, living element. The fact that a person is called Smith is related to life and points to the whole breadth of life. So here we have the soul-spirit, and here the body. The soul-spirit imprints itself in corporeality. But the element that is the same in both of them, the spirit, is a whole, wide world. We do not comprehend the spirit if we only ever regard the soul, just as little as we learn to recognize Mr Smith if we only look at the signet. Nor do we comprehend the spirit if we merely gaze at the material world, just as little as we recognize Mr Smith by staring at the sealing wax.

It is a matter, therefore, of the spirit mediating the interplay and relationship between soul and body. And in our era we are in a phase of humanity's evolution in which it is vital to comprehend this fact properly.

If you consider modern science, you will find that it offers you all kinds of corporeal reality, and really only that. Concepts of the soul and psyche from older times will give you soul quality. But we only comprehend both properly if we raise ourselves to the spirit, since we only becomes citizens of the cosmos—in contrast to the earth citizens we have been until now—by grasping our nature spiritually. As you will see from this we must not only comprehend the human body as we regard all outward corporeality, but must enlarge the scope of this view to properly survey human nature. I will try to illustrate what I mean with an example.

Ordinary science only considers the human being as a creature whose life ends at death. All it can observe thereafter are the bodily remains, and how these are cremated or returned to the earth, becoming dust. Now it would be possible to study the constituents in this human dust, the residue of the human organism. Science will say that human substance decomposes and rejoins the earth. Well this is not even a fraction of the truth: it isn't true at all. You see, what is given back to the earth, irrespective of whether the body is cremated or buried, once had human form and had this also by virtue of the fact that before birth, or before conception, a being of spirit and soul descended from worlds of spirit and worked within this physical body until death. Then this physical body is given to the earth; and the nature of human form works on in the earth, irrespective of whether the body was cremated or buried, and continues to collaborate with the earth. To the earth is continually imparted something that it would not have if human bodies were not given up to it at death; the earth benefits from this. Otherwise, if it did not receive human bodies, the earth would only possess earthly substances.

A being of soul and spirit lived in this human body, descending before birth or conception from worlds of soul and spirit, and configuring this human body. This configuration remains as something essential in every grain of dust, enters the earth or the atmosphere at cremation or burial, and with this human body the earth receives what descended from spiritual worlds. This is not without significance. It is not even an ordinary, everyday truth but has very great significance. You see our earth is no longer evolving, and it would have long been the case that no human being could dwell upon it, perhaps not animals either—or perhaps animals could—if it did not continually receive rejuvenating, soul-spiritual forces in the form of human bodies. The earth is still habitable for humankind because it continually receives human bodies which keep refreshing and rejuvenating it. Since the middle of Atlantean times, the earth intrinsically has already been withering, and no longer has forces of uplift any more, which it did possess in the ancient Polaric time and in Lemurian times and so forth. Since the middle of the Atlantean period, the earth as such only has forces of withering, and is refreshed and sustained only by receiving the formative powers of human bodies which work on in the earth. Only they make the earth a place still habitable for human beings.

You can see from this that on the one hand the inner forces of the planet are active within us, [and] the forces of the atmosphere. But we also give back soul-spiritual forces to the earth; we supply the earth with soul-spiritual forces. When we are born we bear soul-spiritual forces from the spiritual universe into the earthly realm, and use them as long as we need them, until death; then we give them to the earth as formative powers and so become collaborators helping to shape the future earth. If asked what the human being signifies for the earth, proponents of the external scientific outlook would say, roughly: 'If the human being had never arisen on the earth, everything would still have evolved as it did. The only difference would be the absence of man. Houses would not be there either, of course, nor cities and so on, in other words whatever human culture has produced. But otherwise everything else would be the same.' But spiritual science teaches us that the human being is not just an observer here on the earth but, through his very existence, a collaborator, a co-shaper of it; and that he does this also through the body he gives up to the earth at death, becoming a mediator between the world of spirit and this physical world of earth.

Intrinsic to this also is the awareness of being more than a citizen of the earth, of being a citizen of the cosmos. The earth citizen is born to mother and father, bears inherited characteristics, acquires various qualities that he passes on as inherited traits and so on. Someone who knows himself to be a citizen of the cosmos realizes that by entering this existence at birth he bears into this world a soul-spiritual element, and that at death, when he departs this earth, he also continues to contribute to the edifice of future earth existence. Only as a citizen of the cosmos does a person recognize fully how his existence is connected with earthly existence—how he is *one* being with it, and by being so basically endows the earth with its spirituality.

All these ideas that we can acquire from spiritual science should not be acquired or assimilated in the same way as ordinary knowledge. Although it may be a little paradoxical to say this, knowledge is not especially valuable. What is valuable is what we become through knowledge. This also applies to education. To teach a child geography does have a certain outward significance but not initially great inner value. Outwardly its significance lies in knowing, later, that when you're travelling from Dornach to Zurich you don't mistake Bern for Zurich, or suchlike. But its inner value lies in what the soul becomes through learning geography. The soul acquires a capacity to orientate itself in the world. Certain spiritual forces are released from the depths, from the roots of the soul, and the release of these spiritual forces is the important thing.

Now if we consider the period that began in the middle of the fifteenth century, it is a time when people were least inclined to release these soul-spiritual forces within them. They adhered more to the impress, to the sealing wax. Since the middle of the fifteenth century, people have entered the age of materialism; but now we are at a point when we must become aware of this and must return to the spirit, connecting the spirit with matter.

Why did all this occur? To superficial appraisal it might seem that the Lord God could have made things easier for himself. He could simply, without more ado, have given humankind a life of spirit in the fifteenth century, avoiding the whole arduous detour we have made through materialism. Perhaps he could have done so. The Protestants get offended if you suggest he couldn't have. But that is of little interest now. The truth is he didn't avoid this detour but allowed human beings to delve their way deeply through materialism, to wrestle their way through it. In the nineteenth century they reached the nadir of materialism. If they were now to wend their way back to spirituality they would need a strong inner impulse. This strong inner impulse is released by freedom, is released by the fact that a person turns to spirituality out of himself and not through divine inoculation as it were. If we had not delved deeply into materialism, we could not wrestle our way through to spirituality out of our own freedom. This arduous penetration of material reality invoked in humankind the urge to autonomy. This wrestling with and penetration of matter was so strong that even the religions and theology became material in nature. A modern theologian, even, finds it hard today to comprehend something spiritual—perhaps even harder than anyone else. Recently I was discussing something with a Catholic theologian, and as fate would have it we were standing beneath the well-known picture by Raphael, *The Disputa*. In the course of our conversation, I tried to illustrate something by relating it to this painting. I said that anyone who seeks to cultivate the life of spirit must come to the point of recognizing why Raphael, in the consciousness of his time, painted *The Disputa*. Above we see the heavenly worlds with the Trinity, below the sacrament on the altar, and the Church Fathers and theologians. But on their own none of these things are the most essential aspect of the painting. What is essential is this: that a theologian with deeper insight—and many no longer had this at the time—who took his theology seriously, as Raphael did, so that its soul imbued his painting, would know that when the host, the sacrament, has been consecrated, and one gazed through it, one gazed upon the world that Raphael painted in the upper portion of *The Disputa*. The consecrated host really is the means to gaze through into the world of spirit; and that is why Raphael painted it in this way. That was by way of example. And what I mean is that we must find the path back to comprehending the true content of such a painting, which was painted out of a consciousness different from our own. I am unable at this minute to conjure before you the grimace this theologian made when urged to see his holiest sacrament in this spiritual manner. Theology itself has been materialized, perhaps more than anything else. It no longer connects with a truly spiritual element, and that is why Christology itself has become materialistic. For the theologian of the fifteenth century it would have been impossible, as yet, to regard Christ merely as the 'simple man of Nazareth'. At that time he still had a vivid sense of the Christ indwelling Jesus of Nazareth, an awareness that has since faded. For theologians today, the 'simple man of

Nazareth', as they define him, is just a figure like Socrates, Plato or Aristotle, albeit a little more elevated. Theology itself has become materialistic.

Out of the inmost comprehension of our humanity we need to accomplish the volte-face of turning to spirituality in freedom. We cannot do this by churning out spiritual phrases, just talking of spirit; we can only do so by *thinking* spiritually. And it is to think spiritually if we say that knowledge is connected with the forces of the sun, and will with the forces of the moon. As human bodies are created here on earth through the stream of heredity, a solar quality, not an earthly one, acts in the male energy, while a lunar quality acts in the female energy. The earth sows and strews itself with solar-lunar power also in human reproduction, and this human reproduction is in turn related to forces of cognition and will. The spiritual penetrates the physical, the physical creates a spiritual reflection. The synthesis and interplay of soul and body is what we must still seek today, as something absolutely essential. This cannot be done by resorting to the shadowy concepts that have developed in modern times since the mid-fifteenth century—they only go back that far. Instead of these inwardly devised concepts we need an inwardly experienced life of spirit. But only the life of spirit truly experienced leads at the same time to practical actions. Our cultural and spiritual life has been impractical for long enough. For long periods now people have been discussing how to be good, how to be brotherly, how to practise love for one's neighbour and so on. But the ideas devised in this way remained in their confined sphere, and did not have the power to impact on practical life. If you think of a modern businessman, a real modern industrialist or, let's say, a civil servant—so that we have all three types—it is possible of course for him also to be a pious man. But there is a considerable difference between the businessman's inner faith or confession and the work of his that comes to expression in his accounts! What lives in his religious life has no power to enter the account books. And the civil servant is not educated to be a human being so much as a servant of the state. How is what he learned in order to be a clerk or civil servant related to the inner faith he may have? Religious life is one stream while so-called practical life is another, divorced from it. Since concepts and ideas have lost their potency and cannot impact on practical life, we can no longer develop ideas vigorous enough to really affect the life of society. They need to be reinvigorated by spiritual science so that they grow strong enough again to be more than Church sermons—which may elicit warm feelings in the heart, giving pleasure within, but do not find their way into the work that comes to expression in business accounts. Ideas and concepts need to push on further into practical life, and can do so if they are drawn from the spirit. You see, ideas are *not* spiritual if they do not, by virtue of their inner vigour, delve down into the deepest essence of matter. You can discern the spirituality of an idea by the fact that it penetrates into the deepest stratum of material life.

And this is what we need if we are to bridge the gulf that yawns still between modern humanity today, with all the legacies it possesses from an earlier era, and future humanity, which absolutely must create a synthesis and interplay between the material and the spiritual. To be either materialist or spiritual in outlook is simply to fall back into older modes of human feeling. Only if you can be both, so that both livingly interpenetrate, can you become equal to the contemporary needs of human society.

LECTURE 4

DORNACH, 10 OCTOBER 1919

OVER these days I want to explore some of the aspects of what is needed firstly to comprehend and secondly to act practically within society today. It is fairly easy to see from ubiquitous and salient facts that our modern civilization shows symptoms of decline, that there are forces of decline at work in it, and that in the face of this we need to consider how to endow this civilization with new forces. If we survey this civilization of ours we can primarily discern three kinds of decline, three forces that must over time inevitably lead to its downfall. All the dismal occurrences we have already experienced in the course of humanity's evolution and are still experiencing—and some of them are only in their infancy—are just diverse symptoms of the overall phenomenon of decline occurring in our era.

If we expand our view beyond what is happening at present in society today and in the last three to four centuries, and consider the larger course of human evolution, it can become apparent that older cultures had a foundation, also in their daily life and existence, that nowadays we only wrongly believe we possess. These ancient cultures, especially pagan ones, had a certain scientific character: people were aware that something of the whole universe lived in their souls. You need only think how alive still were the worlds of thought of the Greeks, their conception of the world of gods and spirits beyond mundane reality and behind the sense world. And you need only recall something that vividly entered into the daily life of those times and gave these people of ancient cultures a certain connection with a world of spirit of which they were aware. In everyday life the people of these ancient cultures certainly knew they stood within a world that is not limited to mundane experience alone, but into which spirit beings work. Daily actions were undertaken under the promptings of spiritual powers. Thus especially if we look back to pagan cultures we find a certain fundamentally scientific tone, which we can describe as a cosmogony or sense of cosmic connection. In other words, people then knew themselves to be a part of the whole cosmos—not simply lost beings that gambol about here on the earth's green grass like lambs, but connected with the whole broad span of the universe, which shaped their destiny.

There is no real impetus in our civilization to create cosmic connection. We do not have a genuinely scientific way of thinking in the true sense of the word. We itemize the diverse facts of nature and we have a conceptual framework of ideas, but not a genuine science that connects us with worlds of spirit. The science cultivated today and affecting our daily life is very impoverished compared to the powers of the world of spirit that a person in ancient times knew were pulsing through him as he acted. He had a cosmogony; he knew he was membered into the whole universe. He looked up to sun, moon and stars not as to alien worlds but recognized his inmost affinity with them. Thus ancient civilizations possessed a cosmogony, which our civilization has lost. A person cannot be strong in life without this. That is the first thing driving the decline of our civilization, what you might call the 'scientific' element.

The second element driving its decline is the lack of a real impulse for freedom. Our civilization lacks the capacity for comprehensively establishing freedom. Although many speak of freedom, only a few people today have a real idea of what it means, and still fewer gain a true inner impulse towards it. In consequence our civilization gradually succumbs to something that cannot possibly sustain it, to fatalism. Either we have a religious fatalism, where people give themselves up to religious powers of one kind or another, offering themselves in its service as if they were puppets on strings pulled by these greater powers, or we have a scientific fatalism. This comes to expression in a gradually developing view that everything is governed by natural necessity or economic necessity, which allows no room for freedom of action. When people feel harnessed by the economic or the scientific world, fatalism is the only word for it. Or, as I said, we have the fatalism accompanying modern religious confessions, which really also excludes freedom. There are many hearts and souls today who would best like to give themselves up to what Christ or some other spiritual power may do with them. In fact a frequent objection to anthroposophy is that we do not place enough value on being redeemed by Christ, but instead seek to redeem ourselves. People wish to be led, governed; really they want fatalism to be true. And in the recent years of misfortune one has often heard people asking why God or Christ does not help a particular nation. Surely, they believe, there must be divine justice; and they want this divine justice to be meted out, enacted as fate, instead of being inwardly empowered by the impulse of freedom. A civilization unable to cultivate this impulse of freedom weakens people and condemns them to decline. That is the second thing. The lack of a sense of cosmic connection is the first, and the lack of a real impulse for freedom the second of the powers of decline at work in our civilization.

And the third is that our civilization is unable to produce any new impulse for true religious feeling and will. Really it only wants to continue to cultivate the old confessions, keep warming them up again. Our civilization lacks the strength to bring new religious impulses to life, and it lacks the strength, also, for really altruistic action. A strong altruistic impulse can only come from a spiritual world-view. Only when we know ourselves to be a part of the world of spirit do we cease to be so terribly interesting to ourselves as to make ourselves the very centre of the whole universe. At that point egoistic impulses cease and altruistic ones begin. Our era has little inclination to develop this great interest for the world of spirit, but this is what must increase if we are really to feel ourselves part of the spiritual world.

And then the impulses of reincarnation and karma have, as it were, come raining into our civilization out of the blue. Yet how have they been taken up? Even those who embraced them have done so in a very egoistic fashion. It has been said, for example, that a person *earns* his destiny in each life. Even otherwise intelligent people can be heard to say that ideas of reincarnation and karma are an answer to the question of why human suffering exists, and the social question is therefore irrelevant. Otherwise intelligent people have said that poverty is the deserved outcome of a former incarnation, that if someone is poor they must simply expiate something they brought about in their past life. So even ideas of reincarnation and karma are not capable of working into our civilization as an impulse for altruistic feeling. What matters is *how* we introduce ideas of reincarnation and karma into our era. If they only become an impetus for egoism, they do not raise our culture to a higher level but push it still further downwards. Reincarnation and karma actually become unethical or anti-ethical ideas if many people think they must become good so that their next incarnation is a good one. This drive to become good in order to have as pleasant an experience as possible in our next life is a kind of double egoism, a step beyond even straightforward egoism. And this is precisely what ideas of reincarnation and karma have come to mean for many. Our society today has so little real altruism and religiosity that it cannot even comprehend ideas such as reincarnation and karma in a way that would make them an impulse for altruistic and not egoistic actions and feelings.

These three things, therefore, make up the forces of decline in our culture: the lack of a cosmogony, the lack of a real foundation for freedom, and the lack of altruistic feeling. Where there is no real sense of cosmic connection, no true science exists either, no real knowledge: knowledge ultimately becomes a kind of cosmic or cultural diversion or pastime, and has largely become so in our civilization, except where it is of purely utilitarian moment in outward culture, external technological culture. In our era freedom has become little more than a phrase since our civilization lacks the strength to found and establish it thoroughly, and hence to spread its impulse. Nor, in the economic realm, do we have the capacity to progress in a truly social sense, since our civilization has no altruistic impulses but only egoistic, thus anti-social ones, and these anti-social impulses can never enhance social abilities. You see, truly social dynamics depend on creating a structure in society in which one person acts in the interests of another. Can we see this happening anywhere in our civilization? The whole social order is founded on each person acting only for himself, and everything is geared to this.

So how can we progress beyond these symptoms of our civilization's decline? We can't whitewash over them. Let us look these realities in the face and avoid all illusions. The powers of decline are here, and there is no point in thinking we might somehow fix things, repair the problem. Against the forces of degeneration that we have described, we must turn to something from which we can draw regenerative powers. Theories cannot help—people can invent the finest theories, the best principles, but they will get us nowhere. We will only get somewhere by invoking powers that really exist on this earth. If this civilization were only as I have described it, we could do nothing other than let it go under, and share in this downfall. And this is because it is absurd to attempt to correct the symptoms through mere ideas.

But is there perhaps a deeper cause of social ills? There is indeed. People today—as I have often characterized from other angles—are too driven towards the absolute. In asking about truth, they want to know what is an absolute truth and not what applies to a particular era. When they ask what is good, they mean this in an absolute sense, not what is good for Europe, or for Asia. Not what is good for the twentieth century, or the twenty-fifth. This urge for absolute goodness and truth prevents them from enquiring into humanity's actual, tangible evolution. But we must ask the question differently, look at actual reality and, in accordance with it, ask a different question—often in a way that elicits apparently paradoxical answers compared to the views which a superficial observation of things inclines us to. We must ask this: is it possible to develop a cosmological way of thinking again? Is it possible to develop a truly socially effective impulse for freedom? Is it possible to develop an impulse that is simultaneously a religious and a fraternal one, and therefore provides a true foundation for an economic social order? And if we ask these questions with a true eye to reality, we will also find real answers. You see, the important thing is this: that in the modern world not all of humankind is disposed to arrive at the whole, comprehensive truth; across the globe, different branches of the human race are disposed to arrive at partial areas of truth and its practical realization. So where, in the modern world, can a cosmogony develop? Where can the impulse of freedom really come into its own? And where does an impulse exist to develop religious and fraternal social community?

If we start with the latter, unprejudiced appraisal of our global circumstances shows that an outlook, a mode of thinking that cultivates a truly fraternal impulse on earth is to be found amongst the people of Asia, especially in Chinese and Indian culture. Although these cultures have already succumbed to decadence, and although what I say seems to contradict a superficial assessment, it is in these regions that we can discern impulses of love proceeding from the inmost human heart towards all other beings; and only this can provide the foundations for religious altruism, firstly, and secondly for a truly altruistic economic culture.

But the curious thing is this: although the Asiatic peoples have a disposition for altruism, they do not have the means to realize it. They have the right stance or outlook for it, but not the capacity, the talent, if you like, to create conditions in which the beginnings of altruism could be outwardly realized. For millennia, the Asiatic peoples knew how to cultivate altruistic impulses in human nature. And yet they also made it possible for great hunger and destitution to be rampant in China, India and elsewhere. This is the curious thing about Asiatic culture: that the disposition is there, that it is also inwardly authentic, yet there is no talent for realizing this outlook in outward life. Inwardly, it possesses a hugely significant altruistic impulse, but no capacity to realize this outwardly. On the contrary, if

Asia were to remain alone, the fact that Asia has an inner capacity to develop altruism but no gift for outwardly realizing it would lead to a terrible devastation of civilization. Of these three things, the impulse for cosmic connection, the impulse for freedom and the impulse for altruism, Asia has the latter most of all in its inner outlook and disposition. And yet it has only one third of what modern civilization needs if it is to pursue an upward path again—the inner disposition for altruism.

And what does Europe have? It has the most urgent need to solve the social question, but it has no inherent disposition to do so. Really it would need the Asiatic outlook if it wished to solve the ills of society. Social imperatives mean that all the preconditions exist in Europe for solving the social question. But to do so Europeans would first have to imbue themselves with the way of thinking that comes naturally to those in Asia—who, however, have no talent for really outwardly perceiving social misery. In fact, this often even pleases them. In Europe there exists an outward impulse to deal with social problems, but without the inner disposition to do so. On the other hand, Europeans have to the greatest degree a talent, a capacity, to establish the impulse for freedom. Specifically European talents exist to develop and configure the inner feeling of freedom in the most eminent sense. We can say that coming to a real idea of freedom is a specific European gift. But there is no one amongst these Europeans able to act freely, to realize freedom. Europeans are magnificent at comprehending the idea of freedom, but just as the Asiatic peoples would immediately know what to do if they acquired the unsullied idea of European freedom, without other European disfigurements, so the European can elaborate the loveliest idea of freedom but without any political means of directly realizing it amongst the peoples of Europe; and this is because the European only has *one* of the three conditions for civilization—the urge for altruism, for freedom, for cosmic connection. He only has the impulse for freedom without the other two. And therefore he has only a third of what is needed to really bring about a new era. It is very important for us to finally start to understand these matters, as the secrets of our civilization. In Europe, we may say, we have the finest preconditions for thoughts and feelings about freedom, but no means to advance this freedom. For instance, at a time when all Germany was suffering under the tyranny of Ludendorff[10] and others, there were people who composed the finest essays on freedom. In Europe we have a talent for conceiving the impulse of freedom but at present this impulse is only a third, and not the whole, of what is needed if our civilization is really to surmount its problems.

We do not understand the secrets of our civilization today if we do not know how to apportion the three impulses involved in the resurgence of our civilization to the different regions of the globe: if we do not know that a quest for cosmic connection lies in the talents of the Anglo-American world; that the quest for freedom is inherent in the European world; and that the quest for altruism—and for an outlook which, when truly applied in reality, leads to socialism—is found only in Asiatic culture. America, Europe, Asia: each has a third of what is needed for a real resurgence, a rebuilding of our culture.

Anyone who earnestly and honestly seeks to help rebuild civilization today must draw on these foundations. It is no good nowadays sitting in an ivory tower and reflecting on what the best programme for the future might be. You have to go out into the world and draw from it the impulses that exist there. As I have said, if you look at our culture today with its symptoms of decline, inevitably you will gain a sense that it is beyond salvation unless people acknowledge that the three things needed are present in different regions, unless they start to collaborate with each other more broadly across the earth and recognize that one region alone does not have the inner, absolute resources to accomplish this. Each must contribute the gifts to which it is, if you like, predestined. If Americans today wish to draw on their own resources to develop not only cosmic connection but also freedom and Socialism, they cannot do so. Nor can Europeans, besides establishing the impulse of freedom, also find cosmic connection and altruism. Likewise people in Asia cannot realize anything other than the altruism deeply inherent in them. We will only make real progress if other populaces of the globe adopt this same altruism and penetrate it with the element that is their own inherent gift. Humanity today needs to collaborate across the globe in order for its different talents to come together.

We have to acknowledge that our civilization has grown weak, and needs to strengthen once again. To give a more tangible sense of these abstract things, I'll say the following. As you know, the ancient pre-Christian, oriental cultures created great cities. We can look back to widespread oriental cultures with their magnificent cities—but a certain outlook reigned there. In the great cities of all oriental cultures, an outlook developed that if human beings did not reach beyond the physical to the superphysical realm they would live in a void, in a nothingness. And this is really how the great cities of Babylon, Nineveh and so forth could develop—because the people living there were not constrained to think that what these cities produced was truly real. For them reality lived behind all this. Not until Rome did city culture become the standard of reality. The Greek cities are inconceivable without the countryside surrounding them, which nourished and sustained them. If our history were not the *fable convenue* that it is, a story we have agreed upon, but if instead it conveyed to us the real shape of former times, we would see how the Greek city was rooted in the land. Rome was no longer rooted in the surrounding land in this way. Rome's history involves making an imaginary world into a real one, turning an unreal world into reality. In Rome, really, the 'citizen' was invented, this ghastly caricature beside the true human being. You see, the human being is a human being; and that he is also a citizen too is an imaginary matter. That he is a citizen is a fact found somewhere in church statutes or legal statutes. Apart from being a human being with certain intrinsic capacities, he is accorded a registered property, an entry in the land register. And all this is Roman, an imaginary addition alongside reality. Indeed, Rome achieved a great deal more too. Rome learned how to falsely convert into reality everything that arises from the separation of the cities from the land, from the land's reality. For instance, Rome was able to introduce Roman legal concepts into ancient religious ideas. If you look back to the ancient religious ideas and examine their actual nature, you will find nothing in them of the Roman legal terms that later infiltrated them. Roman jurisprudence pervaded religious ethics. What Rome made of religious ethics is basically as if there were judges seated on high in the supersensible world—like the judges that sit in our own Roman-influenced law courts—who passed judgement on human actions. Indeed, because Roman legal concepts still influence us, whenever anyone mentions karma most people who acknowledge such a thing imagine it to be dispensed by some law of justice in a world beyond, rewarding what a person has done in this way or that, with this punishment or that, in line with earthly concepts and in accordance with a Roman view of justice. In such ideas, all saints and supersensible beings embody Roman legal concepts that have seeped through into this superterrestrial world.

Who today, for instance, still comprehends the great idea of Greek fate? We cannot understand a figure such as Oedipus in terms of Roman legal concepts! Under the influence of these ideas founded on Roman jurisprudence, in fact, people have entirely lost the gift for comprehending tragic greatness. These legal ideas from Rome have infiltrated our modern civilization and live there everywhere, have largely created a false reality from what was at first imaginary—not imaginative, but imaginary.

We have to be very clear, therefore, that we are sundered from reality in our thoughts and ideas, and that we need to re-imbue them with reality. Since our concepts are, basically, empty, our civilization still lacks the awareness that people must work together across the globe. Views remain superficial, and no one really wants to look at the underlying cause of phenomena.

I'd like to give you an example of this too. As you know, two parties evolved in the various parliaments of the world in former times, let us say in the first half of the nineteenth century, and somewhat later—a conservative and a liberal party—and so far these have enjoyed a fairly high level of respect. Other parties only emerged later, in addition to these original two. But listen, it is so important today that we get beyond phrases to realities, and that instead of always asking what those who represent a party say about their policies we examine what lies in their subconscious. If you do this you find that those who belong to more conservative parties have more to do in some way with agricultural concerns, with care of the land and soil, that is, the founding origins of human culture. Of course all sorts of other, secondary factors can appear on the surface as well. I am not saying that every conservative has to be an agriculturalist, for of course all sorts of other people join these parties, people who, persuaded by mere phrases, adhere to some principle or other. But all in all we can see that those who are interested in maintaining certain structures and forms of the social order as they are, and not allowing them to slip too suddenly away from them, are people who belong to the agrarian population.

Liberal, progressive movements emerge from the industrial element, from labour that has become more sundered from the land. Thus these two types of party are rooted in something deeper; and we should always try to go beyond the phrases they utter, delve beyond words into actual realities.

And ultimately all these things tell us that we have been living very much in a culture of words. Instead of which we must work our way forward to a culture of reality, a civilization of realities. No longer being so impressed by words, programmes, well-formulated objectives, we must come to the point of understanding reality, and above all realities that go deeper than either rural or city culture, agrarian or industrial culture. And a deeper aspect today lies in the impulses of different parts of humanity across the globe: of American culture in its quest for cosmogony, of European culture in its quest for freedom, of Asiatic culture in its quest for socialism.

However, such quests have been realized, initially, in some curious ways. Anglo-American culture is conquering the world. As it does so, it is essential that it assimilates what it can from the parts of the world it conquers: impulses of freedom, altruistic impulses—for it only possesses the impulse of cosmic connection. It owes its success to the capacity to think in universal thoughts, as we have frequently discussed during the war years. The successes of Anglo-American culture have arisen from certain kinds of supersensible impulse which other cultures refuse to comprehend. This element of cosmogony must not remain isolated but must interpenetrate with the realm of freedom.

To understand what this means we naturally have to distance ourselves radically from mere phrasemongering and instead reach realities. If you cling to phrases you will of course say that in recent years the Anglo-American world has been at the forefront of the impetus for freedom. It has of course, in terms of copious words; but what is important is how things are in reality, not how they are propounded in words.

As you know I have repeatedly had to speak of the phrase-mongering of Wilsonism, which has long been spreading across the western world. From October 1918 onwards, in fact, it even took hold in central Europe. The illusion of empty phrases did not endure for long here but it did take hold for a while. I had to keep pointing it out,[11] and I recall a small movement emerging in response to my frequent reiteration of how empty, abstract and futile was everything related to the name of Woodrow Wilson. But even in America itself now, people are in a small way beginning to see through the vacuity and abstract nature of Wilsonism. Here it was not a matter of turning the people as such against Woodrow Wilson, of European antagonism to his project; but rather it was an antagonism that emerged from insight into the powers at work in our civilization. I wanted to characterize Wilsonism as the embodiment of abstract thinking of the most unreal kind. Wilsonist thinking has exerted such a one-sided influence because it assimilated the American impulse without really possessing the impulse of freedom—just talking about freedom is no proof that the freedom impulse is really present—or the impulse of true altruism.

The life of central Europe is out for the count, has more or less sunk into a terrible sleep. At present, Germans are compelled to think of freedom—not to speak of it merely in fine phrases as happened when people were sighing under Ludendorff's unfreedom. Urgent need of course brings to light some real understanding of the idea of freedom, but with souls and bodily forces lamed, with the impossibility of people really bestirring themselves to think keenly. In Germany we have all kinds of attempts to create democratic structures, but no democrats; we have a Republic but no republicans. All this is a phenomenon that emerges very especially as a characteristic of central Europe.

And turning to eastern Europe, the proletariat of the whole world has been praising the fruitfulness of Marxism. Lenin[12] and Trotsky[13] were able to put Marxism into practice—which has been plundering civilization, and signifies its downfall. And we're only at the beginning of these things.

Nevertheless, in Europe there lives a gift for ideally, spiritually establishing freedom. This Europe must truly enlarge itself by collaborating with the other peoples of the earth.

In Asia we can see the ancient Asiatic spirit dawning again. The leading cultural personalities in Asia—you need only think of the example of Rabindranath Tagore[14]—reveal in their whole manner of speaking that the old altruistic spirit is not dead. But there is now less possibility than there was in earlier times of achieving civilization through this third, only, of human civilizing impulses.

Because of all this, people today speak of so many things that really belong to the culture of decline, but they represent them as some kind of ideal. For years we have heard it proclaimed[15] that every nation must have the means to live in some way—I really don't know how—that accords with its own nature, or something similar. But now let me ask you this. What is a nation for people today, if they are honest? In reality it's just a phrase, not a reality. One can speak of a nation, of a people, if one speaks of a folk spirit as anthroposophy does—when this is founded on an underlying reality, but not when something purely abstract is meant. And those who speak of the freedom of peoples and so on, are speaking in the abstract, for they do not believe in the reality of a national spirit or character. Here lies the deep, inner untruth to which people pay homage: to have no belief in the reality of the national spirit and yet to speak of the freedom of the nation as if this nation were a reality for modern, materialistic people. What is the German people? Ninety million people that can be enumerated one by one! People do not believe in any self-contained nation as such, and yet they speak of these things, and think they are talking about realities, while all the time they are lying to themselves.

By contrast it *is* a reality to identify in Anglo-American culture a quest for cosmic connection, in European culture a quest for freedom, in Asiatic culture a quest for altruism. And now we should attempt to comprehend these three partial forces within a cosmic consciousness and, drawing on this consciousness, to say that the old culture, striving out of its partial element, must go under, and that to seek to sustain it really means to act counter to one's time rather than in harmony with it. A new civilization is needed, and must arise upon the ruins of the old. The ruins of the old are shrinking before our gaze, and we only properly understand our time if we have the will and the courage for something new. But what is new should not come from a merely Grecian or Roman sense of nation, nor from the global consciousness of modern people, but from a cosmic consciousness of a future humanity, in which we gaze upwards from the earth again to the cosmos. And this cosmos must not be seen in merely Copernican or Galilean terms. The Europeans learned to see earth's place in the cosmos in terms of mathematics, but they failed to acquire a true science and knowledge of this cosmos. In his own day Giordano Bruno[16] was certainly a great figure, a great individual; but today we need an awareness that where he saw only mathematical order, in fact a spiritual order reigns. The American does not intrinsically believe in a merely mathematical universe. From within his civilization he strives for knowledge of supersensible forces, albeit on a mistaken path. In Europe people learned to pursue all kinds of knowledge. But when Goethe characteristically asked what the nature of knowledge is, no further progress was made, and this was because Europe proved unable to enlarge its findings, for instance about the human being, into a greater cosmogony. Goethe discovered metamorphosis: the metamorphosis of plants, of animals, of humans. In his view of the skeletal system, the head is a transformed spine and spinal cord. This is a fine discovery. But all this must be developed further into an awareness of the fact that this head embodies the transformed human being from a last incarnation, while our limbs are a preparation for a subsequent incarnation. True science must be cosmic or will otherwise not be worthy of the name. Without incorporating the cosmos, as a cosmogony, science cannot provide us with inner, human impulses that sustain us through our lives. In today's world we cannot any longer live instinctively. We have to become conscious. We need a cosmogony and we need true freedom. We do not just need phrases about it, mere talk on the subject of freedom, but a real incorporation of freedom into our immediate existence. And this can only come about on paths that lead to ethical individualism.

And it was of course characteristic that the moment my book *The Philosophy of Freedom* was published Eduard von Hartmann,[17] who was one of the first to receive a copy of the book, wrote to me to say that the book should have a different title. Not *The Philosophy of Freedom* but 'Epistemological Phenomenology and Ethical Individualism'.[18] Well and good. It would have been a long-winded title, certainly, but not bad to call it 'Ethical Individualism'. Ethical individualism is nothing other than a personal realization of freedom. The best people simply failed to grasp that something such as I was urging in *The Philosophy of Freedom* was drawn from the actual needs and impulses of the time.

And if we look towards Asia, then Asia and Europe need to learn to understand each other. But if things continue as they have been, they will never do so. Asians look towards America and see that really there is only a kind of external mechanism of life at work there, of the state, of politics and so forth. The Asiatic does not have a sense for these outward mechanisms, but only for what emerges from the inmost impulses of the human soul. And the Europeans have to some degree concerned themselves with the nature of Asiatic spirituality, but so far, one can say, without much understanding. Nor have they come to unified agreement, and the way in which they have been at mutual odds has shown they did not know how to incorporate the real impulses of Asiatic culture into European culture with any understanding. Think of Blavatsky:[19] she sought to introduce all kinds of aspects of Indian and Tibetan culture into Europe. In another way Max Müller[20] tried to bring Asiatic culture to Europe. There are things in Blavatsky that are lacking in Max Müller, and vice versa. Simply in the judgement Max Müller has made about Blavatsky we can see how little real mutual engagement there has been. Max Müller thought that Blavatsky failed to bring a true Indian spirituality to Europe but only an imitation of it. He offers this metaphor: If people were to see a pig that just grunts they would scarcely be surprised; but if they saw a pig that speaks like a person, they would be astonished indeed.[21] What he meant by this surely was that he, with his version of Asiatic culture, was grunting like a pig, whereas Blavatsky was like a pig uttering human speech. It seems to me, though, that it is not of much interest when a pig grunts, but that it would awaken a good deal of interest if a pig suddenly ran about talking human language. The metaphor itself shows the search for a comparison that very much remains in the sphere of phrasemongering. But people today pay no heed to this; and if one accentuates the genuinely ridiculous aspect of such a statement, they object to the impropriety of doing so in regard to an acknowledged authority such as Max Müller. But the time has come to speak honestly and without dissembling. To do so requires us to place the secrets of civilization fairly and squarely before people: Anglo-Americanism has the gift for cosmic connection; Europe has the gift for freedom; Asia has the gift for altruism, for religion, for a fraternal socio-economic order.

These three dispositions must merge for all humanity. We must become people of the cosmos, and act from this standpoint. And then what the times really require can eventually arrive.

Lecture 5

DORNACH, 11 OCTOBER 1919

It is so late now that I will keep this lecture short, and leave for tomorrow the main point I wish to make in these three lectures. Tomorrow the eurythmy will come earlier on in the day and then the lecture can be of the proper length.

Last time I suggested that to counteract the forces of decline in our society today we need to differentiate between different populations across the globe and really recognize what lives in these different swathes of the earth's people: in the Anglo-Americans, in the Europeans and in the people of the East. We saw that the disposition to establish a modern cosmogony, a connection with the cosmos, is found above all amongst the Anglo-American peoples; that the capacity to develop the impulse of freedom lives in the European peoples; and that the impulse to develop altruism, religiosity and what is connected with this as human fraternity, is discernible amongst the peoples of the East. A new civilization can only be established if people across the globe find ways to really work together. For real collaboration between them to become possible, various things are necessary. We must open our eyes to the great lack in this modern civilization, to the forces of decline at work there. But we ought not to see everything at work there as bad. This would be unhistorical, firstly, and secondly would not lead to any positive outcome. The impulses within our civilization were once justified, and had their proper place and time. But everything that leads to decline in humanity's history does so because something that was right for a particular time and place survives into a different and now inappropriate place and time, and because, under certain ahrimanic and luciferic inspirations, people stay with what they have become accustomed to instead of seeking to participate in humanity's real progress.

Our era is proud of its scientific rigour. And yet from this science proceed the greatest social errors and disfigurements of our time. We must therefore shine a clear light upon the mechanisms of thinking, and on action too in so far as it is of course very much dependent on modern thinking.

In the context we were considering yesterday we saw how the earth's whole culture is composed of three strands: of scientific culture, political and democratic culture, and the culture of economic altruism, the latter basically looking back to an altruistic religious element. When people today—as I have already indicated—observe the forces at work in our social structure, they stay on the surface and are disinclined to penetrate deeper. In universities professors lecture on the economic wisdoms of the day in a way that is based on modern scientific methodologies. But what lives in human beings and human sensibilities is seen, more or less, as an indigestible gruel. No account is taken of the real facts.

Let us stay for a moment with European culture. What is its most salient trait? To understand this we have to go back a fairly long way and see how this European population, with all its religious, political, economic and scientific impulses, gradually emerged from more ancient Celtic origins and impulses when diverse later strata of the population interwove themselves with these origins—which are still, basically, present in the depths of our European culture. In contrast to the American West and the Asiatic East, a certain intellectualism reigned always in Europe. What I described yesterday as the intrinsic nature of Roman culture, the Roman element, could never have gained such sway if the underlying trait of intellectualism had not already existed within European civilization. Now intellectualism possesses two characteristics. Firstly, it is unable to bestir itself to entirely dismiss religious impulses. Under the influence of intellectualism, religious impulses acquire an ever more abstract character. And equally, intellectualism is unable really to develop the impetus to engage with practical economic life. You will see from the experiments currently underway in Russia how impossible it is for European intellectualism to bring order into economic life. What Leninism develops is the purest intellectualism. It is all conceptual, a social order constructed out of thinking. And the attempt is being made to foist this social system spun from thinking upon actual conditions existing between human beings. Over time it will become apparent in the most dire way how impossible it is to graft an intellectual conception on the social structure in this way.

People today are not yet willing to grasp the full import of these things. In the European populace lives the dire trait of somnolence, this inability of the whole human being to participate in what we so much need to stream through European society. But first and foremost we must grasp what underpins this European civilization, and the origin it has emerged from really. In its own intrinsic nature this European civilization has produced only a culture of intellectualism, a culture of thoughts. In our science reigns the sedate aridity of thinking, and this holds sway also in our social institutions.

We have experienced this intellectualism for many, many decades in the parliaments of Europe. There has been a palpable sense in all these European parliaments that they are informed by the intellectual and utilitarian perspective, an element lacking in energy, without any impetus for religious impulses, nor any either for economic impulses! Just think for a moment how we acquired our religious life. We can see from the whole historical development of this religious life that Europe itself possesses no intrinsic religious impulses. Consider how prosaic, infinitely prosaic was the world as the Roman Empire expanded—sober and prosaic in the extreme. And all this was just the beginning. Consider what Europe would have become if Roman culture, with its prosaic sobriety, had simply continued without the impulse—a religious impulse—that came over from the Asiatic East, if it had continued without the Christian impulse. What sprang forth from the womb of the Orient, and could never have emerged from the womb of Europe, this religious impulse, came towards us as a wave of culture, of civilization from the East. Europe after all at first did nothing other than stuff Roman legal concepts into this religious impulse arriving from the East, pervading it with sober, abstract, intellectual, juristic forms.

The eastern religious impulse was basically alien to European life, and remained so. It never entirely amalgamated itself with the European character. And in Protestantism, in a curious way, it has in a sense been separated out as though in a test tube. In a test tube you can watch how substances separate out from each other, and the same thing happened with the religious character of European civilization. In the sixth, seventh, eighth, ninth and tenth centuries there was something like an attempt to configure an inner unity between religious feeling and sensibility and scientific and economic thinking. But then, really in the same way as two substances separate out in a test tube, the two—the prosaic thinking of intellectualism and the religious impulse—diverged, and at last we had Protestantism, Lutherism: science on the one hand as one truth, and faith on the other as the other truth. The two are now irreconcilable! In fact it is seen as sacrilegious to try to imbue the contents of faith with the contents of thinking, to warm up the content of thought with that of faith. And then came the most prosaic thing of all, that most intellectual Kantianism, which set its critique of pure reason against a critique of practical reason, of ethics against science, creating the most terrible, yawning gulf between two things that must be felt and experienced as one within human nature. And European civilization still really continues to live with these circumstances, under which it will increasingly decline. The religious impulse from the East was assimilated as something alien, and did not unite organically with the rest of Europe's cultural and physical life. It is important to note this.

Look, enough misplaced praise has been heaped on the progress of modern civilization. This praise kept on flowing until millions of people had been murdered within our civilization and three times as many had been made cripples. Sanctimonious speeches were intoned from pulpits until the blood flowed freely and unendingly. This much-vaunted progress was proclaimed from pulpits until it showed itself to be a void. No salvation will come until we look these things squarely in the face. And now come all those of Leninist and other persuasions, reflecting on socialism and economic doctrine, and they imagine that the ideas that have long proven inadequate for governing European civilization will reform our economic order, our social order, without the need for any new ideas, for any new thinking.

I have, I think, previously spoken of the fine ideas that our scholars and academics arrive at in these fields. Very fine. And so I'd like to air these matters once again here. There is a famous economist called Lujo Brentano who wrote an article a while back entitled 'The Entrepreneur'.[22] Brentano tries to construct the concept of the capitalist entrepreneur and for this purpose gathers together various traits. The third such characteristic which he cites is that the entrepreneur uses the means of production in the service of humanity at his own risk, at his own peril. And now our good Lujo Brentano examines the function of the ordinary manual worker in society, and says that the manual labourer's means of production are his own physical capacity for work, and that he uses this in the service of society at his own risk and peril. Thus the worker is an entrepreneur, and there is no difference between them! And so you can see how completely confused scientific or academic thinking has become: people create concepts in which they can no longer make any distinction between two opposite poles.

But this isn't as apparent in Brentano's work as in that of a professor of philosophy in Bern,[23] who has written such an extraordinary number of books that he cannot have had enough time to think exactly what he was writing. Nevertheless he gave lectures on philosophy at Bern University. And in one of them we can read the following sentence: 'Civilization can only develop in the temperate zone, not at the North Pole—where it would freeze solid—nor at the South Pole, where it is hot compared to the North Pole, and civilization would burn up in the heat!' Strange to say, there really is a proper professor of philosophy who wrote so much so quickly that his writings include the idea that it is cold at the North Pole and hot at the South Pole!

The economic errors of our good friend Brentano are born, basically, from the same superficial appraisal of things as much else in Europe. What exists already is regarded as a given, and one's conceptual schemas are simply related to that. People learn this from scientific methodology: scientific institutes teach it, and people in our day—an era, supposedly, when no heed is given to authority any longer—simply parrot it back. When told that someone is an authority on something, they think this a reason to assume he is telling the truth. Rather than insight into the truth of a statement, people accept it because the person who made it is a supposed authority. And so economic realities are all regarded as equal in importance alongside each other, whereas in fact they are interpenetrating elements that must be examined separately.

Just as European civilization received the religious impulse flowing towards it from the East, so something else was necessary for its economic structure. As the fifth post-Atlantean era approached, towards the middle of the fifteenth century, this was also a time when events occurred that were to affect the whole of modern civilization and give it its basic character and countenance: the discovery of America, the discovery of the sea route past the Cape of Good Hope to the East Indies. This formed and determined our subsequent civilization. And Europe's whole economic development cannot be studied in terms of Europe alone. It is nonsense to think that studying economic factors in European society will reveal the economic laws at work there. We only unearth these laws if we continually recognize that Europe was able to expel or export countless things to America. And the whole structure of Europe only arose by virtue of the fact that there was a new world to be found over there in the West, to which Europe dispatched its economic impulse, just as it had received the religious impulse from the East. Its own economy developed under the regime of this current, this flow, just as its spiritual and cultural life developed under the influence of religious impulses from the East. European life, the whole background to the development of European civilization, developed in the context of these two streams over past centuries. Here you have European civilization in the middle, and from the East you have an influx of the religious impulse [see drawing, purple], while towards the West flowed the dispatch or discharge of the economic impulse. These things lived in the developing civilization of Europe.

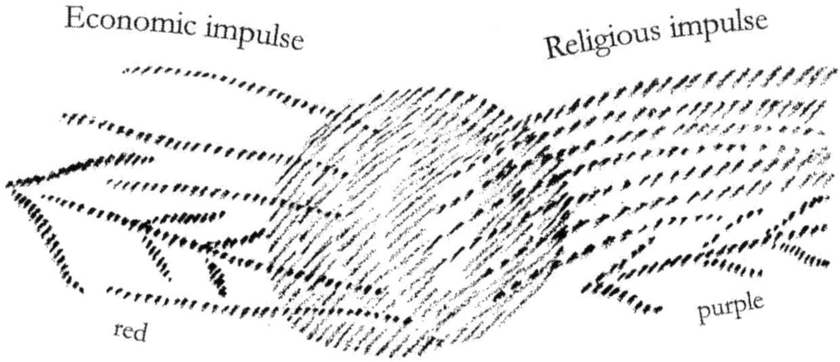

Board drawing 4

Now at the end of the nineteenth century this reached a certain crisis point: it started to falter, becoming more sluggish than it had been in the past four hundred years. Today we are still affected by this faltering, still live with its consequences. The religious impulse entered Europe as something alien, and gave rise to our cultural and spiritual life. And our economic life arose by continually diluting itself. If America had not existed, and our economy had been compelled to emerge by its own laws alone, it could not have continually scattered abroad what it could not use, and could not have developed in Europe as it did. Now this comes to a standstill, and so an inner escape must be found. From within, a means must be found to introduce into the proper channels what can no longer be effected by shipping things off elsewhere.

This must happen through threefolding. This must happen by really organically membering things that have become haphazardly interwoven. There is more than just one reason why the social organism should be membered in a threefold way—there are all kinds of reasons for it, scientific, economic, historical reasons. To make a proper assessment of the justification for a threefold social organism we must be able to survey all these diverse reasons.

It is important to say this today since modern people suffer from such conceptual poverty, one that has assumed really dire proportions. Anyone with a sense for ideas finds a really very small sum of ideas holding sway in our cultural life today. Wherever you look you find the same ideas, whether you're studying a work on physics, on geology, biology, psychology or whatever field you like: different facts but precisely the same ideas. The facts of psychology, for instance, consist really only of words, since people know the psyche only as a sum of words. If they speak of the will, it is just a word, and nothing is known of the real nature of the will. If they speak of thinking, they know nothing of the real nature of thinking, since they think only in words. Nor do they know anything about feeling. The whole field of psychology is a game of words today, spliced together in the most varied ways. Just as in a kaleidoscope the little pieces of glass assume different shapes and patterns, the same is true of our concepts. In our different disciplines they are cast into different arrangements, but there is only a very small sum of ideas that you continually encounter, which are grafted onto the facts. People do not try too hard to find concepts that correspond to reality, the ideas that really belong to the subject of enquiry. But these things go unnoticed.

A little while ago in a city in central Europe, radical socialists held a congress.[24] They were trying to work out a social structure for Europe, roughly the same as you can read about at present in a series of articles in the Basel journal *Vorwärts*.[25] The characteristic thing about this social structure, which people consider very ingenious and perfectly conceived, is that it was created by people who have never really had anything to do with economic life, who have never really acquainted themselves with the actual sources and driving forces in economic life. It was created by people who participated in politics in recent decades. And how did they do so? Well, either by being a voter or an elected representative. As a political candidate you were either elected in a first or second ballot. If you weren't elected in the first ballot, you might run out of election funds. These sums had been spent. During this first round of the campaign, the parties would have castigated their opponents, accusing them of being rogues and deceivers, or something still worse. Then came the second ballot. So far no party would have had a majority and now, in the second ballot, it was a question of electing one of the parties with a relative majority. At which point a different procedure came into force: you got your opponent, who until then had been a rogue, a deceiver and so on, to pay you back a third of the election funds spent in return for your backing of him. Suddenly your opponent, the rogue, was a man who needed to be elected. You got a third of your election funds back and, in the interests of recouping this sum, you became a supporter of the one who had previously been dismissed as a charlatan and so on. Someone had to be elected after all, and your candidate had no prospects of being elected; so you cut your losses by recouping a third of the funds you had spent.

So this is the kind of political life in which people participated. The political administration was subject to this kind of string-pulling, and people learned to exert political influence—they became adept with this whole political machinery, but didn't have a clue about economic life. People sought to graft the political ideas they acquired in the process—ideas which were of course very corrupt but were after all still political concepts—onto economic life, impose them on it. When realized, this would give rise to an economic life with a purely political structure. Today people confuse the structure of economic life with political structure, and are unable to keep separate things that have gradually become fused and entangled. But what we need today is growing insight everywhere into real conditions, something people are very averse to developing.

But it should not be thought that the true reality we seek through anthroposophically oriented spiritual science can be discovered under the influence of a civilization that tyrannizes over external reality with a few dogmatic concepts, rather than actually observing it. Anthroposophically oriented spiritual science aims to uncover true reality, and therefore it cannot be founded on the model provided by religious confessions of the past.

This was the enormously painful aspect of the old theosophical movement. What else was it really but the desire for a kind of extra religion? It did not consist of a new impulse arising amidst European civilization itself but only of feelings that had already existed in the old religious element. People had grown weary of these old religious concepts and feelings, and so they turned to something different; but what they turned to was pervaded by the same atmosphere as that of the old confessions. People wished to be pious in the same way as Protestants or Catholics, rather than finding what was really needed: a truly new religious impulse alongside other impulses; and this was because the European population had become accustomed to a life imbued with an alien, Asiatic religious impulse. That is the important thing. And until spheres that have only been artificially fused become organically interwoven, European civilization cannot make progress. This is a very serious matter. And this sense must imbue what needs to live in science, in economics, and in religiosity and political life.

Lecture 6

DORNACH, 12 OCTOBER 1919

In these observations I have suggested from all kinds of different angles that what is commonly regarded as the history of humanity is in many respects a superficial view of things. To understand contemporary circumstances, it is very important to avoid all illusions about the superficiality of this view of recent historical developments. We should not for example assume that what holds true as the latest phase of history in the fifth post-Atlantean era applies to the whole course of human history. We should not think this. But what I am about to say does hold true for this latest phase.

Socialists suggest that the reality of all human history is to be sought only in economic processes, in the dynamics of economic life, in class warfare that arises from these economic processes. In this view, these economic realities are the foundation for the superstructure of law, ethics, cultural life altogether, thus also art, religion, science and so forth. In terms of the whole of humanity's history this is of course nonsense. But we still need to ask what has given rise to this nonsensical view. It is due to there actually being some truth in this, if we consider only the latest phase of human evolution, our recent, modern era. Amongst the occurrences that inaugurated this new era we can refer, as yesterday, to upheavals in evolution that arose through the discovery of America, the discovery of the sea route to the East Indies. But we also see this latest phase of human evolution in terms of the Reformation, that great cultural upheaval that occurred at the beginning of the new era.

It is necessary today to recognize the real nature of the Reformation. If we draw on everything discussed yesterday by way of preparation, which can give us a deeper view of history, not a superficial one, we find that what was apparently a cultural transition at the beginning of modern times in fact arose from factors that were very largely economic. And insight into the economic foundations of the Reformation has led to the narrower view propounded by socialism that in fact all historical developments were only the result of class warfare and economic factors.

If we shed the light of truth and not illusion on what happened, and on the metamorphosis occurring at the beginning of modern history, we must discern a mighty shift in the population, one that occurred fairly rapidly at the beginning of the new era. This shift involved a change in ownership of land and territory. The leading figures who dictated and determined the structure of society prior to the Reformation lost this dominance during it. Far more than people realize, all ownership of land and estates was in the hands of the Church. This theocracy very largely dominated economic conditions in general prior to the Reformation. Those who owned lands and estates held it in a sense on behalf of authorities in some way connected with the Church.

If we study the course of history with a less idealistic and more truthful eye, we discover that almost everywhere in Europe estates were taken out of their old ecclesiastical ownership and transferred to worldly rulers. This was very much the case in England, and later on also in Germany to a large degree. Later on in Germany a large number of territorial rulers joined the Reformation. This was not however invariably due to wild enthusiasm for Luther or the others driving the Reformation but to a hunger for Church land, the longing to secularize Church estates and properties. Huge amounts of Church estate were transferred to worldly rulers, to regional barons. In England a large proportion of those who owned properties and estates were divested of these and emigrated to America. A large number of those who emigrated to America—and yesterday we looked from another angle at what underlay this—were expropriated owners of land in Europe. In other words, the changes and developments usually referred to as the Reformation were greatly influenced by economic factors. A superficial view sees this as a new spirit entering human souls resulting from the old Church incorporating too strong a worldly element into its spiritual outlook, sees this as the need to find a more spiritual path to Christ again and so on. But if we delve somewhat deeper, we see that an economic shift occurs with the transfer of ecclesiastical property to worldly people.

But this is connected with a very far-reaching fact of world history, and we only understand the diverse facts of modern history by looking back on a broader scope of human evolution. Here we need only look back to the phase of human evolution which we call the Egypto-Chaldean, which as you know ended in the mid-eighth century BC when the Graeco-Roman era began, and in turn lasted roughly to the middle of the fifteenth century.

If we go back to ancient Egyptian, ancient Chaldean culture, the ruling powers at that time were of a quite different kind from what they later became. Today people give little thought to the great upheavals that occurred in the course of history. In those times, which ended roughly in the middle of the eighth century BC, the rulers were people whom one could call initiates within the older traditions of spiritual science. The Egyptian pharaohs up to a certain point in time were definitely initiates: they were initiated into the secrets of cosmology and regarded what they had to do on earth in a cosmological context. If you state such a thing today you encounter difficulties of understanding, for the simple reason that modern people, with their modern consciousness, object that these initiates, the Egyptian pharaohs, and also the Chaldean rulers, did things that were highly questionable. Of course we might say that modern, uninitiated rulers also do some things that do not exactly accord with the highest moral standards, but this would be a misplaced objection here of course. We have to point out, though, that beyond the confines of the sense world there are not only good gods but also gods that act counter to human interests as these are usually regarded. This means that someone who is a real initiate will not inevitably act only out of good motives. In saying, as I do now, that the pharaohs were initiates, you only need recognize that they acted out of spiritual impulses. Spiritual impulses, sometimes very bad ones, lived in their will, and this cannot be disputed by anyone who has come to understand through anthroposophy that all kinds of divine, spiritual powers, supersensible powers, lie behind the world of the senses. Until the middle of the eighth century BC, the real rulers were those who could incorporate into their will, and not just their awareness, what divine, spiritual powers gave them. Then a time began during which, if we strip away all the illusions that our ordinary history veils it in, the real rulers were the priests. The worldly rulers themselves, even someone like Charlemagne, were more or less dependent on the priests. Military might in ancient times up to the middle of the eighth century was placed in the service of the initiates. In the fourth post-Atlantean era, the Graeco-Roman period up to the middle of the fifteenth century, soldiers were the mercenaries of the priests. And basically, campaigns such as the Crusades were essentially military expeditions on behalf of the priestly rulers. What was done had some connection or other with this ruling class of priests.

Thus in Egypto-Chaldean times rulers were from the initiate class, then from the mid-eighth century BC to the middle of the fifteenth century the class of priests ruled; and from this time onwards 'Homo economicus' became dominant in history. The names themselves don't matter much. As we move forward through history names matter less and less, but what underpinned and sustained the process of ruling and governing was the ability to engage in economic affairs. The important thing about the priests and initiates of olden times was that these dominant rulers could engage in economic circumstances, although they did this from higher perspectives. And then, in more recent history, the economic type likewise involved himself, really, in all aspects of social structure.

But this is connected with something else, which I pointed to already in relation to the initiate as ruler. The ruling initiate class worked through their will by incorporating into this will the spiritual impulses of higher worlds. This was no longer so in the priestly class. The priest type does not embody spiritual life in a full, fundamental sense and, for this reason, in civilizations where the priest was dominant, in European civilization, the intellect became the primary quality instead.

In Asia, in the Orient, spiritual life rather than intellectual life is the essential thing. You see, the civilization that still exists there has succumbed largely to decadence, but nevertheless there are remnants of something that was once initiate culture, spiritual culture. When the religious impulse of the Orient was carried over to Europe, it passed into the intellectual outlook of the priests. Initiation into realities, into the world of spirit, grew to be theology, an intellectual assimilation of the realities of the spiritual world. Theology is an intellectualized assimilation of the realities of the world of spirit. But this priest class, which intellectually assimilated spiritual realities and proclaimed them in an intellectual form, gave way at the beginning of the new era to the class of economists, to 'Homo economicus'. We can identify specific phenomena that show the emergence of this type of economic human being. And we will speak of this in a moment.

But we must of course first ask this: what causes such changes and transformations throughout history and evolution? It is due to something that in turn requires us to go deeper than a merely superficial view of history. It becomes clear, if you read what they write, that historians see no great changes occurring in the inner life of human beings during the course of history. Materialistic thinkers hold the view that an apelike being once wandered about on the earth, and from this the human being emerged—very slowly, of course, but modern science likes to see things developing slowly. Once the human being was here, his mind, consciousness and inner state underwent no great change. Today we may imagine ancient Egyptians to be a little more childlike than ourselves, not yet as 'clever' as we have become; but in general people think that the ancient Egyptians had an inner sensibility roughly resembling our own. In fact, if we look back to the time preceding the mid-eighth century BC, this sensibility and state of mind was quite, quite different from what it became after that period.

If you examine the soul configuration of modern people, and are only aware of this frame of mind, you cannot form any picture of what lived in someone prior to the eighth century BC. These people still had a living connection with their preceding incarnation. For the broad swathe of so-called pagan peoples other than the Hebrew-speaking peoples—for whom things were a little different—inner soul experience was very much the outcome of their preceding incarnations, preceding lives on earth. It was quite apparent to them that an experience of worlds of spirit filled them inwardly. They had no doubt at all that their essential aspect was not passed down to them by father and mother, but had descended from worlds of spirit to unite and combine with what came from their parents. The inner sensibility of these people was very much rooted in their spiritual culture. And therefore their society could be governed by initiates: by those who to some degree had been initiated into spiritual realities, and not only in thoughts, intellectually. In speaking of spiritual realities to people in those times, you were speaking of something they were wholly familiar with. Really all human beings saw themselves as centaurs: they saw their physical body as arising from physical heredity, and overlaid upon this was what had descended from worlds of spirit. Everyone knew this; everyone pictured themselves as a kind of centaur.

Then came the time that began with the eighth century BC, roughly the time when Rome was founded. Real spiritual connection was lost during this era—we have considered this previously from other points of view. But a certain spiritual connection remained with worlds of spirit through human intelligence. The human being no longer pictured himself as a centaur; he no longer felt that a higher, spiritual entity had descended and united with what came through heredity. Instead he had a clear awareness that his intelligence, his world of thoughts, was not dependent on his blood or physical corporeality, but that it was instead of spiritual origin.

We do not properly understand the great philosopher Aristotle if we do not know that in calling the highest aspect of the human soul *dianoetikon*[26] he was very much aware that this highest part of the soul, which is intellectual in quality, has filtered down from worlds of spirit and soul. Aristotle was fully aware of this, and indeed people continued to be fully aware of it during early Christian times. This awareness that human intelligence has a divine, spiritual origin, was only lost during the fourth century AD. At that point people gradually stopped believing that their faculty of thought filtered down to them at birth from soul-spiritual worlds. A great change occurred within the human soul. If we go back to the first three Christian centuries, we find that people then knew both that they were descended from their parents but also—in the same way that their eyes knew light directly, without cogitating on it—that their intelligence came from the gods. This was immediate awareness for them, like the immediacy of a sense perception. Only in the course of the fourth century AD did people increasingly gain a different feeling: of their head as a bony cavity—which it is, of course, as we have discussed in the past—containing the organs of intelligence, in turn connected with physical heredity, with blood relationship. Only in this era, with the transition from belief in the divine nature of intelligence to physically inherited intelligence, could intellectualization of the religious impulse, as one might call it, be accomplished by the dominant priest class. And once this intellectualization was far advanced, and the view of intelligence had become inseparable from the human body, the dominance of the priests also came to an end. The priests could only continue to rule while it was still possible to communicate old traditions of the divine nature of intelligence. 'Homo economicus' emerged in history at the moment when belief in the divine nature of intelligence had faded and people increasingly saw the physical human being as the essential bearer of thinking, as its organ.

But we must not forget how the priests fought to maintain their dominance and still do so today. Those familiar with Catholic theological literature, for instance, know how the class of priests still battles with all possible philosophical arguments to prove that the intelligence within us is something given to us from without. Read any of this literature, and you will find no denial of something regarded as incontrovertible by people today—that all other faculties inhere in human corporeality except intelligence. Catholic theology seeks to retain intelligence as something divine and spiritual that has no intrinsic connection with human corporeality. In general the human mind does not accept this. In general people feel that the body is what enables us to think, the basis of intelligence. Thus increasingly people have come to regard themselves as really only a physical being. 'Homo economicus' could only emerge under the influence of a kind of spirituality that assumes we are only physical beings.

There are therefore deeper spiritual reasons why 'Homo economicus' rose to the surface. And 'surface' is about right, since this was something narrowly and superficially interpreted in socialist theories. The human being as economic species has been predominant since the Reformation. And so you can see what spirit holds sway in the faiths and confessions that have arisen since the Reformation. Let us have no illusions about this spirit. On the one hand we have mundane science, with the technology penetrating ordinary everyday life and its rejection of all faith—religious matters are not supposed to disturb the sphere of this externalized science. Faith, meanwhile, is meant to be prettily conserved in a separate compartment, as far as possible from the realities of life! Science in one compartment, with its own accounts; religious faith in another compartment, likewise with its own separate accounts. Ne'er the twain shall meet! The economic human being desires faith, desires even to be pious, the more pious the better. You can see him heading for church on Sundays, prayerbook demonstrably in hand. But religion must never muddy the ledger of financial accounts, except of course for the sacrilegious phrase ('With God') that precedes them.*

* Translator's note: The words 'With God' were once used on the first page of German bookkeeping ledgers.

Religion must be kept at arm's length from financial matters. Otherwise one might easily conclude that in many respects the Reformation was only a roundabout way of secularizing and confiscating Church assets, a means whereby worldly rulers could seize them. A German prince or an English lord could not have baldly stated the intention of creating a new era in world history by dispossessing those who once owned all property. Modern socialists say it of course: we are expropriating the owners of land and property! But this was not something said at the beginning of the modern era. They did it but drew a veil across their actions by saying they were establishing a new religious confession. People are then ignorant of what underlies their piety. But they take pleasure in this illusion under which they hide the real reasons for their pious faith. And in this way 'Homo economicus' rose to the surface.

The sense of experiencing a spiritual reality within gradually faded. That is the deeper, spiritual cause of what happened. If we go still further back, to before the third post-Atlantean epoch, which ended in the mid-eighth century BC and started in the third and fourth millennium BC, we arrive at a structure again entirely different. However paradoxical it may sound to modern ears, no one in the fourth or fifth millennium BC believed that his descent from mother and father was of essential importance. In those days people were still sure that their essential being had descended from the heavens, if I can express it like that. They did not think of themselves as having an earthly origin but a spiritual one. And the Jews spoke of the epoch when people began to feel their human nature in their physical flesh as the Fall, as the beginning of 'original sin'. This first took hold of them at the beginning of the third post-Atlantean era, when they began to attribute a part of themselves to physical heredity, to father and mother and to blood relationship, thinking only that a spiritual element overlaid this physical matrix. It took hold of them again a second time when they began to regard the element of intellect as something inherited, as something connected with corporeality. And other 'Falls' will come in future.

In our own time our task is to return to spirituality in a different way. To do so we must be able first to regain a spiritual intellectualism. It must be possible for us to give our earthly life a meaning within which something spiritual becomes discernible. If for instance we consider things contained in my book *Occult Science*, it cannot be said that the intellectuality used to comprehend these is bodily in origin. Using bodily reason we cannot arrive at what is said there about the cosmos and the human being. This therefore involves re-educating ourselves to comprehend an intellectualism that is spiritual. Modern humanity will have to first reconcile itself to seeing intellectualism as something divine and spiritual again. And after this it will be possible to embark again on a return to spirituality as such. This is a task that humanity must take up consciously: to return to spirituality firstly by spiritualizing intelligence. Human beings must learn again to think in a way that is imbued with spirituality. The best way to begin to do this is to comprehend ethical matters and to lead ethical concerns back to moral imagination, to the kinds of moral intuitions I described in my *Philosophy of Freedom*. If—as I expressed it there—one sees in the moral sphere something that draws its impulses directly from the world of spirit, this is the beginning of spiritualizing the intellect. I first expressed this quietly and cautiously in my *Philosophy of Freedom*, since at that time, in the nineteenth century, one could not expect people to countenance much in the way of spirituality.

'Homo economicus', who emerged with the Reformation, really saw his task as being to make all intellectualism into a physical, bodily matter. This 'Homo economicus' in the age of the Reformation quickly sundered himself from a spiritual understanding of earthly human life. I can cite a few examples to show this. In the first part of the sixteenth century, Thomas Cromwell[27]—not to be confused with Oliver Cromwell—was living in England and was highly influential in the introduction of Reformation principles into that country. James I[28] wished to save the old priestly dominance; and we best understand him if we see him in this light—as the preserver of priestly influence and rule. But others thwarted these plans, among them Thomas Cromwell, an early representative of 'Homo economicus'. We can only understand Thomas Cromwell if we know that he is one of those who tarried only briefly in the world between death and rebirth, before being reincarnated on earth. Amongst ruling, leading individuals in more recent times there are an extraordinary number who spent only a short period in the world of spirit before their present life. As I have often mentioned, one of the most significant phenomena in recent history is the selection of the least fit as rulers. I've been saying this on various occasions for many years. Our rulers and leaders are not the best of the bunch. The times have led to a situation in which the best today remain in the lower echelons whereas those promoted to high positions are often not the best by any means. And this 'selection of the unfittest' is due to the fact that they had only a very short intervening period between their last life on earth and their present one. We find this to be true of a great many of the leading personalities of modern times: a speedy return to earth after only a short period in the world of spirit. This means they are little imbued with spirit: they have assimilated few spiritual impulses in their life between death and rebirth. In consequence they are impregnated instead all the more with everything that only the earth can endow them with.

The 'Homo economicus' types are those who had lived only a short time in the world of spirit, and were entirely pervaded by what only the earth as such can give. This is not to say that there have not also been important figures in modern times who spent longer periods between death and rebirth; but they were kept under. This was something dictated by the destiny of historical developments, by the general karma of humanity.

And these facts have influenced humanity's culture today. It really is woeful to see the very common phenomenon in modern times of people who are far, far inwardly superior looking up to certain authority figures who are far, far worse in nature. This is a general phenomenon today. Revered authorities are truly not the elect, not superior types of human being. A time has arrived when the adulation and acclaim of modern civilization should fall quiet so that we can instead perceive and engage with actual, unvarnished realities. People must try to accustom themselves to regard life in terms of the inner configurations of souls rather than superficial glances. And one of the facts that plays in here is the need to distinguish between people who spent a longer period in the world of spirit between death and rebirth, and those who tarried there for a shorter period.

We need to perceive human beings from a spiritual perspective. Only when we do so will it become possible to bring conscious harmony into our social structure. Deeper insight into what is needed in society today can only be gained if we seek this insight on the basis of spiritual perceptions and knowledge.

During these three days I felt it my duty to show you how we must consider modern civilization in regard to the possible further evolution of humankind. You see, our earth, with everything on it, has entered upon its period of decline and decadence. I have often mentioned that insightful geologists are already pointing to this. In the context of a very rigorous, precise study of geology, purely external, physical evidence can show that the earth is already crumbling away, that earth's ascending path of evolution has come to an end, and that we are, really, wandering about on earth's fragmenting lump of rock and soil. But it is not only earth's mineral realm that is crumbling but organic nature too, organic creatures, are declining. The bodies of plants, animals and human beings are no longer in a flourishing phase of evolution but are now in decline. We no longer have the organization we had until the fourth century AD, or in the ancient Greek period. Our organization is degenerating, and the earth has entered into decadence along with us. The physical earth is declining and degenerating. I first pointed to this phenomenon many years ago in a lecture in Bonn,[29] but mostly people do not pay sufficient attention to such things. We inhabit brittle and perishable bodies. But at the same time we must consider what goes hand-in-hand with this: it is precisely because our bodies are brittle that we can develop spirituality all the more if we dedicate ourselves to this.

If I can draw this schematically, the bodies of ancient times [left-hand drawing, white] were fully pervaded by their spirituality [red]:

Board drawing 5

the body sucked up spirituality everywhere. Nowadays our body is largely brittle, in decadence, and spirituality [right-hand drawing, red] sprinkles out of it everywhere, becomes free of the body.

If we consider this carefully, it is apparent that we can grasp the spirituality inwardly in our soul precisely because of the brittleness of our bodies.

Because of this brittleness, however, we must not rely on the physical but instead turn to the spiritual element. Everything physical is growing brittle, is already in decline on the earth, and we should not place our hope any longer in this physical level of things. Instead we can only expect something of what—to put it trivially—is sprinkling out precisely because the physical realm is in decline: the spirit and soul.

From this you can see one thing: through our bodies we are connected with earth's physical conditions, which come to expression in society in economic conditions. Since all now is growing brittle, all is in decline, economic conditions are likewise growing decadent. It is idiotic to think that economic circumstances can be regenerated without more ado by economic circumstances. To dream today of some economic paradise on earth brought about by purely economic factors is like trying to galvanize a corpse into life again. If therefore you take all that exists today as purely economic theory, and let people tell you how economic life should be established on economic principles, in accordance with the laws intrinsic to it, how production relationships should be configured, how we should pass from private ownership to common ownership and so on, you will find that it is all based on the false belief that economic life can be regenerated through economic life itself. In fact, everything physical in nature is in intrinsic decline, also in economic life. If something is in intrinsic decline, it can only ever be healed for short periods. In other words, we need instead a remedy for this economic life that is continually inwardly collapsing. If economic life were left to itself, and if people made of it what Lenin and Trotsky seek to make of it, it would just go on waning, declining and collapsing. For this reason we need instead to heal economic life with its opposite pole: that is, the autonomous life of spirit which is its reverse. If you have a patient or someone who might fall ill at any moment, you must keep calling on the doctor. If you have an economic life that is continually on the point of collapse because of the very nature of earth's evolution, you need to counteract this continually with the healing quality of an inner life of spirit. That is the inner connection. Acquiring an independent life of spirit is connected with a healthy cosmogony, or connection with the cosmos. And without an independent life of spirit, as a continual healing wisdom alongside an economic life with its continual tendency towards decline, humanity will not progress. It is idiocy to try to regenerate economic life only through economic factors. We must instead draw on the healing potency of an autonomous spiritual life and set it alongside this economic life, with the bridge of the neutral life of rights spanning these two. Unless we can recognize that the earth's physical life is already degenerating we will never properly understand what our modern era requires. It is a failure to recognize this that leads to so many people today believing that economic life itself can conjure forth the means to regenerate economic life. This can't be done. Only an independent life of spirit set alongside economic life will keep economic life in motion. And this mysterious connection in life can be properly understood only by those who can perceive it from the point of view of a truly modern cosmogony.

Consider what a serious position we are in if people run headlong towards ruin because they still think that economic life can be regenerated by its own powers—because they cannot recognize what sprinkles from the brittleness of physical existence, becoming autonomous, and becoming available then as continual powers of healing. People ask what means can be employed to counteract revolutions. Well, the revolution will come once enough crises have accumulated their impulses of demise and destruction. You can only counteract revolutions by continually employing the strength that works against them. If you do not balance economic life with a continual healing life of spirit, economic life will gather and compress itself into revolutions.

It is essential to realize the full gravity and significance of these things, and not to think one can simply play around with spiritual science. One can't. A Sunday sermon cannot be bodged together from true spiritual science. The kinds of habit that people acquired from their old religious confessions, seeking only to develop an inner, voluptuous enjoyment through all sorts of doctrines about reincarnation and karma, is not what these teachings allow if one takes them seriously. These teachings seek to engage with life, to become deeds by virtue of their very nature. Thus it is not some pleasant subjective mood to shape what lives in spiritual science also into all sorts of social ideas, but instead really a self-evident necessity, intrinsic to all this. Of course, anyone who speaks of evolution in the modern, scientific sense and in fact has no inkling of the fact that an ascent and flourishing first occurs which later gives way to a process of decline, will likewise be unable to understand that we have already entered the phase of decline in earthly evolution. He will seek to elaborate forces of regeneration from degenerating processes, and this can no longer be done.

What I wanted to impress on you above all in these three lectures was the profound gravity of spiritual science. It is not something to be played around with. Yes, people may dilute it into all sorts of mystical sectarianism, but playing around with it like this is a very bad idea. You cannot play around with spiritual science.

There are many opponents of what we stand up for in this anthroposophically oriented science of the spirit. Almost all those who dabble their toes in 'mystical' matters will be opposed to us. If they want to dabble merely, they will not find spiritual science to their liking since they have no desire to feel the full seriousness of life. This is why there are so many opponents of spiritual science, especially those who like dabbling their mystical toes in all kinds of puddles. A new anti-spiritual science impetus has come about recently, driven by people who object to what they say is its scientific character whereas, in their view, true experience of spiritual worlds must emerge from direct, immediate experience of the spirit, unsullied by anything scientific. Likewise we have recently been opposed in an area, Munich, where we have in fact accomplished much work but from which something murkily mystical is now increasingly emerging. A mystical book has been published in Munich, albeit by a different publisher, which basically seeks to embody such an impulse, and is entitled 'Of the Living God'.[30]

To apprehend these things at a time in which society is in such a parlous state shows us how much spiritual frivolity and cynicism exist today. We must give serious attention to the way spiritual life is being sucked forth from the decline and degeneration of our times. We must be able to set ourselves keenly and without prejudice against the decline of the earth, since what dies physically gives birth to living spirituality. But at the same time, as anthroposophically oriented spiritual scientists, who really feel and sense the nature of spiritual things, we must develop a fine sense for all superficial dabbling in spiritual matters; and nothing should be less worthy of our sympathy than any kind of sectarianism, any kind of mystical dabbling. For this does not penetrate worlds of spirit. On the contrary, it bars the way to the spiritual world. But ways into the spiritual world are exactly what we need if we are also to make social progress. That is why the time has come now to consider the most important question of life with full seriousness: what can we actually do to energetically take up impulses that truly accord with our times?

Look. This building stands here.[31] It stands and waits for the world to take it seriously, for people really to see that it was consciously constructed, placed into a time of decline, in such a way as to capture and absorb the spirit from our era. No belief should hold sway here that it is possible to preserve the old, all that is ripe for decline and decadence. Rather, the belief should reign here that a spiritual element, which must in no way resemble the past, can be drawn forth from ongoing degeneration. This cannot be accomplished through small cultural metamorphoses. Only great cultural impulses can bring about necessary human progress towards the future. Let us study how to become strong enough to really absorb the new impulses. We must have the courage to tell people clearly what it means that the earth is in decline, and that the civilization surviving until now is accompanying this decline. But from it we should save a new spirituality, which can be taken over into other worlds once the earth has fully succumbed to its downfall.

With this building must be connected the endeavour to work in full consciousness towards a renewal of art, science and freedom. Embodied in the forms of this building is an attempt, if you like, to scorn everything from the past. Thus we should really have the courage to take hold of the sustaining fact that this building stands here. We will not succeed by merely tinkering with things instead of working consciously and publicly to present to humanity the need for a new culture of the spirit. This alone will be the true point of departure for a new, social culture. Social impulses will no longer be drawn from economic factors but can only be implanted from the spiritual realm into the economic domain. And we have to realize that the time of 'Homo economicus' is past, that another type of human being must come: the cosmic human being who knows that besides physical, earthly heredity there lives in him also the forces of the sun, of the moon, the starry heavens, of the supersensible world. We should impress this on people in forms in which they can understand it, and only then can we make a fitting contribution to humanity's real progress. Simply passing on mystical teachings will get us nowhere at all. Our mysticism must become a real, active life of spirit.

That's what I wanted to draw to your attention. Really, without being immodest, we should regard this Dornach building as the starting point for a great world movement, a truly international one encompassing all areas of spiritual and cultural life. This building here should become the point of departure for stripping away any inclinations we might still have for declining, waning culture, instead encompassing an impulse truly focused on a renewal of humanity's consciousness. If we could realize in the world a new point of departure for capturing spirit from the decline of the physical earth, and if we could establish this Dornach building as a monument to this new impulse, trying to direct people's attention to what is intended here, then we would fulfil the true aims of anthroposophically oriented spiritual science. But we must bestir ourselves to create something that really speaks to humanity in a way that it can hear, that says: Look, what we are doing here really does seek to cultivate the further development of scientific, artistic and religious consciousness. If we are able to speak of this positive impulse, we will accomplish far more than if we simply attempt to accommodate ourselves to all kinds of things that others want. We should keep in mind that something new must enter our will and intent. If we can do this we will fulfil a worthy task. But in this respect we should sometimes speak with our souls, in this way really seeking to take up the task of anthroposophy.

Lecture 7

DORNACH, 17 OCTOBER 1919

TODAY I want to speak about some fundamental insights of initiation science, and this will provide a basis for our further reflections tomorrow and the day after. Firstly I want to point to something that lies in every human mind but is not usually grasped with sufficient clarity. In speaking of such things, we are always starting from a modern perspective in the sense I have often referred to here: that knowledge and insights hold true for a specific era, and even for a particular geographical region, rather than universally and forever. So, for example, certain angles on knowledge apply to European civilization while others are relevant to the Orient. Now I am sure that we are all aware that our knowledge lives between two poles. On the one hand every person is aware of the knowledge we acquire through sense perception. In a simple, naive way we come to know the world through our senses, but then we also combine what we see and hear, what we receive through any of our senses. And basically what science provides in the West is nothing other than a combination of the sensory information available to us.

But every person will also feel that there are other kinds of knowledge, and that we cannot possibly be whole human beings in everyday life if we do not add another form of knowledge to this first kind. Besides the ideas we develop through natural perception, and by means of which we explain various phenomena in nature, we also possess ethical ideas, moral ideals, upon which we feel that our actions are based. We allow these ideas to rule and govern us in our everyday life. And surely every person feels that the one pole of our knowledge, that of sense perception and the rational insights connected to it (for rational understanding is only an adjunct to sense perception), usually does not rise to the level of moral ideas. Moral ideas exist; but as we pursue scientific enquiries, for instance, we cannot derive these moral ideas from our observations of the plant world, of the mineral world or in any other branch of science. This is the tragic aspect of our time, in fact, that people seek to discover ideas for social action by employing scientific methodology. Healthy common sense can teach us that we can never succeed in this. Moral ideas exist in a different sphere of life. And our life really is subject to the sway of these two streams: of natural perception on the one hand, and of moral perceptions on the other.

If you have read my *Philosophy of Freedom* you will know that the highest ethical ideas that we need as human beings can come to us by grasping moral intuitions, and that these ethical ideas, once we possess them, are the foundation for our freedom. On the other hand you may also know that certain philosophers highlight a kind of gulf between natural knowledge on the one hand and ethical knowledge on the other. The philosophy of Kant[32] is based on this same gulf, this abyss, which it cannot completely bridge. This is why Kant writes a 'Critique' of theoretical reason, or of 'pure reason' as he puts it, in which he engages only with the knowledge of nature, with what he has to say about this knowledge of nature. And on the other hand, he offers a *Critique of Practical Reason* where he writes of moral ideas. We can say that he sees all human life as springing from two separate roots, each of which he describes in his two major 'Critiques'.

Now it would of course be a poor outlook for humankind if there were no bridge connecting these two poles of our inner life. If we give serious attention to spiritual science on the one hand and to the challenges of our time on the other, we are inevitably led to ask where this bridge between moral ideas and natural ideas can be found.

In this lecture today, in relation to discovery of this bridge, I will start from what I will call a historical perspective. From our reflections here you will know that in ancient times people had a state of soul and sensibility that was different from what it later became. The emergence of Christianity really represents a deep incision in humanity's whole evolution. And only if we understand what emerged and developed in human evolution as Christianity arose can we begin to understand human nature at all.

Before this emergence of Christianity we find, if we overlook Judaism (as we mentioned here recently[33]), the whole scope of pagan culture. Judaism was after all only a preparation for Christianity. This whole pagan culture was very different in kind from our present Christian culture. The further back in time we go, the more we find it to be a unified culture, one primarily founded on human wisdom. I know that people today feel offended if you suggest that the wisdom of ancient times was more advanced than they themselves are nowadays. Nevertheless, it was so. In ancient pagan times, across the whole globe, a wisdom existed that lay closer, far closer to the deep origins of things than our modern knowledge, especially our modern science. And this old, very ancient knowledge was of a very immediate and specific kind: a knowledge deeply connected with the spiritual reality of things. In knowing the reality of things, human beings at that time received something into their souls. An especially distinctive aspect of this ancient pagan wisdom they received—passed to them by the initiates of the mysteries, as you know—at the same time contained both natural and moral knowledge. People today overlook this very significant truth in the history of humanity's evolution only because the outer records of history do not delve far enough back into fully characteristic periods of ancient pagan wisdom. Historical knowledge does not reach far enough back to comprehend times when people, as they looked up to the stars, received from there wisdom which firstly explained to them the course and passage of the stars themselves but secondly also taught them how they should conduct themselves in their lives here on earth. Somewhat metaphorically, but also to a good degree objectively, we can say that in ancient Egyptian and Chaldean culture people read natural laws from the course of the stars but also read there precepts governing what they should do on earth. The codicils of the ancient Egyptian pharaohs, for instance, contain precepts about what should become law. It is true to say that over many centuries prophecies were made of what should later become law, and that everything these codicils contained was read from the stars' trajectories. Thus in those ancient times there was no such thing as the astronomy we know today, which consists only of mathematical laws of the movements of stars and planets, but instead a science of the cosmos which was at the same time a science of morality and ethics.

The questionable nature of modern astrology, which in some cases is very amateurish, is that it often lacks a sense of the whole—of the laws it identifies being at the same time moral laws. This is a very significant thing, extraordinarily significant.

As humanity developed, this primordial knowledge, this ancient wisdom, was largely lost. And to this is due the fact that certain secret schools (which really ended in any serious way at the end of the eighteenth century, certain secret schools in the West also) continually pointed to a lost science, to what they called the 'lost Word'. Usually later followers no longer even knew what had been meant by the word 'Word'. But this was based on a certain reality, and if you read Saint-Martin[34] you can still find echoes of what was felt very clearly up to the eighteenth century—that in ancient times people had possessed a spiritual knowledge they received at the same time as natural laws, and that this contained their moral science too, and that this had been lost already in the eight centuries preceding the emergence of Christianity. In fact we might say that more ancient Greek history is largely that of a gradual loss of ancient wisdom.

Nietzsche[35] called the pre-Socratic philosophers the 'philosophers of the tragic age of the Greeks': Heraclitus, Thales, Anaximenes, Anaxagoras. I wrote about them in my book *Riddles of Philosophy* in so far as one can write of them for humanity today in outward terms. If you read their works you find, in sentences that have survived—like oases in a desert—the last echoes of a great, comprehensive knowledge and perception that existed in the ancient days of humanity. What Heraclitus says, and what Thales, Anaxagoras and Anaximenes say, feels like humanity's loss of memory of its ancient, primordial wisdom, with only the odd, fragmentary phrase surviving from it. The few sentences that we still have of the works of these philosophers, from the seven sages of ancient Greece,[36] are like fragments or shards of memory.

And then, in Plato's works, we find still a kind of clear awareness of this primordial wisdom, while Aristotle transforms this all into external human wisdom. The core of it increasingly vanishes in the works of the Stoics and Epicureans. The ancient wisdom survives only as a kind of legend. This is how it was in Greek times.

The Romans, who were by nature a prosaic, hard-headed people, lacked all sense of this primordial knowledge, which they turned into abstractions. That this should happen—loss of primordial wisdom—was necessary for humanity's evolutionary journey. People could never have developed freedom if the *ur*-wisdom they received by means of their atavistic clairvoyance had remained in them with its original intensity and significance. But bound up with it were all the moral impulses with which humankind had been endowed from divine heights. This had to be preserved. Human beings had to preserve their moral impulse.

And among the many things we have already expressed about the Mystery of Golgotha is this: that the divine principle descending to the earth through the human being Jesus of Nazareth sustained the moral fabric that had gradually been torn to shreds as primordial wisdom faded and died away. However paradoxical it may seem to people today, an ancient wisdom existed [see drawing on page 95, white] and it was bound up with the human being's moral power, moral wisdom. This [red] was an intrinsic part of it. Now the old primordial wisdom grew dim and could no longer be the bearer of the moral impulse.

This moral impulse had in a sense to be taken under the shield and protection of the Mystery of Golgotha [see drawing on page 97, yellow] and it was further transmitted for western civilization as the

Board drawing 6

Christ impulse that sprang from the Mystery of Golgotha, into which was infused a kind of moral essence of the ancient primordial wisdom.

It is very remarkable to trace the science, the wisdom living in western civilization until the eighth or ninth century AD. If you look at my *Riddles of Philosophy* you can read there a brief account of western knowledge up to that point. And really there is nothing in this development of thought that we would still describe as 'knowledge' in our own time. This latter-day knowledge has emerged since the mid-fifteenth century, since the time of Galileo—no longer inwardly intuited, inwardly experienced primordial wisdom but external traditions of knowledge passed down. I have often told you the story about Galileo. It's a true story not fabricated. Galileo was having difficulty persuading a friend of the truth of something he was stating.[37] Like other people at that time, his friend was used to accepting whatever Aristotle or other traditional authorities said. Everything people learned in those days was based on tradition—what Aristotle had written was simply passed on. Well, this learned friend of Galileo believed, with Aristotle, that the nerves proceed from the heart. Galileo was trying to show him that empirically the corpse would tell a different story: that the nerves issue from the head, from the brain. Galileo's Aristotelian friend would not believe this, so Galileo showed him a corpse, pointed to the fact that nerves issue from the brain and not the heart, and expected his friend to believe the evidence of his eyes. But instead he said that this only 'appeared' to be true. Appearance suggests that the nerves issue from the brain but Aristotle, he said, tells us the opposite. And if compelled to decide between the appearance of things, the evidence of his eyes, and what Aristotle says, the man insisted on crediting Aristotle rather than nature! This actually occurred. And in our time we are experiencing something similar, except it is the other way round.

You see, the knowledge in those days was all tradition. New knowledge only arose in the time of Galileo, Copernicus and such figures. And through these centuries, a moral impetus was sustained by Christianity, was largely bound up with the religious element. This was not the case in pagan culture, where people knew that by receiving cosmic wisdom they also received a moral impetus at the same time.

Then came the middle of the fifteenth century with a new impetus which broke entirely with all forms of ancient wisdom, even if the latter had been present still only in the form of tradition. It is extraordinarily interesting to see the fury with which figures such as Giordano Bruno raged at old, traditional wisdoms. Bruno really gets furious and lambasts the traditional memory of ancient wisdom. Something entirely new arises. We have to see this new element as a whole new departure unless we are to relinquish almost all understanding of humanity's evolution.

If we indicate the Mystery of Golgotha here [drawing, yellow], we can say that the moral impetus continues [red]. So what was sustained from an older time, carried forward into a newer era through the Mystery of Golgotha, in the direction indicated here [arrow pointing right]? It was an end. And as we approach these later times, the ancient wisdom fades away, even in the forms handed down as tradition. Though it bubbles on in waves as tradition [white] something new begins with the fifteenth century, a new beginning.

It is true to say that we are still within this beginning phase. The few centuries that have passed since the mid-fifteenth century have

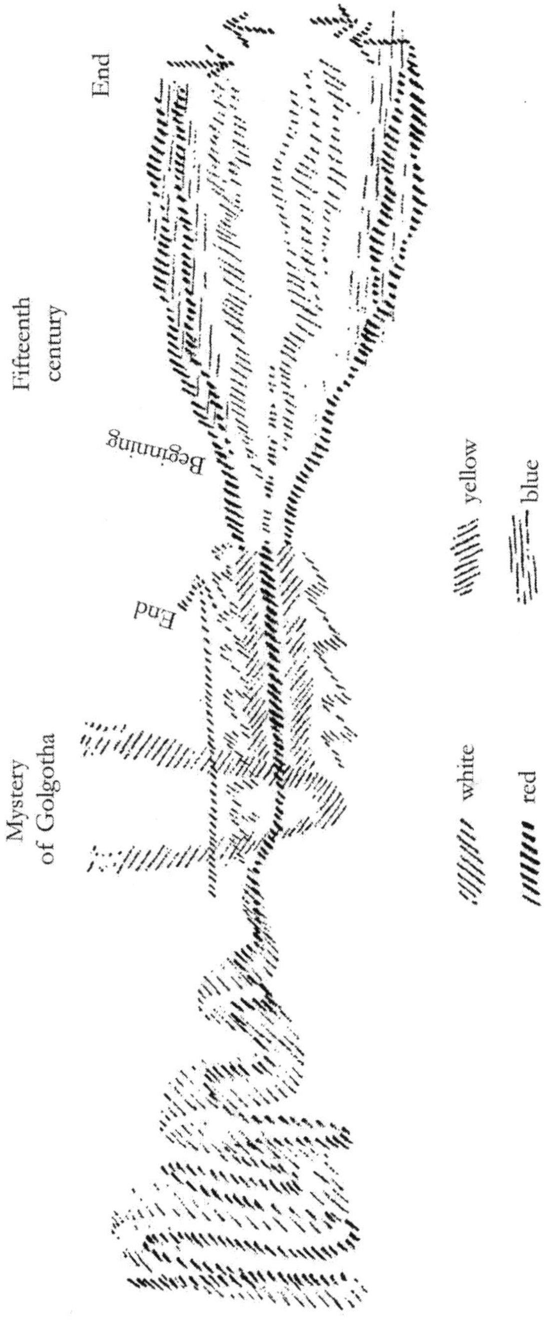

Board drawing 6/7

brought us modern science; but nevertheless we have not yet got far beyond these beginnings.

But what kind of wisdom is this? Well, in stark contrast to the ancient pagan wisdoms, it characteristically contains no moral impulse. However much we study these new wisdoms, these Galileo wisdoms in various branches of science such as mineralogy, geology, physics, chemistry, biology and so on, we will never draw from this knowledge of nature any kind of moral impetus.

It is a great illusion to believe that we can found the 'social sciences' on science. We will never be able to squeeze an ideal for human action from the kind of knowledge of the laws of nature we have today. This knowledge is still in its infancy, and we can only hope that, as it keeps evolving, it will come to a point where it can once again incorporate moral impulses as such. But if it were only to evolve in the way so far characteristic of it, this could not give rise to moral impulses. Instead this knowledge of nature must now also develop a new, supersensible knowledge [blue], which can in turn contain the beams of moral will [red]. And when the beginning that arose in the mid-fifteenth century comes to its end at the end of the earth itself, then supersensible knowledge will be able to flow together with sense knowledge [white] so that a unity arises from both [arrows].

When someone versed in ancient, pagan wisdom, or someone who acknowledged this wisdom, received it from his mystery initiates, he received simultaneously both natural knowledge and cosmic knowledge, a knowledge of humanity's origins and of morality, and this gave him a moral impetus for his actions. These two were one.

Today we must try to see that we gain knowledge of nature from one direction and supersensible knowledge from another. Science as such is void of moral impetus, and the latter must be won through supersensible knowledge. And since, ultimately, social promptings must be moral in nature, true social insight and understanding, and even just a sum of social impulses, are inconceivable unless we raise ourselves to supersensible cognition.

It is important for people today to see that we must take a different path to develop social insight from the one scientific methodology offers. But at the same time as I say this, I must also point out a curious paradox. I have often said here that the profoundest truths of initiation science can appear paradoxical or strange to ordinary everyday consciousness, and to a confirmed materialist may even seem crazy. But today we need to engage and acquaint ourselves with these seemingly paradoxical wisdoms. In our time it remains true to say that many things humankind regards as foolishness are nevertheless wisdom before God.[38] It wouldn't go amiss if people today who either smile dismissively at anthroposophy or condemn it out of hand were to recall this biblical phrase from time to time. They might realize, then, that what they regard as foolishness might be wisdom before the gods. It would do some people a great deal of good—and by 'some' I mean a very large number, and in particular those who carry their prayerbooks to church but fulminate about anthroposophy—to study the creeds of Christianity a little more closely and see what they actually contain, rather than arrogantly vaunting their beliefs about it. It really is worth acquainting ourselves today with things that initially seem paradoxical, rather than just dismissing them.

For instance, to put it a little starkly, two paths are possible today. We can for instance absorb all that the sciences of chemistry, physics or biology teach us. We can study Darwinian evolutionary ideas with commitment and industry. Studying all this we may develop a materialistic outlook. It is undeniable that in this process we may become materialists. People today are so quick to pass judgement and so they become materialists if they identify themselves fully with contemporary views of nature and its laws. But there is another route one might pursue. Besides attending to what is offered by physics, chemistry, mineralogy, botany, zoology and biology, and all that is taught in these disciplines, we can also attend to actual empirical experiments; can pay attention to *how* one conducts oneself in the chemistry lab, *what* one does there; *how* one studies plants or animal development.

You see, Goethe's scientific insights are based on his engaged preoccupation with how others gain their knowledge. The greatness of Goethe is that he did this, studying how other people arrive at their findings. It is very illuminating indeed to properly study a treatise by Goethe such as his 'The Experiment as Mediator of Object and Subject'.[39] Here you discover how Goethe attentively observed what happens as the scientist engages with natural phenomena. He very attentively observed what we might call 'research methodology'. If you read my 'Introduction to Goethe's Scientific Writings' you will see the magnificent results that Goethe arrived at by studying scientific methods. In a sense we can continue what Goethe began in the nineteenth century, and apply it to scientific achievements in the twentieth, which Goethe of course could no longer study.

So, as I say, two paths are possible, Let us keep this in mind for a moment. Either we stop with the results science offers, or we also study how people conduct themselves in order to arrive at them. But now let us consider the human striving for knowledge from a different angle. As you know, besides mainstream science there is another kind of knowledge—which we can pursue in the form, for instance, of cosmology, anthropology, anthroposophy, insights into human nature—leading to findings such as those I have described, say, in my *Occult Science*. Here we have positive insights concerning the world of spirit. Just as we gain positive insights in science, in mineralogy, geology and so forth, so we also gain positive insights relating to the spiritual world. It was very important to me as our anthroposophic movement developed also to offer positive insights into the world of spirit in the various books I have written. But here again we can proceed not so much by arriving at results but by considering *how* we arrive at them: how the process can be described whereby we move from outward to inward observation; how we not only undertake research in laboratory conditions, or in clinical trials, or with a telescope, but also how through inner soul development we can arrive at higher spiritual vision by mystical means. This would be something parallel to studying scientific methodology itself, to examining how results are obtained. So we have these two things: a concern with findings and results, and a concern with how we arrive at them inwardly.

But now let us hypothetically assume something that will seem a little paradoxical. If we assume that someone, like Goethe, concerns himself in science chiefly with studying scientific method, we will find that he does not become a materialist at all but comes to acknowledge a spiritual world-view. In modern times a sure way to overcome materialism is to gain insight into the methods of research used in science. People in fact only become scientific materialists because they either do not concern themselves with how they conduct their research, or do so insufficiently. They stay with the results, with the findings they gain in the lab, in the clinic, from the observatory. They do not pass on to Goetheanism, to studying the nature of the research they are doing. You see, if you allow the scientific approach to the world, its way of relating to things, of developing knowledge, to work upon you, you become at least an idealist; but more likely still, you develop a spiritual view if you pursue this far enough.

But if one tries to avoid arriving at the positive findings of spiritual science, if one finds it tedious to concern oneself with the details of spiritual science, and instead only ever wants to read accounts of how the human soul becomes mystical—if, in other words, one focuses attention largely on the methods used to arrive at spiritual findings, this can be the greatest temptation to become materialistic. The greatest temptation to become materialistic lies in the reluctance to concern oneself with the actual, palpable findings of spiritual science, instead repeatedly accentuating mystical enquiry, mystical contemplation—the method used to enter the world of spirit.

This is paradoxical, as you see. By observing natural science, scientific enquiry we become spiritual; but if we disdain to arrive at real spiritual insights, and speak only of mysticism—that is, what is undertaken to arrive at spiritual insights—we will suffer the great temptation of becoming a real materialist. We must know such things today, and we get nowhere without them. For there are, you see, bands of monists today[40] whose supposed leaders broadcast a superficial world-view: they compile the external materialistic results of science into a superficial world-view which modern people find illuminating since they do not wish to exert themselves too much. They prefer going to the cinema to anything else, and therefore love a kind of cinematic knowledge—which is what materialism is—rather than something they must elaborate inwardly themselves. These leaders of the monist fraternities thus offer a kind of superficial materialism. They are pests, really, for they spread errors. It is not a good idea to give them oxygen for they turn people's heads towards materialism. And yet they are less dangerous than another kind, for they are largely honest at least. This honesty doesn't prevent them spreading errors, but at least they are mostly honest and modest, and their errors will be eventually be overcome—they will only be of passing importance.

But there are other people who—systematically and knowingly—refuse to lead others to the palpable, positive findings of spiritual science. Indeed they encourage the modern, rather easygoing and comfort-loving disinclination to engage with the positive, detailed findings of spiritual science. They know that things such as those published in my *Occult Science*, which one needs to study for a couple of years if one is to get somewhere with them, are not comfortable for people today. They may of course send their sons to university or college to qualify them as chemists or what have you, but think that a knowledge, a spiritual grasp, of the heavens and the earth is something you can get in the twinkle of an eye in one evening's reading. They think a single lecture on the supersensible world should give them the whole span and scope of cosmic wisdom. People find detailed findings from positive spiritual enquiry uncomfortable. There are certain individuals in modern culture who make use of this disinclination to persuade people there is no need to concern themselves with actual, positive spiritual realities. They say, for instance, 'What's the point of first learning then talking about higher hierarchies? Why go on about Saturn, Sun, Moon, Earth, Jupiter, Venus, Vulcan and so forth? All this is superfluous.' Instead they advise people to go deep into themselves, to make their souls mystical, and then they will come to the God within. They teach this, give their followers generalized ideas about how the material world relates to the supersensible, encouraging the disinclination in people to penetrate into detailed spiritual realities. And why do they do this? Seemingly they wish to disseminate a spiritual outlook, but in reality they want something else: by this means they want to properly cultivate materialism. And that is why the proponents of monism are less of a danger, while those who propound mysticism, who talk of all kinds of mystical things, are often the real cultivators, refined cultivators of materialism. They teach some vague way of entering worlds of spirit, but avoid giving details, keep their words very general, and, if they are successful, will ensure the world becomes material through and through in two or three generations. Today, the surest, subtlest way of developing materialism is to teach mysticism to those who disdain to engage with positive, spiritual-scientific findings. Many of the things that nowadays spring up from the soil of so-called 'spiritual' literature cultivate materialism much more vigorously than books, say, by Ernst Haeckel.

People find such things very uncomfortable because it makes demands on their capacity for discernment. They dislike this. They would far rather revel in an inner enjoyment of all things mystical. And this is also why there is so much opposition particularly to honest spiritual endeavours that disdain to encourage people to dabble in vague mysticism. If you present a spiritual science worthy of the name you will inevitably meet opposition. And this is because there are numerous people and groups of people today who seek at all costs to prevent the true spiritual elevation of humanity. Instead they make use of the fact that rambling on about vague, mystical subjects is a sure way to cultivate materialism. They consciously employ this tactic; and for this reason also they are hell bent on opposing authentic means of guiding people towards spiritual science.

I am referring here to a wealth of literature available today. Anyone who picks up a mystical book today, of whatever kind, will absolutely need to call upon his capacity of discernment. One should not be misled by the fact that a lot of mystical dabbling published today is easy to understand. Naturally it is easy to understand someone telling you that you need only look deep inside yourself and you will find a god dwelling within—your own god, found only by following your own path, which no one else can show you, since each person speaks of their own, different god. You find such things presented in a really extremely seductive way in many books published today.

I would ask you to be fully aware of these things, keep them vividly in mind, for you will only achieve what our anthroposophic movement seeks to achieve by becoming at least a small band of people who really endeavour to develop this capacity of discernment I have spoken of. It would be a poor outlook for humanity if people did not make this effort, and develop this capacity. Today, amidst all the confusion and chaos, it is important to stand fully upon one's own two feet. The causes of so much of the confusion reigning today are almost palpable in small realities, if we are able to judge them aright.

To end, I would like to tell you of one such small reality which I became aware of just a couple of hours ago, and which is well able to cast some light on the mood of soul and sensibility of people today. My publisher in Leipzig, Altmann, wrote me a letter which I received a couple of hours ago. He told me that an article fiercely critical of anthroposophy has been published in a theosophical journal in Leipzig.[41] Well, this is of course permissible! But this disparaging article appeared in the same issue in which my *Calendar of the Soul* and my 'Appeal to the Civilized World' were also published: first the *Calendar of the Soul*, then my 'Appeal to the German People and the Civilized World', followed by an article fiercely attacking me and disparaging anthroposophy, 'Rudolf Steiner's Appeal to the Instinct of Mediocrity'.

In such matters we see some characteristic aspects of the nature of a modern human soul, albeit here in grotesque caricature. It is uncomfortable of course to discern the many forms in which such traits appear. Many grotesque contradictions surface not only in such distasteful ways, but are also present everywhere in the life of humanity. Today it is essential that we develop real clarity, discernment sharp as a razor, if we are to stand our ground. That is the important thing.

Lecture 8

DORNACH, 18 OCTOBER 1919

We have been reflecting in all kinds of ways on how a healing of our social conditions, and other circumstances affecting human community, can only come about if, from within, we allow other modes of thinking to take hold of us than those which have become dominant over the last three to four centuries. One such especially influential mode of thought, scientific thinking, ought no longer to hold sway over us. Nowadays it is difficult to speak of this scientific thinking completely impartially because it is undoubtedly true that humanity has made enormous advances by means of it. At the same time, though, we must realize that modern advances of this kind have suppressed a true life of spirit and culture. Gradually progress has come to involve aspects of human knowledge that could subsequently be utilized in external technology. And the rest of cultural life was then touched also by this tendency always to orientate human thinking to what can be utilized in external technology.

It would be quite wrong to think that I am referring here only to everything in modern culture that is directly dependent on the scientific mode of thinking. No. What I mean is that the whole way of thinking of modern humanity—except where old ideas, old elements have been grafted onto this thinking from the past—is of a kind which comes to expression in an extreme form in scientific thinking. Not only people directly affected by science think scientifically. In fact, though paradoxical, it is true to say that people directly involved in, and influenced by, science are furthest from the type of thinking I am here referring to. A general mode of thought has come to particularly characteristic expression in science, so that in a sense we can best see through the scientific lens how modern humanity thinks. We have often spoken of the influence of this manner of thinking which comes to especially characteristic expression in science.

And now I want to point to a peculiarity inherent in our thinking, our whole mind, our whole modern sensibility in general because the soul is so much informed by scientific impulses. The peculiarity is this: that as modern human beings we have in a sense lost the ability to observe things impartially. People believe that they do so, but they do not. Our very education today inoculates us with a large sum of predetermined ideas that colour the way we see things so that we no longer have a vision untainted by these concepts.

You might well think that this fact—that we do not have an untainted vision of things—would be most apparent and injurious in scientific enquiry, in science. One might well think this. But on closer inspection something more becomes apparent. Scientists are saved from the ruinous and devastating fact of not properly seeing things by increasingly directing their attention to the external sense world alone, to what is presented to our outward senses. These outward senses are not governed, you see, by predetermined ideas, and so they continually correct and adjust what arises from such views, thoughts and opinions, especially from preconceptions. Observation itself continually corrects the views and judgements we otherwise impose on perception. And this is why we do not notice all kinds of preconceptions that do, also, inform scientific observations. If we take scientific findings in their context, we find that scientific observations bear the imprint of predetermined ideas and views.

And yet this lack of capacity to see any longer is particularly injurious when we start thinking about social conditions. Here the realities in no way correct or amend the preconceptions that people impose on them. Ultimately therefore we have come to the point when people can claim and assert whatever they like about the social realities of life. Nowadays all kinds of opinions are asserted: on the one hand that social reality consists only in economic processes, that all spiritual life is only a kind of superstructure, a sort of smoke that rises from it, an icing on the cake of economic factors. That is one extreme. The other is this: since people have no sense of real spiritual agencies alive in the world, they talk of prevailing, abstract ideas, ideas about things and so forth, and claim that these ideas, perhaps through human agency, shape the external realities of economic and other factors.

Two opposite views, as you can see. Now when it comes to proving one view or the other you can cite indisputable evidence for either, of equal validity in both cases. It can be proven that everything is governed by prevailing ideas; and equally that this is pure fantasy, and that in reality all ideas are only reflections, only a superstructure overlaid upon economic factors. One person can neatly refute what the other claims. In both cases the proofs are perfectly valid.

This phenomenon has been ignored far too much in the culture of our day. People divide themselves into factions or parties, and propound a particular maxim, some programme or other. They are convinced they are right, and that their mottoes and programmes are backed up by proof. Others propose quite different maxims, a quite different programme: they too can back up what they say with evidence, and it is not possible to say that the reasoning of either is better or worse. We really should take note of this phenomenon in political life, since it is the most typical trait of our time. Ultimately it leads to the gravest anti-social factors and moods. You see, if you are convinced by a particular motto, and have good reasons to offer for it, you easily regard someone else of a different persuasion as an idiot or rogue, or in some other way dishonest. It is a tragedy of our time that this is not really understood. On top of this comes the fact that people today believe that the human soul has always been constituted as it is today. And as soon as you draw attention to the phenomenon I described, it is fairly predictable that someone will reply that this has always been so in humanity's history: that all opinions have always been able to coexist with equal logical coherence. But if people would only take the trouble to inform themselves about the real nature of human evolution, they would not assert this. In truth, such a state of affairs did not always prevail. Well-proven views, maxims and programmes did not always stand in such clear definition alongside each other as they do today. Nowadays, if you're as clever as some left-wing socialists, you can easily and clearly prove the tenets of Marxism. Or otherwise, if you wish to adopt a different perspective, you can prove equally well that Marxism is complete nonsense. It is important to be aware today that excellent proofs can be offered to back up very opposed standpoints.

Children today are taught to prove things: they are as it were inoculated with this capacity, and in fact this is something immensely sad—that everything can be proven so clearly and rigorously, and in consequence people can be so strongly persuaded something is true. Of all the ways of persuading someone, offering proof is the easiest today. There is no easier way to persuade someone you're right. And precisely through this ability to prove things, people have completely lost their proper sense of the need to work hard, to struggle to acquire one's convictions in life: that a battle must be waged within, that one has to overcome oneself, if a real conviction is to take hold in the soul.

To what is this due, this fact so incisive in our lives of being able to prove things so easily? It is because we are accustomed to confining our thoughts only to the surface of things. Nowadays people ensure their thinking lies strictly upon the surface of things, and they make no efforts to delve deeper. And the more superficially one thinks, the easier it is to prove whatever you like. It is very important indeed to recognize this. The thinner our concepts are—and at the surface of things all concepts become thin and abstract—the more easily these concepts seem to offer evidence for whatever one wishes to think and believe, which arises in fact from quite different subterranean origins: feelings, hidden intentions and suchlike. Our whole factional politics ought to be studied and described from this perspective I have just described.

But what can least be achieved as we study things only in this superficial manner is real insight into human nature. And that is why so many people today are now urging that we deepen our ideas, at last, developing for instance self-knowledge, or in other words insight into our own being. Countless books, lectures, briefings and campaign leaflets speak of the need for such insight. But this in turn requires a sound basis! You cannot acquire it from any random point of departure. To get beyond the miserable plight of resorting to evidence and proof, we need to learn to see things with an open mind: simply to learn to see things in outward life as they actually are. Learning to see things as they are is especially necessary for our healthy sense of things, for a healthy view of the world; for this is what we have most lost sight of. We can prove how things ought to be, but we don't perceive their reality, see them as they are, since truly seeing is harder than proving them to be a particular way. Certain assertions made today, in the social domain for example, are only arrived at by proving things. If, instead, we develop an unprejudiced eye for reality, we cannot arrive at such assertions. The thing of most importance is to develop real perception of things, really to see them.

If you read Goethe's scientific writings, and also his writings about art, you will see that in his day already he was trying to strongly urge the practice of open-minded seeing. He recognized how the sciences all work out of concepts reliant on proof, and he thought this, especially, was something that needed to be overcome. What he wanted above all was to acquaint himself with the phenomena themselves, the archetypal meaning of facts and realities, really to acquaint himself with them as they are. His efforts largely fell on deaf ears: today this foundation on which Goethe attempted to let realities themselves speak to him, the foundation of his theory of colours, for instance, is still a field where his right to contribute to our understanding is hotly contested.

But for insight into human nature it is especially necessary to develop true sight of the realities of life, of subjective life. People today, for instance, speak a great deal of external and internal phenomena in relation to human experience. It seems to me that if you were to ask many people today whether the colour red, or a particular tone, or something else they perceive in their surroundings is an inner or outer reality, they would say it is an outer one, external to them, in contrast to inner experience. And then if you ask them whether they can articulate the difference between outer and inner, they will say with some assurance that they are very clear about it: that what the senses perceive is outside them, and what is within, and belongs to the human being himself, is inner. You may pursue these questions further and ask a person about these external things, the green grass, the blue sky, the rising sun and so on: people can express what they observe in these terms, describing each phenomenon separately and specifically. But if you then ask someone to itemize what they call their inner experience in the same way, the great majority of people will find it hard to offer any clear answer, or at least one involving detailed facts and realities. They have the illusion that they know this inner life very well compared with outward realities. But if you probe a little and ask them to describe their inner life in as much detail as they describe outward things, you will find they don't get very far. If, however, someone does really succeed in describing inner experience it becomes apparent this is nothing other than a reflection of external reality, everything that has arisen and developed in relation to the outer world, preserved in paler form in a person's memory. It will be little different from the outer phenomena he has described. A person today is unlikely to be able to tell you more about his inner life than, at most, how he feels in response to the green of the grass and the blue of the sky; he will find it very difficult to describe a real contrast and distinction between inner and outer.

This has considerable consequences: it means people are unable to properly grasp the distinction between inner and outer experience in any meaningful sense. You see, scientists, from their modern perspective, try to investigate the human organs as supposed bearers of inner processes. They try to prove things without really perceiving them, saying for instance that a table is outside us and inner life is within. And in referring to inner experience, especially in science, they point to the interior of the skull, equating it with inner life. Here they transpose ideas gained from unclear perception into the human body and say that inside there, somewhere behind the eyes, is inner life [see drawing]. Some who delve deeper may perhaps question these concepts, but unconsciously at least people do think that the outer world is under their fingertips while inner life sits behind their eyes. This however, with the consequences drawn from it for the bodily organs, is founded only on imprecise perception. In fact, everything that you are entitled to call your interiority is what you experience in the so-called outer world. You are continually interwoven with the outer world, and what you apparently experience within you, you in fact experience with the whole wide world outside.

Board drawing 8

In one of the 'Eight Meditations'[42]—you can find it there—I pointed out that as we observe the outer world we continually grow together with it, and that it is quite mistaken to distinguish between an outer and inner world as such. If we were really to articulate what we see, we could only regard as our inner experience what our mind experiences as surrounding us. That is what constitutes our inner experience. Many mystics feel uncomfortable with this idea, for they place much emphasis on inner contemplation. But this inward contemplation is usually nothing other than referring to certain corporeal ideas of the outer world as 'inward' and even renaming them as our divine interiority and suchlike. These are favoured ideas which we borrow from the outer world. We ought really to designate as 'inward' what we can see without preconception and usually call outward. In a sense we are within ourselves in what comes before our gaze. And then, ultimately, we are also really far more at home, let us say, in the moment when all of you are sitting here, in this hall, than in your so-called inwardness, especially when you refer to what is inside your skull, behind your eyes, as your interiority. However you may think about this interiority, apart from a few concepts, really very sparse ones, that you have taken from anatomy or physiology, you know very little about what lies behind your eyes or goes on inside your skull. And if you ask which is more inward—what is going on around me in this hall or what lies under my skull—you will be able to recognize that what is around you in the hall is doubtless more inward than what is happening under your skull. At least at this moment your inward life is touched far more by the apparently 'outer world' in this hall than by processes occurring under your skull. The latter are very external to your experience, and do not really impinge at all on your interiority. And when you objectively relate what you see, you will acknowledge that the outward is really inward, and the inward is, for the human mind, very much outward.

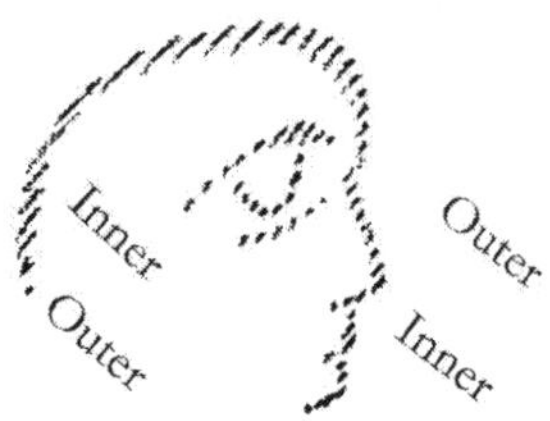

Board drawing 8

Now you may say that these ideas are mere hairsplitting. Well, not initially, since they derive from elucidation of what is really perceived as opposed to theoretical deductions or proofs. This is what one can actually perceive, actually see. It is immediately present to consciousness, and would be regarded as true if people only attested to what is actually present to the mind, rather than reconstructing reality in terms of preconceived notions. This is the point of departure. But it has an important consequence. As long as you hold to the notion that things outside you are external, and what is within you is internal, you cannot arrive at what I describe as acknowledging spiritual-scientific realities through healthy common sense. You see, spiritual-scientific realities can only be perceived and comprehended if we start from a mode of seeing without preconceptions. Then these realities can be recognized, long before we develop any clairvoyant capacities as such. Employing the tangled concepts of modern daily life makes it very difficult, by contrast, to recognize reality.

That we see the outer world—or what we usually call the outer world—as we do, in a way that if truly seen and defined encompasses our inner life, is due to our senses and is connected with the way they are fashioned. We live in the immediate present through our senses. We experience what occurs around us in the present moment through our senses. They makes us witnesses of the present moment. But, as we are given up to the outer world, our ideas arise from our sense perceptions, and we bear these onward in our memory. We recall later what we experienced in a present moment now gone, and carry it on within us. This largely composes our concepts. Human concepts are mostly memory pictures of what we have drawn from the so-called outer world. But these pictures, ideas, concepts are mediated, not engendered but mediated, by what we otherwise know as our interiority and which we have now come to see is outward. What lies behind your eyes, of which you really know nothing, mediates ideas and concepts. This is quite definitely the case. It mediates concepts and ideas. But what is actually occurring within your head?

If you observe what actually occurs inside the human head, it cannot be said that in so far as we think or picture we are likewise a witness of processes in the present, as much as is the case in our sense perceptions. In our thinking this is not so. In the activity of thinking, the activity in which we engaged prior to birth or before conception works on within our head. In other words, what occurs within the head [see drawing] while you are thinking or picturing is not an activity you engage in by virtue of living in the present moment. Instead you think by virtue of the reverberation of an activity that you engaged in between death and rebirth, or conception, in the supersensible world.

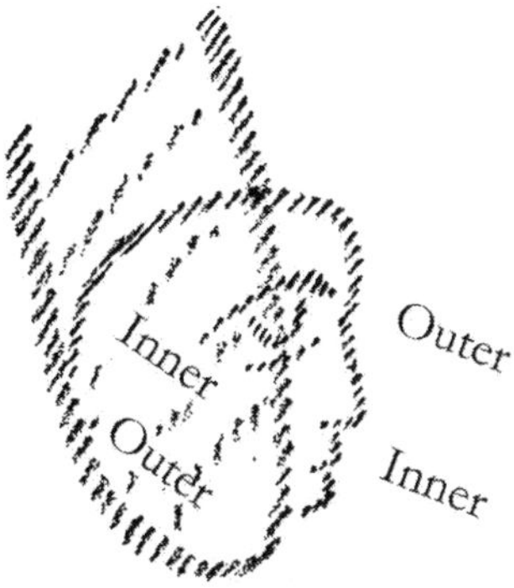

Board drawing 9

You are only a contemporary human being by virtue of perceiving with your senses. As you open your senses to the outer world, you perceive the present moment and live as a contemporary with the external present. But the moment you begin to think, something plays into your skull that is not what you presently are as a human being: the reverberation of what you were in the world of spirit before birth, or before conception. If you wish to imagine this more pictorially, you can say: I strike a tone that goes on reverberating long after I struck it. Now imagine that during the whole period between your last death and this birth you were engaged in an activity in the world of spirit which I can draw schematically as follows [see drawing, red]. This activity goes on reverberating; and this reverberating activity is one you engage in when you think in the present. When thinking, you are not engaging in an activity of your present human nature, but it is, rather, a reverberation of the activity you engaged in between your last death and latest birth.

You are only a person of the present in your sensory nature. In thinking you practise an activity which is a reverberation of what you engaged in before birth in the supersensible world. It simply is not

Board drawing 9

true that in thinking we practise an activity that originates in the present. If you examine what is occurring in the present in your brain, study it scientifically, you will of course only find material processes since what is at work in a non-material realm in your skull is a pre-birth quality which is only echoing on. The fact that a person not only *emerges* from the supersensible world but, in living here and now in the present, re-experiences what he engaged in during his existence in the supersensible world is living proof for someone who can see truly.

If you imagine that you experienced a severe pain here in this physical world, and that, as it goes on reverberating in you, it no longer has a physical cause, you can say, similarly, that your thinking in the present is the echo, the reverberation, of what you experienced in a far more intensive manner before you were conceived and began to develop your sensory nature.

Thus only in sense perception are we people of the present. If we were this alone, we would never think, since thinking is not given us by virtue of being born into this physical world but by our ability to let reverberate the activity we exercised before birth, or conception, in the world of spirit, and by applying this activity to the sense world surrounding us.

We can never understand this if we start from ordinary concepts of 'outer' and 'inner'; and least of all will we understand the true state of affairs if we start from a foolish mysticism reigning in so many minds today, and teaching that the realm of supersensible human experience is in some way to be found within. What we should seek, rather, is the pre-birth condition. In pointing beyond the outer world of the senses you ought not to point inwards but instead back to the time you spent prior to conception and birth. From this present person you should go out into the pre-present person and then you really are entering the supersensible realm. That is the important thing. Because of a reluctance to work their way through to this sound concept, people speak in words that have no real content: of all kinds of divine interiority and suchlike. The inner nature people seek in this way in their present being should be sought instead in what we were before we were conceived for our present life.

And when we act, when will passes into action? Let us consider the simplest kind of action: we walk around a room. That's an action, isn't it? First we see ourselves walking about. People are unaware of how will is connected with walking, just as little as we are ordinarily aware of what we experience in sleep. Just as we see the colour blue, or a tree, or stars, we can outwardly observe what this individual of flesh and blood is doing as he walks about. We can observe ourselves. But we know nothing of *how* we will. All we know is that someone is walking about, and this is us. And since we must identify this person walking about as ourselves, we say, 'I *want* to walk about.' But how exactly this wanting is connected with the walking about is something quite definitely removed from our ordinary awareness.

Well, this in turn is closely related to what we usually call 'externality' and 'interiority'. As you walk about, and therefore are moving your legs, you can observe your legs moving [see drawing, p. 118]. You can watch this fellow walking about and can discern what he wishes. You see an outer occurrence. But here you can gain a far greater sense of an actual human interiority, for although you cannot perceive how the will is connected with the walking, nevertheless you infer your will from this walking. You can see this more easily here than in the sense world. You can more easily think of this walking about as having an inner quality than you can the content of the sense world. Where will passes into action, it is easier to see that there is an inner quality at work.

Naturally this is not something that modern mystics care for in their view that outward action is an outward matter, and that we must penetrate into inner, divine nature within, which is the true human being, and so forth. But just as we have here [see drawing, p. 118, top] something inward in sense perception, and something outward within the supposed interiority of the human head, so here this interiority [drawing, bottom] contrasts with our limb system.

And now we arrive at this remarkable thought which cannot easily be reconciled with things that people prove today, but which, curiously, is true if we consider the matter without preconception. However, I believe that the mood of soul prevailing today is of a kind—forgive me, I also have to speak of such things—where numerous philistines think that the region of the cosmos unfolding below their diaphragm is very much connected with their interior nature. People regard it as something related to their inner life. In fact it is the most external of all within us.

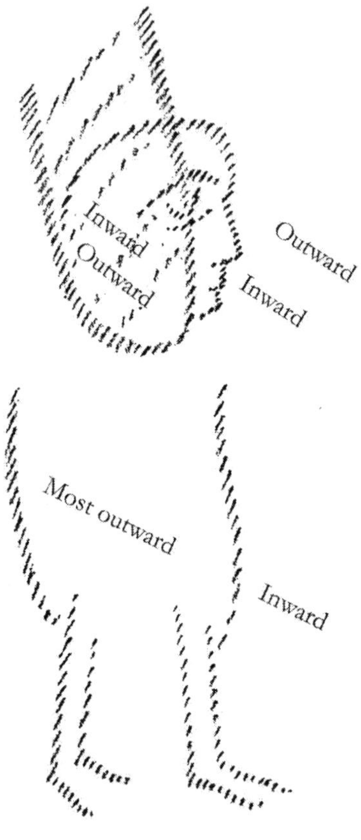

Board drawing 8

If we call this [see top drawing] outward, we can regard what lies below the diaphragm as the most outward aspect of the human being [bottom drawing]. What lies below the diaphragm, the human abdomen, is the most outward aspect of all in us. Every tree, every stone we see is inwardly closer to us than our abdomen, which is the most absolutely outward aspect. Our sense perceptions are our true interiority, what we perceive as our actions. The content of our head is already outward, and most outward of all is what lies below the human chest. This is to really acknowledge what can be seen. It can be seen.

Look, this in turn has a very specific significance. Since we have been developing anthroposophy we repeatedly say, don't we, that when a person is awake his I and astral body are within the physical and etheric body. This is true; and when someone sleeps, while he is asleep, his I and astral body are outside the physical and etheric body. I have often pointed out what the nature of this 'outside-ness' largely consists of: the aspect of the I and astral body normally within the head submerges itself in what lies below the diaphragm. You can even get something like empirical proof of this. Imagine you're dreaming of the loveliest snakes; this is because you have just awoken from your immersion in your own abdomen, where you perceived the intestines. This memory of a perception of the intestines conjures your dream of beautiful snakes. If we are talking from our own perspective as human beings, 'outward' and 'inward' only acquire palpable reality if we know what is really outward, what is really inward in us.

And in turn, only when we can acquire such ideas, rather than ones that can be 'proven'—ideas instead that can be seen—then it becomes possible for us to comprehend spiritual-scientific insights with our healthy common sense. This is because whatever we initiate through the will springs in a certain way from the most outward aspect of our nature.

Now let us consider the healthy nature of an idea that must replace a really very pathological one. People believe that when they *will* something, this comes from within them. In fact it springs from our most outward aspect, from what we absolutely do not inhabit while we are awake during the day—the aspect which we may at most inhabit when we are asleep. When we will something, we are not inside ourselves at all but in the cosmos. We accomplish something that is a cosmic occurrence, and by no means merely our own subjective occurrence.

Throughout my whole writing life I have endeavoured to teach the contemporary world concepts that are, in this sense, healthy ones. You can start with my *Introduction to Goethe's Scientific Writings*, where I sought to draw on Goethe's world-view to replace sick concepts with healthy ones. There I pointed out that certain occurrences in the human being can only be properly considered if we do not think something is merely happening inside a person, that it is simply the person concerned who is doing it. Instead we must regard this so-called human interior as the stage upon which the cosmos enacts human actions, as the stage for cosmic occurrences. On the penultimate and last page of my little book *Truth and Science,* I summed up its whole elaboration of epistemological ideas in the thought that the human being is a stage for what the cosmos enacts within him, and that he does it in connection with the cosmos, not from within. This is the most important section of that book—these last two pages. It was originally my doctoral thesis;[43] but because these two pages are the most important and significant, most keenly grappling with things in modern thinking that need to change, I was only able to shape this little book as it now appears after I had been awarded my doctorate. These last two pages were missing from the original thesis I submitted, since the academic world could not have been expected to countenance conclusions which have some bearing on reconfiguring the whole modern world-view. The original dissertation laid the epistemological ground for this in a relatively inoffensive way, in terms of an objective philosophical treatise. But where it tended could only be added in a later printing.

Only when we really practise this exact seeing I have spoken of, no longer simply succumbing to illusions that are elicited by preconceived views, will one also be able to develop healthy insights into the nature of the human will. What we see outside us when a person walks around, or when we observe ourselves performing the simplest actions, moving our legs forwards, say, is only the inner aspect of the will. The most outward aspect of it, which has meaning for the cosmos, is apparently concealed within us. Yet concealed within our most outward aspect lives something spiritual that underlies what we are reluctant to call inward. What occurs within this, the spiritual aspect—of course not what physically happens, but the spiritual aspect parallel to the physical action—is again not something of the present moment. Of the present moment is what we observe the person doing. But what occurs within is something else, is in fact something only germinally beginning to occur. As you walk about, or as you perform some other actions with your limbs, something occurs in your outward nature that has real meaning after death: it is the prelude to processes that will occur between death and your subsequent rebirth, just as what lives in your thinking is the echo of what you were in the world of spirit between your previous death and latest birth or conception. What resonates in your most outward aspect, which people call the most inward, is the embryo of processes that you will enact between your next death and following rebirth. We only comprehend and perceive human will if we do not, once again, consider the human being at this moment but instead see in him—apparently in him, though it lives in his most outward aspect—the correlate to actions, something belonging to them, that departs through the portal of death, thereafter becoming activity between death and a new birth, developing there too in such a way that it can once again enter us and continue to reverberate in our outward nature.

If we study the human will, trying to find in the person we are at this moment the mystical depths of this will, the divine origins of this will, then phrasemonger mystics usually find that they should not do this only in their belly, since this isn't quite elegant enough for them. They are not actually concerned with truth but with special, unctuous turns of phrase. If we seek the truth instead, we find that something that has, let us say, an unappetizing connection with physical, sense reality is a correlate to what departs through the portal of death and continues into a subsequent existence. Here we must seek our future being. Thus we gain from thinking evidence of our pre-birth existence, and from our will evidence of our life after death, as I have often[44] explained here, and even sometimes in public lectures. These are truths we do really need to become aware of today. It is essential to realize that human thinking is something that cannot actually be produced by us at this present moment with our flesh and blood, our bones and nerves, but that it reverberates from a life before birth, and that will is by no means something that we can produce in our present entirety, in the present moment, but that it has an aspect which survives beyond death. If we really come to recognize what cannot be produced by us in our present form of flesh and blood, then we begin to see the human being before us as eternal in nature. We do not acquire these truths by speculating about eternity, but rather by becoming able to engage really positively with the nature of thinking on the one hand and will on the other.

This is essential: if we seek to develop higher insights today that accord with modern spiritual science, we must regard phrase-mongering mysticism as the most injurious of things.

And this is why certain things one puts in writing from the perspective of authentic spiritual science should be accepted. They often are. But then people start objecting when it comes to the really important thing: to engage with the specific, detailed realities of human life. It's at that point that people turn instead to the chatter of dabbling mystics, who try to conjure an inner world from words. But the society and culture of today are in too grave a crisis for us to luxuriate in such mystic generalities. What we need to do today is engage with matters that configure the human soul in such a way that people can really acquire these ideas and use them to understand society and what lives in it. Will anyone develop truly social ideas if he cannot *see*, if he learns to approach reality with the prejudices and preconceptions of the academic and scientific mode of thinking? We will only acquire a capacity to perceive reality cleanly if we free ourselves through the ideas of spiritual science from the undergrowth of prevailing outlooks, whose ultimate consequence can be found in many mystical aberrations of our day. The mystical aberrations of our time are not signs of a new resurgence towards a better condition. Often they are the last stage in decline, the ultimate extremity of mere empty phrases rather than true insights.

True insights tell us such things as that thinking is the echo and reverberation of life before birth, and will a prelude to life after death. These are specific insights. In speaking of such detailed realities, we speak in a quite different way from those who say merely that something eternal, the divine I, lives in our temporal nature and that if we experience ourselves in this eternal being we encompass our divine nature—the true I as opposed to the untrue I, and so forth. We can spend all day playing around with such ideas and it may engender a great sense of well-being in us, but it will not lead us to real insights.

Lecture 9

DORNACH, 19 OCTOBER 1919

In our reflections I have been highlighting from many different angles the connection between embracing spiritual-scientific insights and the view of society that must increasingly become widespread in humanity. It is likely that in the process you will have felt a need to examine one question more thoroughly: what is the inner relationship between socially committed actions and the sensibility that can develop in us as a consequence of gradually living our way into spiritual-scientific ideas? Spiritual-scientific ideas initially reveal to us a certain inner mood of soul by helping us understand something—human destiny—which we witness in ordinary life and yet must often experience as incomprehensible. This human destiny becomes comprehensible to some degree when we become acquainted with the law of recurring lives on earth and the laws of karma connected with this. We learn to see that our journey through one life on earth is dependent on former lives on earth. We have already spoken, after all,[45] of the forces that play over from one life into another, and have learned in some respects how destiny works, and is shaped and configured by the cosmos.

Now all of you will have a sense that if a person today does not gain higher insights he can only have a dim inkling of how his destiny is shaped by succeeding lives on earth. What we call karma is something that can be understood relatively easily. You can gather this from the last edition of my book *Theosophy*, and the changes I made to the chapter concerning karma. But the real perception of life I spoke about yesterday, that straightforward view of life unobscured by prejudice and preconception, which would immediately reveal the law of karma, is something that very few people as yet possess. If people were to see what happens in life with the straightforward, unprejudiced vision I spoke of yesterday, healthy human reason would speak of the laws of destiny in the same way as spiritual science does. But so far this is not the case for the majority of people. Most people do not have the simple capacity to see that would bring home to them how I consciousness lives within the soul. There are even philosophers today who speak of I consciousness as if this were the most certain, sure and real thing that exists. We can say that this is as true on the one hand as it is one-sided, and indeed almost untrue, on the other. How, in fact, do we actually perceive our human I?

Yesterday you learned how, in respect of inner life, thinking is really only a reflection of life before birth, and how the life of will is an embryonic or germinal prelude to life after death—and in other words how what weaves in our soul does not fundamentally belong to the bodily sheath that encloses us from birth to death. Our extra-physical, extra-temporal being plays into our thinking on the one hand, and into our will on the other. But you know too how we look back on our life and have the sense that our previous life lies behind us as memory. It is very easy for us human beings to think that we have passed through life consciously, and retain it in our memory back to the point where our memory begins. It seems to us as if this here [see drawing] is the present moment, and that we remember continuously back to the moment in childhood of our first memory. You can easily discover, though, that this is very mistaken. If you trace the course of your life back to the moment in childhood of your first memory, and regard this as a continuous current, that is of course completely wrong, for in this retrospective view you really only perceive occurrences of waking life. In fact, each succeeding day is interrupted by a night, when you perceive nothing. Each succeeding day is interrupted by a night.

Board drawing 9

It is therefore completely illusory to ignore the fact that this retrospective memory of your life, this conscious memory, is not a complete current but one in fact continually interrupted by all the periods when you were asleep and remembered nothing. The line of recall is therefore not a continuous but a discontinuous one, a sequence of memories continually interrupted.

To clarify what I mean, I would like to offer a picture at this point. Imagine a white disc within which is a black spot. What do you see? The white disc, and, where there is no white, you see the black spot. Let's leave aside the question of whether the black spot is something real or only the absence of white. You see the black spot, and where you see it no white can be seen on an otherwise white disc. This is an image really of how you perceive your I in ordinary life.

Just as you do not perceive anything here [at the centre] where the black spot is, so you do not perceive your actual I. You do not perceive it at all, but you perceive the experiences you underwent

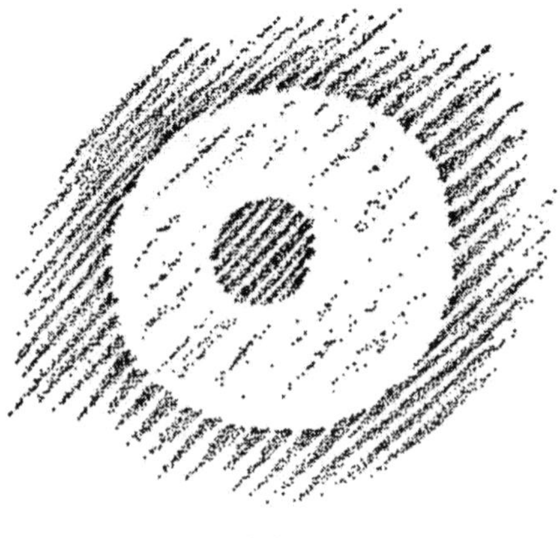

Board drawing 9

each time you were awake. But not your I, not at all. Only by virtue of the fact that, when you survey your experiences, they are not present—just as there is no white here in the black spot—do you perceive your I. As you look back on your life you perceive your experiences, but do not perceive the interruptions. Instead you perceive your I. It is therefore the lack of waking experiences that in reality gives you the picture of your I. In other words, when you say 'I', you are perceiving the period of your life during which you were asleep and unaware.

It is true: the unperceived, the unremembered parts of your life, when you look back, are the cause of your I perception. If you did not sleep at all, were always awake, you would have no perception of your I as you look back. You would appear to yourself as an I-less being swimming in the flux of cosmic existence.

It is extraordinarily important to see these things simply, straightforwardly. Everyone thinks that perception of the I is an experience. No. We perceive the I as a hole or void in our experiences. Please keep this in mind for now.

And now I'd like to ask you to remember, as I have said so often, that we do not only sleep when we sleep but we are also asleep when we're awake. We are only really awake in respect of the world of our senses and thoughts. In respect of our will we are asleep. Just as little as we know what we accomplish during sleep so likewise we cannot perceive the inner impulses of our will. Yesterday I said how a person can observe his own actions, but not see the will itself. We are asleep in our will. In so far as we have will impulses, we are asleep in the daytime too. We are awake only insomuch as we can perceive through our senses and form rational concepts, ideas. But we are only half awake. Even when we're awake, we are asleep in the other part of our being, the part that wills.

And now you will understand how things stand with the I. It does not enter at all as a real entity into your sense perceptions and your thoughts but remains below in the will, continuing to sleep there during waking life. This is why you can never see it as an actual entity, as real presence, but only as the empty spot at the centre. You can have the dim sense that you possess an I, in that something of what you have there as a hole in your soul experiences resounds for you from the will. But your perception of the I is very much a negative one, and it is extraordinarily important to recognize this. We have to recognize the nullity of the superficial picture of the I that figures too in many modern philosophies. You see, only when we comprehend this whole set of circumstances I have described here can we understand, inwardly understand, the relationship between one person and another in life.

I described this relationship between one person and another in new material added to the latest edition of my *Philosophy of Freedom.*[46] Besides perceiving our own I, albeit negatively as I have described, we also perceive the I of another person. We would not be able to do so if we ourselves were conscious of our own I. If the I dwelt in our own consciousness, the relationship between people would be fatally demolished: we would pass through the world and would only ever have I, I, and I in our mind, in our world of sense perceptions and thoughts. We would pass others by and feel them only to be shadows, would be surprised when, on extending a hand, these shadows took hold of our hand. It would be inexplicable to us why our hand did not simply pass through the ghost of another person. This would all be down to the fact of possessing the I as substantial entity and not just as a negative picture in our thoughts and sense perceptions. But we do not possess it like this. We have it only in our will and the feeling that emanates from the will. There the actual I exists, but not directly in our life of thoughts and sense perceptions.

In perceiving another person, we actually perceive him through our will. Those who regard themselves as philosophers today quite often entertain the crazy notion that in meeting another person we encounter a pattern of forms: up above his hair, then a forehead, a nose, a mouth and so on. Since we have often seen ourselves in the mirror, we know that he looks like we do. And since we have an I, we conclude, by analogy, that the other person also possesses one. This is preposterous, complete nonsense! In fact we perceive the other person's I exactly as we perceive our own, albeit negatively. And precisely because our I is not in our mind, our consciousness, but outside it, like will also, we can transpose ourselves into the other person's I. If the I dwelt within our conscious mind, we would not be able to do this, and would perceive the other only as a shadowy existence. Now, how does the perception of the other person occur? A very complex process occurs here. We meet another person, and he commands our attention in some way, and very briefly lulls us asleep. He hypnotizes us, lulls us asleep for a very brief moment. Consequently our sense of our humanhood is very briefly lulled asleep. We defend ourselves against this, and assert our personality. This is like the swing of a pendulum: sleeping into the other, awakening in ourselves, sleeping into the other again, awakening in ourselves. And this complex process of oscillation between falling asleep in the other and awakening in ourselves is what happens when we meet someone. This is a process in our will. But we do not perceive it because we do not perceive our will at all. But this vibrating back and forth nevertheless occurs, as I describe in my *Philosophy of Freedom*.

In this oscillation between falling asleep in the other and awakening in ourselves we have the archetypal element, in a sense the nucleus, of social community between people. This is the *ur*-element of social interaction and interplay. This original element, and thus also all the complex forms of social interplay, therefore dwell in the part of our being that sleeps even when we are awake. The life of society is essentially, at most, a dreaming entity in our waking experience, not fully awake. And this is why it is so hard to grasp social dynamics in ordinary life, since they do not unfold in a fully waking state but in a life of dream, and since in order to maintain ourselves within ourselves we must continually defend ourselves against social instincts, against empathy with the other.

Now just consider how complicated it makes our life to enter into relationships with all kinds of people that involve repeatedly falling asleep and waking up. One person is of one kind, another of another. We fall asleep in the other, and this sleep partakes of the other's nature. We are subsumed by him as we fall asleep in him. If you imagine you have been speaking to various people, for instance during our break in proceedings here, then you must recognize that you slept into all of them and, having awoken again from them, something of them is in turn always within you. Thus you imbibe something of the being of each of these other people. All this vibrates between you, swells between one person and the other. Basically it is a dim, dark element that reigns in this social interplay between people. And our modern consciousness does not partake in much of this social feeling that weaves and swells between one person and another.

The task we have today, in the modern world—as you can see from various reflections of ours—is gradually to emerge from the old blood relationships and raise ourselves to an understanding of the dim, obscure weft of social relationships. It is one of the most important missions of our era to gain insight into this weft and swell of personal interactions. What I have called the 'threefolding of the social organism' basically refers only to a pattern of human community in which the human being gradually might become able, after a number of generations, to take up this interweaving between people with true understanding. Such understanding can only arise if the life of rights and the life of spirit and culture come to exist autonomously alongside economic life, and especially if the life of spirit can stand in complete freedom beside the other two realms of life.

To undertake this threefolding of society is the most vital public task for humanity today and in the near future. Only then can humanity survive and develop a truly social inner grasp of human life. In the modern era, since the middle of the fifteenth century, humanity has begun to develop this understanding. It is difficult today only because the divine-spiritual powers are for the first time calling upon human consciousness. All progress made hitherto was brought about more or less unconsciously. What we first need to do now is to work consciously to create a social structure. Old social structures emerged from blood ties, from the nuclear and extended family, the tribe, the class and so on, and these expanded to become nations. Today humanity flounders about in nationhood because people wrongly believe they can still preserve these old forms and contexts. In fact we have long superseded them, and the need has long since arisen to develop different forms of social community from those embodied in ties of blood and race.

I said to you that the first stage on this journey towards social understanding necessary today and in the near future was heralded by the dominance of economic man since the Reformation.[47] I pointed out that in ancient times the initiate held sway, later giving way to the priest, and how since the mid-fifteenth century economic man has become dominant. Since the Reformation those who previously wore cloaks of purple and pulled the strings of power became the puppets of 'Homo economicus' if they wished to rule. In truth, since the middle of the fifteenth century, economists have ruled—the figures who took care of the economies of diverse regions of the earth. Although others were the titular rulers, they were so in name only, and governments were really entirely pervaded by economic principles. Of course people don't like speaking about everything since the Reformation being done from an economic perspective. They prefer to speak of ideals and so forth, but these are merely masks concealing what the real actors on the stage of history were about. To make sure the veil was not lifted too much on this truth, Ministers of Culture, Education, Justice and so on have gone on being appointed since the Reformation. But in fact they were all somewhat diluted finance ministers. If you examine realities, you can see that at most such roles were a continuation of old traditions but under a largely economic aspect.

In this context, the Catholic Church knew how to be very contemporary, precisely in the era of the Reformation. It ensured that progress was entirely in accord with the new economic principles. To illustrate this we need only consider one among many facts. Up to this point, the Church had succeeded in bringing about a close connection between the loftiest spiritual matters and the most trivial, mundane concerns. In olden times you could make recompense for your sins by all kinds of actions. But gradually it became possible for you to pay for them in cash instead. Faster really than the other, worldly powers, the Pope counted on these modern advances. He began to assure his future income from this penance for sins. If you have the power to make people pay you for absolving them from the sins they have committed, this represents an enormous future income. And if this is assured, as it can be by human faith, the income becomes very secure The biggest Siennese bank therefore thought it was very secure business to purchase from the Pope a given number of such future penances. Making fulsome use of these funds, the Pope drew vast sums from the bank in Sienna; and the bank appointed Tetzel to levy them.[48] He went around the countries of central Europe gathering in the absolution funds for this Siennese bank.[49]

So as you see, the Church became very adept at employing modern conditions to its advantage. These historical facts must be carefully considered.

'Homo economicus' emerged. The Church was there, but ultimately its administration of spiritual matters became, with the help of the bank in Sienna and its debt collector, its agent, only a mask of spirituality. If you study recent history you will certainly find deep significance in the rise to dominance of economic man. The Pope only remained as strong a ruler as he was because he recognized the right moment to become an economist also, incorporating 'Homo economicus' into his position and function.

Yes, 'Homo economicus' came to dominance from the Reformation onwards, succeeding the older figure of the priest. Only in the nineteenth century did humanity in general arrive at the stage which the Church—with its far better understanding of progress—had already come to at the time of the Reformation. But this economist type prevailed only into the nineteenth century, and then gave way to yet another type. In saying that this new type became dominant, we mean that it came to control the structure of society. In the first couple of decades of the nineteenth century, the usurer or banker became dominant. If you seek a true definition of the banker you find that history becomes extremely touchy about it. If—it is mostly avoided—you study real, underlying socio-economic factors to discover a definition of the figure of the banker, whether great or small, be careful to avoid seeking a definition of the usurer too, for in fact the two definitions closely resemble each other, inevitably. And this is a secret that has been carefully guarded in recent times, just as certain secret societies have guarded their 'symbols' and 'phrases' rather than scattering their 'pearls' before humanity in general. This remained hidden in ordinary society.

Bankers became dominant. And if we examine how social structures developed during the nineteenth century, we find that in the first couple of decades of that century the banker, this specific economic type whose economic activity involves only money, came to exert his decisive influence—as 'Homo economicus' had done formerly—on all developing social structure, on all national laws and suchlike. It is very important to understand these circumstances—that 'Homo economicus' ruled from the Reformation onwards, that the banker type becomes dominant from the start of the nineteenth century. And we cannot understand public life in the civilized world in recent times if we do not see in it the history of the dominance of banking. Towards the end of the nineteenth century there arose what I already spoke of in 1908, in my lecture series in Nuremberg.[50] In the first half of the nineteenth century and a little way on into the second half, the owner or bearer of money was dominant as an individual; but then this principle of dominance changed so that money itself became dominant. In the first half of the nineteenth century individuals were dominant as bankers. If you recall, I gave an example to illustrate this. I told you how the King of France once sought to 'tap' money from Mr Rothschild in Paris.[51] Now if Rothschild is going to be tapped for funds by the King of France, this tells us, doesn't it, who was really in charge? Kings don't of course do their own tapping of funds directly. The king sent his minister—'finance minister' as this kind of minster of economic affairs is known—who arrived when Rothschild was just busy with a leather dealer. Rothschild's servant told the envoy from the King of France to wait in the anteroom. The finance minister of the French king regarded this as highly unusual—to be kept waiting while Rothschild talked to a leather dealer. He should wait? No thank you!

Instead of waiting, he pulled open the doors himself and announced that he was there in the name of the King of France. 'Do take a seat a moment,' said Rothschild. The minister could not begin to comprehend such treatment. 'But I am the envoy of the King of France,' he said. 'Well, take two seats then, but please sit down!'

You see, at that time a particular individual banker held sway, but this gradually passed into the reign of shares and banknotes themselves. And gradually we sailed on into the era when individual owners of money are no longer the chief thing, but the abstract accumulation of capital. Someone can be rich today and poor tomorrow. Individuals themselves rise and fall. But the joint stock or public limited company, the abstract, corporate 'person'—as I showed in Nuremberg in 1908—became dominant instead.

And thus human evolution arrived at an extreme, most outward point. You see, as soon as money itself rules or reigns, as soon as it is the driving engine, the time has arrived when the mere cash figure, money itself, must be succeeded by realities. Now money is the most spiritual element in the economy. It is the aspect of the economy that can only be comprehended spiritually. And money only has a spiritual value, one that exists solely in human acknowledgement or evaluation. You can eat bread and meat, but not money. If money is recognized you can acquire useful things by means of it. It has only an inner, soul or spiritual value, a conceptual value, a value in thought. And the time has arrived when something must change in evolution, from the purely economic spiritual value of money to what is really grasped in the spirit. And now the social insights that need to be fostered through threefolding should follow directly from the dominance of the most highly abstract economic entity of money. The darkness and obscurity of social insights amongst people today must give way to illumination. Now imagine [see drawing] that this represents a person from birth to death.

The person gains social insight in this first life into the fact that society, social structure is not founded on the monetary value at work in it, but on social understanding. Then the person passes through the portal of death, passes through the time until his next birth, and

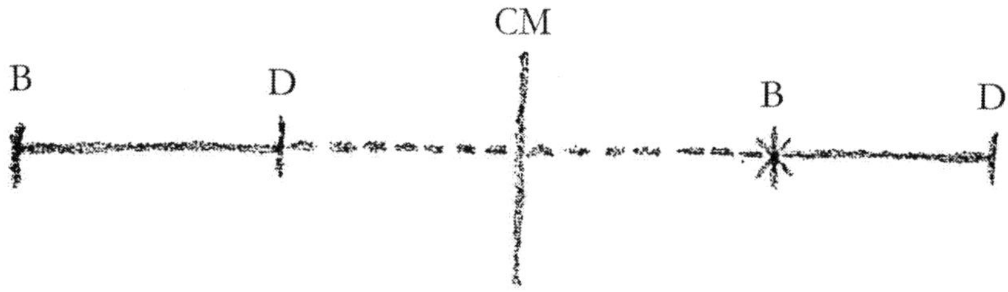

Board drawing 9

then lives from birth to death again. The social insight a person acquires between birth and death also of course lies inwardly in him and above all enters the sleeping will as I described it yesterday; and it is this that is borne through the portal of death. Thus a person bears his social insight into death and through to the moment of cosmic midnight, bearing it then onward through birth and into his next life on earth.

What becomes of this acquired social understanding, these social insights, in the following life? This great question is one we must ask today. These insights become understanding of karma. In other words, the present era of humanity's overall evolution is one when humankind must acquire social understanding, for it brings understanding of karma in a following incarnation. But no one can acquire social insights except by acquiring understanding of the spirit.

You see how things are interrelated, how social understanding is dependent on spiritual understanding, on a spiritual grasp of the world and outlook, and how in turn this social understanding can give rise, as human evolution continues, to the necessary perception of destiny: when people pass through the portal of death with social insights, and subsequently are reborn, they will come to understand their destiny in their following life.

This is the important thing: for us to fully recognize how things are connected, interrelated in humanity's earthly evolution. We live in an era when social insights are necessary; and we will be reborn in an era when individuals will understand their destiny. It is truly no abstract impulse to say that social understanding is necessary today, for it is intimately connected with earthly humanity's inmost evolutionary impulses.

This is what I wished to impress on you today, my dear friends. Next time we will speak further of these things.

The lectures in Zurich—as you know the public lecture tomorrow will be held in Basel—have to be postponed for two days due to a change of lecture hall. The first lecture will take place on 24 October, and then there will be lectures on 25, 26, 28, 29 and 30 October, and then a eurythmy performance in Zurich on 31 October. This means I won't be able to give the lectures here next weekend. For those of you who have the time and inclination for this, therefore, I will continue this series next Thursday at half past seven.

Lecture 10

Dornach, 23 October 1919

We have spoken from various angles about the relationship between a spiritual-scientific world-view and a social outlook. We are discussing these themes because it is so necessary to recognize today that thorough healing of our life and really fruitful developments towards the future are only possible if spiritual-scientific ideas enter human thinking and modes of thought.

Apart from what I said recently in relation to a retrospective view of our biography, something else can be said about it too. I pointed out that when we look back on our life so far, we must also be aware that, in the ordinary mind, we perceive it only discontinuously, and that states of sleep intervene between these discontinuous parts. These states of sleep are not really included in our review, and we easily succumb to a certain illusion in regard to this. We believe that our life is a continuous thread, but it is not. This life of ours shows us only interrupted episodes. But, if we draw on spiritual-scientific foundations, we ought to realize that periods unseen in our retrospective review are nevertheless just as much experience as the experiences incorporated into our ordinary mind and memory.

Now the experiences which the human soul always undergoes during sleep are not easy to describe; and this is because we must liberate ourselves from various things belonging to our ordinary outlook and awareness if we are to form any concept at all of what occurs for us in the periods between falling asleep and awakening again.

In ordinary life we live in space and time. When fully asleep—seen now from the perspective of ordinary consciousness—it is true to say that we are living neither in ordinary time nor ordinary space. When we recall what happens to us during sleep, this memory is a kind of shadow image or we can say a 'projection' of what has been experienced in sleep into the space-time conditions of waking life.

But if you wish to study these conditions more precisely, you will have to consider also that the state of sleep is not simply one of rest in contrast to the waking state. In this respect, particularly, we are at risk of succumbing to a mistaken judgement based more on preconceptions than on actual seeing. If we regard ordinary waking life as our 'normal' state, we can ask when our sleeping rest occurred. This rest is only present really at two points: the moment of falling asleep, and the moment of awakening. Falling asleep and awakening are in a sense zero points compared to waking consciousness. The state of sleep itself is not a zero point, but the opposite. Let's take a metaphor for this from mathematics. You can have a sum of money, let us say 50 francs. You have this sum. When you have spent it all you have nothing. But when you have accrued debts to the tune of 50 francs, you have less than nothing, a negative sum. The zero point relative to waking life is the moment of falling asleep, and that of reawakening; but the state of sleep itself is a negative condition relative to the ordinary waking state. While we sleep processes occur that are the reverse of ones occurring in waking life—processes of a very different kind, ones whose reality is not subject to the laws of space and time like those of waking consciousness.

But something really comes into its own element in this state of sleep, as you may have sensed in a recent lecture: our true I. The I lives in our will, but is asleep there as we know. The true I does not enter our ordinary life of thoughts; we would never becomes aware of it except as a kind of negative space. And as we look back on our life and experiences, we do not include both days and nights in our review, but only the waking experiences of our days. And instead of saying that we look back on our nights, we say 'I'; we feel ourselves to be an I.

Such truths must slowly permeate human beings for otherwise they will be crushed by a merely scientific view of the world, which has of course also, for the majority of people today, come to encompass all other realms of life, all other outlooks. We will only come to know ourselves fully if we can say to ourselves at every moment of our life that we are not only a person of flesh and blood, with consciousness, as most people today are aware of, but also someone who hatches or emerges from his body between falling asleep and reawakening. And that during this time of sleep we live in quite different conditions than in ordinary waking life. Only then, during sleep, is our I in its own, true element—it can unfold and lay claim to its substantiality. During waking life our I is only present in the will. In thinking and even in a large part of our feeling, we only possess images of this I.

This is why it is badly mistaken for some philosophers to claim that there is reality in the I a person addresses as his. Only if we woke to higher consciousness in sleep would we perceive the true I; or if we could see the process at work in the will, then too we could experience our true I in this will.

These things should really pass into our feelings and sensibility if they are to play their due part in life. We must be able to recognize that in our ordinary outlook on the world we are only able to comprehend one half of our being, and that in the other half we are perpetually embedded in supersensible experiences which we are unable to perceive with our ordinary consciousness. A person will only be able to acquire a certain reverence for underlying creative principles at work in us if he can connect with supersensible reality in this way. And in a materialistic age such as ours, not only will a view of the supersensible realm disappear but along with it also this reverence for the creative principles at work in the world. Reverence altogether will vanish from human hearts. There is really very little reverence today, very few of the feelings that can truly lift our sensibility to the supersensible realm. Many of the feelings people still try to preserve are nothing more than a kind of sentimentality—which is always also untrue. Sentimentality is never entirely true.

If we become conscious of such things—and once again I am obliged to mention this—by absorbing them into both our mind and feelings, a fact dawns before our mind's eye: that human life and the life of the world possess something like the character of a great mystery. And without this view, that life and the cosmic order are a mystery, real progress in humanity's evolution is unthinkable. An age like ours, in which no one wishes any longer to believe that life conceals secrets, can basically be only a passing episode. Such eras can exist in order that people cut themselves off for a while from their true depths, so that subsequently, through a counter-reaction to this withdrawal, they delve all the further into a real sense for the mystery of life. But this mystery of life can come home to us neither through sentimentality nor abstraction. It can only dawn on us if we are inclined to enter into the realities of the supersensible world in specific detail. We can make something like a beginning with this if we can really develop a kind of sacred feeling towards our entry into the state of sleep, and likewise a sacred feeling as we look back upon it: that condition when we were, without even really speaking metaphorically, dwelling in the habitations of the gods.

But ultimately we must recognize how far removed modern outlooks are from this, and how thoughtlessly humanity today regards this other side of life. But if the realm that lies behind falling asleep and awaking is not understood, how can anyone encompass what lies beyond the span between birth and death? Beyond this span of our earthly life lives something that also exists between birth and death, although here it is hidden behind a corporeal sheath. If there were a less egoistic religiosity, a more altruistic religiosity alive today—I have spoken of this before[52]—the experiences we pass through from birth onwards would be seen as a continuation of pre-birth or pre-conception existence in the world of spirit. And then we would see occurrences in human life as miracles, as enigmas we must continually seek to decipher. We would feel a longing to look upon human development as a revelation of something that takes shape, configures and embodies itself from supersensible worlds into the sense world. And basically it is already true to say that we can only comprehend post-mortem existence in the right way if we first consider life before birth.

Life is indeed full of mysteries, and in our era evolutionary necessities mean that a number of them must be revealed to humanity. We cannot acquire awareness of the entirety of our being and nature if we do not enlarge our view of ourselves to encompass life both before birth and after death. Without allowing our pre-birth and after-death life to shine into this corporeal existence we will know only a part of our being. It is still extraordinarily difficult to talk to people about these things unless they are previously prepared somewhat through a study of anthroposophy. Either they are keenly interested in preventing the truth of such things from reaching others, or they simply fail to understand them. You need only look around you to discover that most people, in their habituated views of the world, pay very little attention indeed to pre-birth life. They are more concerned with life after death because they would much prefer to survive the decay of their physical body. Religious confessions reckon with this kind of egoism, speaking basically only of life after death but not of life before birth.

Now this isn't the whole picture, but it is still hard to talk about these things today since it is a dogma of the Catholic Church not to believe in a life before birth, and other religious confessions have adopted this too. Most of the Christian confessions now consider it heresy to speak of pre-birth life. But to dogmatically refuse to consider life before birth has an extraordinary impact on humanity's evolution. I am not so much speaking of conscious things but more unconscious factors in human evolution, but there is almost nothing conceivably more likely to cradle people in illusions about their own nature than to withhold from them insights into life before birth. This is because it falsifies our whole outlook on life if we are deceived into thinking our presence here on earth is due only to mother and father. In creating this illusion, the Church has secured itself a hugely powerful means to withhold insight into pre-birth existence. And the

Church will therefore fight ferociously against all teachings concerning it. The Church will not endure them. One should not succumb to any illusions on this point, nor should one think that life is easy to understand without taking account of pre-birth existence.

But there is something resulting from this to which you should give deep and thorough heed. Let us recognize that it lay in the interests of ecclesiastical confessions to withhold important truths about human nature from people, that they more or less made it into their mission to do so. By this means the churches were able to wrap people in dullness and illusion. And now today we must no longer be deceived about this, nor seek a tactful compromise here with all kinds of ecclesiastical confession. No compromise should be made. And let us be clear that it will serve no purpose to try to say that anthroposophy is concerned with the Christ, is not atheistic, nor pantheistic and so on. This will never help, since the Church confessions will not mind in the least if you do *not* concern yourself with Christ. They wish to hold a monopoly on speaking about Christ and they will simply be irritated that *you* concern yourself with Christ. They want to hold a monopoly on the subject, and there is no point in your forbearance, for if you accommodate them you will always be inclined to conceal the most important aspects of life in fog and obscurity. Humanity at present needs to work its way through to spiritual insights, to which the dogmatic Church confessions are most of all opposed, especially those confessions that have gradually developed here in the West. The Church as such cannot be at odds with spiritual-scientific insights—that is impossible for intrinsically the Church ought to be concerned only with human feeling, with ceremonies and acts of worship but not with the life of thoughts. An educated Oriental completely fails to comprehend western ecclesiastical confessions, since he well knows he is bound to the outward rite, giving himself up to ceremonies customary in his faith, but may think whatever he likes. In oriental faiths there is still some regard for freedom of thought, a freedom that the Europeans have entirely lost. They have been raised to subservience in their thinking, especially since the eighth or ninth century AD. And this is why people in the

West find it so difficult to grapple with things I recently said:[53] that it is easy to prove any point of view, that one can prove one thing and, equally well, its opposite. And the fact that something can be proven is no evidence of the truth of what is asserted. To arrive at the truth you have to delve into far deeper strata of experience than those in which our ordinary proofs lie. But such experience is not something that Church confessions wished to bring to the surface, and so they have sundered people from truths such as this: *O man, you stand here! And as your organism develops from infancy, gradually there develops in you what you underwent in your life before birth.*

And what is it that chiefly develops out of pre-birth existence in an individual human life between birth and death?

Well, we can distinguish between a person's individual life and social interactions. Without keeping these two poles of human experience apart, you cannot actually form any idea of the human being at all: individual life (what we possess at every moment as our most intrinsically private experience), and social life (what we could not have if we did not continually enter into an exchange of thoughts and into other kinds of interaction with people). Individual and social factors play into human life. Everything that is individual in us is, basically, the reverberation of pre-birth life, while everything we develop in the social realm is the germ of life after death. Recently[54] we even noted that it is the germ of karma; and so we can say that we contain both individual and social aspects in ourselves. What is individual is the echo of pre-birth existence, and what is social is the germ of post-mortem existence.

The first part of this truth, that the individual element is in a sense the echo of pre-birth life, is something we can see particularly well if we study those with special gifts. Let's go to a radical extreme, which is a good idea here, and consider the phenomenon of genius. Where does the power of genius originate? Genius is an unusual capacity of some kind that a person brings with them at birth. It is always the outcome of life before birth. And since, understandably, pre-birth life comes to expression in childhood especially—for later a person adapts more to the life between birth and death, whereas in childhood everything he experienced prior to birth emerges—the childlike quality is expressed throughout a genius's life. We can say that a genius is distinguished by his ability to preserve something childlike throughout life. The genius maintains his youthfulness, his childlike quality into advanced old age because genius itself is connected with pre-birth existence. But not just genius, all gifts, everything that makes someone an individual, are connected with pre-birth existence. If one therefore insists on the dogma that there is no such thing, no pre-existence, what does this imply? It is a way of spreading the doctrine that no foundation exists for special, individual gifts. You know that if they are entirely honest, ecclesiastical confessions hold that there are no grounds for personal gifts. One can't actually dispute that these gifts exist, but what underlies and sustains them is denied, and so they can be regarded as fairly unimportant.

And this is connected in turn with the fact that Church confessions reigning for centuries have brought about an education in Europe that ultimately led to human uniformity today, to the levelling of people. How do people today regard individual gifts and talents? And what would they be if socialist teachings were made reality? In such matters it is less important to take outward names at face value than to consider inner connections. Someone who is both a Catholic who believes in the dogmas of his faith and at the same time hates the teachings of the Social Democrats lives in a very curious dichotomy. It is like saying that you met a little boy in 1875 of whom you grew very fond,[55] and still like him a great deal today. And if someone objects that the little boy of 1875 has of course become a man by now, and stands before you as a Social Democrat, no longer the little boy he was, it is as if you were to reply that yes, you are still fond of the little boy from back then with the life he had at the time, but you don't at all like what he has become. Social Democracy grew from Catholicism! Catholicism is merely the little boy who grew up to be Social Democracy. Neither the former nor the latter wish to acknowledge this is so—simply because people do not wish to discern a living dynamic in the social realm, but see in it instead just something like papier mâché, something stiff and rigid that retains its form for as long as it does. In fact, what lives in society grows and lives, and it can also be preserved; but then one must distinguish between illusion and reality. Look, you distinguish between illusion and reality if you recognize the following. Catholicism in the eighth century grew to be the Social Democracy of the twentieth! And what survives as Catholicism alongside it is not true Catholicism of the eighth century but an imitation of it; is a Catholicism copied from it, since true Catholicism has in the meanwhile grown to be Social Democracy.

In general this is not acknowledged since people do not wish to take the trouble to see realities, preferring instead to set up illusions, deceptions in front of reality. And that is easily done. You simply give something that has long gone the same name as it once had. But if—to put this in a nutshell—you give the name Catholicism to what is represented in Rome and disseminated through Europe, give it the same name as applied to what Rome embodied in the eighth century, it is like calling a 60-year-old man a boy of 8! The boy was once 8, but he no longer is now.

I am drawing your attention here to something we need to consider since the social realm can be regarded as something living and not dead. And unless we comprehend these things, humanity today will not succeed in gaining insight into the nature of truly social existence. Society's roots lie in spheres into which we usually no longer delve with our externalized nomenclatures, in whatever language. We have most chance of doing so in oriental languages, little enough in European languages, and least of all in English or American English, which is far removed from reality. In other words, our languages are obstacles to understanding the social realm, and humanity will only develop insight into society by emancipating itself from merely linguistic understanding. But nowadays people abhor everything that goes beyond mere linguistic comprehension. And what one most often finds is that when anyone tries to explain something to you they first offer you some verbal explanation. And yet it does not matter at all how you call or name something, what words you use to describe it. What is important instead is to lead people to reality, not to words. Above all, therefore, if we wish to develop social understanding, we must overcome our entanglement in language, and this can happen only if we also overcome the greatest prejudices of our time. In the terrible war years we have recently experienced, we heard the call of 'freedom for every nation!' resounding through the world. The smallest nations today seek to establish their own social structures. A passion and paroxysm of nationalism has come over humankind, and this is as injurious for society on earth as materialism is for our life of thought. And just as we must work our way beyond materialism towards freedom and spirituality, so human beings must work their way beyond nationalism, in whatever form it manifests, towards a universal humanity. Unless we do, we will not make progress.

We will however not find it possible to emerge entirely from nationalism if our languages do not approximate themselves to deeper forms of expression for the spirit. I'd like to close these reflections more or less with a picture, and if you ponder on it a little you can arrive at various things of importance for understanding the modern age. Look at any book today and you see these little devils, printed words, as black words on white paper. They have grotesque forms, and in their juxtaposition they signify the sounds of speech. They can be traced back to other, more expressive forms of writing and script. If we go back a long way we come to forms of writing such as the Egyptians possessed, or ancient Sanskrit, which more or less originated entirely from snakelike forms. Sanskrit symbols are transformed snake shapes, with all sorts of additions. The Egyptian hieroglyphs were still painted or drawn images, picture script; and in their most ancient period were even an imagination of what was portrayed or embodied. Script derived directly from the spirit. Then it grew ever more abstract until it became something that was already bad enough, our own ordinary script, connected with what it signifies only by virtue of our learning its forms.

Then came something still more dire, stenography, which is now the complete death of this whole system that developed out of the old picture script. The declining line of development must give way in turn to an ascending one. We have to return to a trajectory that leads us back from everything that script, especially, drew us down into. And the beginning of an attempt to do so has been made in the form of what stands here on the Dornach hill. Though this building leaves much to be desired, much of it is imperfect, its forms express in a contemporary way the supersensible being towards whom we human beings should look. It is also, I would say, intended as a world hieroglyph. If you really study its various forms you will be able to read in them far more than you can absorb through descriptions of the spiritual realm, or at least that is the intention. The intention is to realize a cosmic script in this building. Script emerged from art originally, and it must return to art. And it must move beyond symbolism to allow the spirit to live directly within it, by becoming again a new kind of hieroglyph.

The building that stands here will only be rightly understood if we recognize that there are various demands upon humanity today that require an answer. Basically, the words of language are no longer by any means sufficient to give this reply. Such an answer has been attempted with the forms of this building. Much in it is imperfect, but this building has been an attempt to give an answer. And if one looks at it in this light, it will be the right way to look at it.

This is what I wished to add to our previous reflections.

LECTURE 11

DORNACH, 1 NOVEMBER 1919

IN speaking during these days of social questions, among other things, this really is not based on any subjective programme, any subjective impulse, but, as I have already characterized from all sorts of angles, on observation of human evolution and of the evolutionary forces at work in humanity in our particular era, and on what they prompt us to develop today and in the near future.

It is a difficult business to unveil the deeper impulses at work in what concerns humanity's evolution at the present time, for today people are disinclined to consider important matters with true and profound seriousness. But thorough seriousness is required in relation to the concerns of humanity in our era. Our time prompts us to free ourselves from very specific prejudices, and in particular from presuppositions. Today I'd like to offer a few perspectives that can enable us to view things we have often spoken of in the past in a deeper way. And here we will certainly have to direct our gaze to a somewhat broader context concerning humanity.

We distinguish the era in which we currently live, our cosmic present, from other eras, by saying that it started in the mid-fifteenth century; and as you know, we refer to this period as the fifth post-Atlantean epoch. And we divide this from the period that ended when this one began, which in turn started in the eighth century BC, and which we call the Graeco-Roman in reference to the peoples informing and sustaining its culture. And then going back further still, we identify a previous Egyptian-Chaldean epoch.

Now if we look, inwardly of course, at this Egyptian-Chaldean epoch, we find that ordinary history falls far short. Even if we study historical records for this period, we cannot delve very far back into the evolutionary history of humanity. And yet it is only when we can properly understand the distinctive character of this third post-Atlantean epoch that we can draw on it to see things of significance for our modern era.

You are aware of one thing above all: in ordinary history, the culture and civilization of the then known world is referred to as 'pagan'. Judaic-Hebrew culture sits amidst it like an oasis, and must be seen as a preparation for Christianity. But if we overlook the pre-Christian Judaism isolated amidst the quite different culture of those times, we can consider the nature of this widespread pagan civilization. What is distinctive about it? It is primarily a culture of wisdom, one of perception and vision of things and occurrences in the world. Even if our 'clever' contemporaries regard the pagan view of the world, issuing from the ancient mysteries, as being of 'mythic' and pictorial character, it must nevertheless be said that all such images and myths passed down to us originate in profound insights into the nature of things and processes.

We need only recall what we sought to characterize as the supersensible wisdom arising in various regions in these ancient times, and we will see that we are concerned here with a primordial wisdom underlying all the thinking, feeling, and sensibility of these ancient peoples. Until the end of the eighteenth century, and even through into the early nineteenth century, a certain echo of this primordial wisdom, a tradition that encompassed it, existed and thrived in some secret societies. During the nineteenth century this fount more or less dried up, and what remained came to serve the interests of particular groups, and especially particular nationalities. What still exists in ordinary secret societies today can no longer be regarded as authentic and fruitful pagan wisdom originating in ancient times.

This store of pagan wisdom has a particular quality that we ought never to overlook if we wish to understand what is really at work here. It has a quality that necessitated the smaller oasis of Judaism establishing itself, as preparation for Christianity, within this larger expanse of pagan wisdom.

If we properly perceive this ancient pagan culture, we find that it everywhere contains great and sublime stores of wisdom, wisdom that profoundly penetrates to the very essence of things. And yet this pagan wisdom contains no real moral impulse for human actions. In a sense these ethical impulses for human action were not needed then, since unlike the human knowledge that exists in our own time, this ancient pagan wisdom really gave people a sense of being rooted in the whole cosmos. The human being dwelling and walking upon the earth did not feel himself constituted only of the substances and forces present outside him in earthly life in the mineral, animal and plant kingdoms. The human being felt how forces or powers play into him that also circulate in stars and sun and so forth. He felt himself to be part of the whole cosmos—not only in an abstract way, but his mysteries gave him points of reference for undertaking actions, for his whole conduct, in accord with the course of the stars and planets. The ancient star lore was nothing like the computational astrology to which people today assign importance. This ancient star wisdom was regarded by the leaders of ancient pagan mysteries as the source of real impulses for the actions and conduct of each individual. The human being knew himself to be safely embedded in the cosmos, not only in terms of a generalized wisdom. What he was to do from morning to evening on any day of the year was read for him from the stars and given to him as directives by those he acknowledged as initiates in the mysteries. But in Chaldean and Egyptian lore, nothing of what the initiates deciphered in this way from the mysteries contained any kind of moral impulse for humanity. Moral impulses as such were first prepared through Judaism, which was later developed and elaborated further by Christianity.

And now we must ask this: why is it that this glorious ancient pagan wisdom, which came to the loveliest artistic and philosophical flowering in ancient Greece for example, contained no moral impulses?

If however we were to go further back to the third millennium BC, we would find that the impulse of wisdom is at the same time accompanied by a moral impulse too, and that this is absolutely as I have already described:[56] that this impulse of wisdom simultaneously embodied what ancient peoples needed as their moral and ethical principles. But a separate and distinctive ethos and moral impulse, as appeared in Christianity, did not as such inform pagan wisdom. Why? This was because during the millennia immediately preceding Christianity this pagan wisdom drew its source of inspiration from a place far to the East in Asia, from the very remarkable being of Lucifer who was actually incarnated in the third millennium BC in far-off eastern Asia.

To the knowledge we have gained about humanity's evolution, we must add the fact that, just as Christ incarnated at Golgotha in the human being Jesus of Nazareth, so Lucifer also actually incarnated in the third millennium BC in Asia. And a great portion of ancient culture was inspired by this earthly incarnation of Lucifer in a living human being of flesh and blood. Indeed, Christianity, the Mystery of Golgotha, as it first unfolded amongst human beings, was originally comprehended in a way inevitably informed by what people had received from ancient, luciferic wisdom. Even the otherwise extraordinarily profound Gnosis had limitations that were due to the fact that this luciferic incarnation exerted its influences across the ancient world. We cannot understand the full significance of the Mystery of Golgotha unless we know that it was preceded, not quite three millennia earlier, by an incarnation of Lucifer.

The Christ incarnation came to add to this Lucifer inspiration what redeems it from one-sidedness. And thus came also what now creates the educative impulse for humanity in regard to the development of European civilization and its American adjunct. But since the middle of the fifteenth century—since the impulse arose to develop, primarily, individuality and individual personality—this process of evolution also includes the forces that again prepare the incarnation of a supersensible being. Just as there was a bodily incarnation of Lucifer, and an incarnation of Christ in the flesh, so, early in the third millennium since Christ's advent, there will be an actual incarnation of Ahriman: Ahriman in the flesh. This bodily incarnation of Ahriman is not something earthly humanity can escape. It will come. And it is only a matter of earthly humanity finding the right stance towards it.

In everything of this kind that happens, when such incarnations are being prepared, we must consider what gradually leads towards them in the evolution of humanity. An entity like Ahriman, who is seeking to incarnate in the western world at a certain point after this current time of ours, is already preparing his incarnation. As he does so, he guides and governs particular forces in human evolution in such a way as to be very specially advantageous to him. It would be a bad thing indeed if human beings were to sleepwalk towards this and fail to recognize in certain phenomena occurring in human life these preparations for Ahriman's corporeal incarnation. People will only find the right outlook by perceiving in this or that sequence of events informing human evolution how Ahriman is preparing his earthly existence. It is high time that individuals should recognize which of the events and occurrences unfolding around them are the machinations of Ahriman, and may be advantageous to him as he prepares his forthcoming incarnation on earth.

It would doubtless be most advantageous of all for him if the great majority of human beings had no inkling whatsoever of the things that favour and prepare his coming incarnation, if the great majority of people went about their lives with the view that these unfolding preparations for Ahriman's incarnation were good, progressive, of benefit to and appropriate for human evolution. If Ahriman could sneak into a slumbering humanity, this would give him the greatest pleasure. And this is why we must identify the events and occurrences within which Ahriman is working towards his coming incarnation.

One of these evolutionary realities in which we can clearly discern the ahrimanic impulse is the spreading belief amongst humankind that a mechanical, mathematical comprehension of the cosmos, which first arose in the form of Galileism, Copernicanism and so on, can enable us to understand the life and workings of the cosmos beyond us. This is why anthroposophic spiritual science so keenly emphasizes the need to seek spirit and soul in the cosmos, rather than merely what Galileism or Copernicanism seek in the form of mathematics, mechanics, as if the world were a great machine. We would succumb to the ahrimanic temptation if we stopped short at merely calculating the orbits of planets, if we studied only astrophysics rather than delving beyond the physical constituents of heavenly bodies, discovery of which is regarded as such a proud achievement today. It would be grave indeed if we did not counter this Galileism and Copernicanism with knowledge we can gain about the permeation of the cosmos by soul and spirit. But Ahriman, seeking favourable conditions for his incarnation, most definitely wishes to avoid such an outlook. He desires to keep people as dull-witted as possible in the sense of only comprehending the mathematical aspect of astronomy. For this reason he seduces many into affirming their commonplace rejection of the existence of spirit and soul in the universe. This, however, is only one of the seductive forces that Ahriman infiltrates, if you like, into human souls.

Another of these seductive ahrimanic forces connected with his forthcoming incarnation—and one might say that he collaborates accordingly with Lucifer—is his endeavour to sustain amongst human beings the already widespread sense that an economically satisfactory existence is all that is required in society. Here we touch on something that modern people are disinclined to acknowledge—which is that modern, mainstream science no longer offers anything in terms of knowledge of the spirit and soul. The methods employed in modern, mainstream science are fit only for grasping the external characteristics of nature, the external nature too of the human being. Consider how disparaging the average citizen is today of anything that strikes him as idealistic, or that in any way suggests to him a pathway of some kind towards the spiritual realm. He will continually ask what use this is, what earthly benefit it brings. He educates his sons at a grammar school or some other institution, then sends them to university or college. But all this serves only really to prepare them for a profession, or in other words to procure the material goods they require or the food they eat.

Consider for a moment what we touch upon when we touch on this question. So many people today no longer accord the spirit or the soul any intrinsic value. They take from mainstream culture and knowledge only what they have been told is useful, that has some utilitarian value. And here we must recognize a very important, mysterious fact that holds true today. A solid, average, modern citizen who works at the office industriously from morning till evening and then participates in the normal evening formalities or customs will absolutely refuse to engage in the kind of 'irrelevancies' presented in anthroposophic spiritual science. These seem to him superfluous, since after all, as he sees it, these things procure him nothing material. He can't eat them. He believes—though people may often be reluctant to concede this—that all really useful knowledge should ultimately serve to put food on the table.

Yes, a curious error that people today so often embrace: they think that the spirit is not something they can eat. And yet the very people who say this are the ones who actually do! You see, to the degree that you refuse in any way to absorb spirit, which would otherwise be assimilated *as* spirit, you devour spirit with every bite you introduce materially into your mouth and stomach, and conduct it down channels other than the ones it would need to take if it were to be wholesome for humanity.

It seems to me a cultural advance that we can safely say most Europeans are not cannibals! But, with their American adjunct, they are nevertheless devourers of soul and spirit. Material substance devoured unspiritually means that the spirit slides off on an erroneous path. It is hard to say such things to people today. But try to really grasp for a moment how much of modern culture must be characterized once one knows this fact. And maintaining the human being in this kind of soul- and spirit-devouring state is one of Ahriman's impulses to support and prepare his coming incarnation.

If we succeeded in shaking people awake to recognize, alongside a merely material economy, the autonomous, free life of culture, which really possesses spirit, as a part of the social organism, we could await Ahriman's incarnation with a stance and outlook that accorded with our full humanity.

Another strand in our life today which Ahriman needs to further his own incarnation is what comes to such prominence today in the 'national principle'. Everything that can sunder people into different groups and classes, and distance them from mutual understanding across the globe, everything that divides and separates them, at the same time furthers Ahriman's impulses. The call for national liberation, even of the smallest states, and suchlike, is one in which we ought to discern the voice of Ahriman. The times have passed when blood ties and national traits should come to the fore. And where such outmoded things are preserved, this furthers what Ahriman seeks to further.

Likewise we further what Ahriman seeks to further if we do not energetically reject what I have often characterized here in the past: nowadays there are all kinds of people with the most diverse party political views and outlooks. All these outlooks can equally well be proven correct. You can prove the truth of what some socialist party states just as much as what an anti-socialist party adheres to, and you will have equally valid grounds for doing so. If people do not recognize that this mode of proof is very superficial, and that our present mode of intelligence can prove whatever it likes, both for and against anything—and this is very useful for mainstream science but useless for another kind of knowledge—then people will fail to see that this superficial intelligence of theirs, so serviceable for science, is something that should not be applied to the life of society, to the life of spirit. Then different groups will prove opposite things to be true, and since both will be valid it will lead people to hatred and bitterness—of which we have plenty already in our era. These are again things that Ahriman seeks to promote in order to further his own incarnation on earth.

Something that will serve Ahriman especially well in furthering his earthly incarnation is a one-sided grasp of the Gospels themselves. You know how necessary it has become in our time to deepen our understanding of the Gospels through spiritual science; but at the same time you are aware, too, how widespread is the view that understanding of them should not be spiritually deepened—that we ought not to express things relating to the Gospels that issue from a true knowledge of the spirit, of the cosmos. We ought apparently to 'simply accept' them as we meet them today. I have no wish at all to discuss the fact that the true Gospels are not in the least available to us, since what we possess today as translations from the ancient languages of the Gospels are not the Gospels. But let's leave that to one side altogether. Instead, I'd like to speak of the deeper-lying fact that we cannot come to a true comprehension of Christ if we seek only—like most confessions and sects today—to engage with the Gospels in what these confessions call a 'simple' way, which actually means easily and comfortably. At the period when the Mystery of Golgotha took place, and for a few centuries after it, people comprehended the true Christ because they could grasp what was said of him with the aid of luciferic, pagan wisdom. This wisdom receded, and what people today draw from the Gospels in their diverse confessions and sects does not lead them to the reality of Christ whom we seek through our science of the spirit, but only to an illusion or, at most, a hallucination, a soul or spiritualized hallucination of the Christ.[57]

It is not possible to reach the reality of Christ if we do not draw on spiritual science to fathom these Gospels. Without this we delve only as far as a hallucination of Christ's appearance in world history. This has become thoroughly apparent in modern theology. Why are modern theologians so keen to speak of the 'simple' man of Nazareth, and to regard the Christ really only as the man Jesus of Nazareth, someone just a little loftier than other historical figures? It is because people have lost the capacity to approach the reality of Christ, and because what they have drawn from the Gospels takes them only as far as a kind of hallucination, something illusory. They cannot truly encompass the reality of Christ through the Gospels, but only an idea that is hallucinatory or illusory. Think how many theologians speak of Paul's experience near Damascus as 'only a vision'. This is a subliminal recognition, really, that their view of the Gospels can offer them only a vision or hallucination. In this they are not mistaken, but are inwardly aware that their experience has no connection with the reality of the Christ being. I am not using the word 'hallucinatory' in any disparaging way, but I want only to characterize how theologians grasp the Christ being only in the same manner as an inward hallucination is produced. If people were to get no further than this, if they did not work their way through to the reality of Christ but only gained a hallucination of him, Ahriman would find his purposes best furthered.

(The Gospels likewise amount to a kind of hallucination if we engage only with a *single* Gospel.)[58] We have worked back against this principle of seeing the Gospels in isolation by considering the four Gospels from four different angles. Here it gets us nowhere to take each Gospel literally, for they outwardly contradict each other as we have often seen. There is a great danger in taking a single Gospel literally. The sects that swear by the literal content of a particular Gospel, of John or Luke, develop a sort of delusional idea, a kind of twilight consciousness. The dimmed consciousness that would develop precisely through a one-sided engagement with the Gospels, without spiritually deepened understanding, would produce people best fitted to help Ahriman prepare his incarnation. Such people would develop a stance towards him that perfectly served his purposes.

This again is an uncomfortable truth for people today. Within their confessions they think they have no need for anything like anthroposophy, for they keep close to the 'simple' message of the Gospels. Out of humility—they think—they adhere to the simple Gospels. In fact this is the worst arrogance conceivable: it consists in seemingly taking the Gospels literally, but then overriding the wisdom they contain with judgements they were endowed with by birth, ideas that eddy from their blood. The 'simplest' and most 'straightforward' people are usually the most arrogant, especially in the realm of religiosity and religious confession. Ahriman's coming incarnation is best prepared by people who repeatedly preach the need merely to read the Gospels and nothing more.

Remarkably, two very divergent parties work together here: those I described earlier as soul and spirit devourers, and those who further Ahriman's incarnation as I just characterized, by simply accepting the literal words of the Gospels. The two very much go hand in hand. If nothing came to light other than the world-view of the soul and spirit devourers on the one hand and of the literal Christians on the other, who do not wish to fathom the depths of the Gospels, Ahriman would be able to make everyone on earth an Ahrimanian! The positivist Christianity disseminated through the world today is preparing Ahriman's incarnation. In a great deal one can hear today that claims to represent the orthodoxy of the Church we ought really to discern a preparation for the works of Ahriman.

You see, things today are not as people assume them literally to be. As I have often said, people today live far too much in words, and we need instead to depart from words and enter into realities. We can say that words do in a sense sunder people today from the real nature of things. And people are divided most strongly from true being if they bring what is often called 'straightforward' or 'modest' understanding to bear on ancient texts, including the Gospels. It is actually far more modest or humble to really delve into the spirit of things, and the Gospels themselves, seeking to understand them from a spiritual perspective.

As I have said, Ahriman and Lucifer will always work hand-in-glove with each other. It is only a question of which of them gains the upper hand in human consciousness at any time. A strongly luciferic culture held sway until some time after the Mystery of Golgatha, from the incarnation of Lucifer in China in the third millennium BC onwards. From this incarnation a particularly strong influence was exerted until the early Christian centuries, and has still gone on working in our own era.

But now the signs and traces of Lucifer are growing fainter since an incarnation of Ahriman is approaching in the third millennium, and the signs of Ahriman are becoming particularly discernible in things such as those I have described. You can say that Ahriman has signed a contract with Lucifer, the words of which can be put as follows: 'I, Ahriman, consider it especially beneficial for me to claim use of the canned preserves, leaving people's stomachs to you. This latter on the condition that you will allow me to keep their stomachs—that is, human awareness of their stomachs—in a dulled and twilight state.'

What I mean by this is that the people I referred to as soul and spirit devourers remain unaware of the stomach, and what they introduce into their stomachs they lead directly into the luciferic stream unless they bear spirituality in their human nature. What they have eaten and drunk without spirituality goes straight through the stomach to Lucifer!

And what do I mean by the canned preserves? I mean libraries and suchlike which store academic knowledge undertaken without true interest; knowledge that does not live in people but in books in a library. Take a look at these academic pursuits, these disciplines that are undertaken without reference to human experience. There are huge numbers of books in libraries everywhere. Whenever a student has to write a scholarly thesis or a doctorate, these are sent off to as many libraries as possible. But quite apart from this, people write, and write and write nowadays, and only a very little of what is written is read. Only when people have to prepare themselves in some way for something do they resort to the library shelves and in turn quote whatever they find there, what is preserved there. These 'preserved cans of wisdom' are highly beneficial to Ahriman and further his preparations.

Things are done like this in every field: things are introduced into the world that would have meaning and purpose if people were actually interested in them, but they are not. And so in all fields we find things that are in a sense separate from the human being. It is enough to make one despair, if one were inclined to despair. Imagine you're involved in a court case and you need a lawyer to manage it. And then at some point you go and see the lawyer to discuss the case with him. He has no end of relevant papers in a file, for the documents multiply, but if I go to discuss these matters with him, he hasn't a clue about them. He opens the file and looks through all the documents, and gets nowhere: he has no real connection with his files. Here is one file, here another. The files grow. But there is absolutely no interest in them. It is enough to make you despair if you have anything to do with professionals who work like this. They have no connection with the matter in hand, and in reality know nothing about it, since everything is in the files themselves: little cans of preserves, while libraries are the big cans of spirit and soul preserves. People have no wish to connect with these things, to penetrate them with understanding or interest. And ultimately this gives rise to the mood prevalent today which fends off anything that requires the head. A little of the head is needed to understand something after all. People wish to refer their confession, their world-view, back to the heart alone. Naturally the heart must be involved; but the way in which people today often speak of their religious confession reminds me of a proverb common in the area where I grew up: 'It's a funny thing, is love. When you buy it, you're buying nothing but the heart, but you get the head thrown in for free.' That, roughly, is the mood that expresses what people today like to absorb as their world-view. They want to have it directly through the heart, as they say, without exerting their head—except that the heart doesn't beat without the head. But a lot can be absorbed through the heart if you actually mean the stomach. And then what the head ought to accomplish for humanity is meant to follow for free, it's meant to be thrown in as an extra, especially in the most important aspects of life.

It's important to take note of these things, very important. If you do, you see the seriousness required in relation to human life today, and the need to learn even from the illusions that can proceed from the Gospels, to learn from the predilection for illusions that people have today. The kind of knowledge for which people often seek today will not lead to truth. Using numerical calculations people think they can supply statistical evidence on which they can rely. Ahriman has an especially easy time with statistics and numbers, and he is very pleased indeed if, say, an academic demonstrates that the population of Macedonia consists of a certain number of Greeks, a certain number of Serbs, a certain number of Bulgarians, for people believe in numbers. And Ahriman does his sums with the numbers people believe in, as I explained to you today. But afterwards you realize how 'certain' these numbers actually are. Certainly, numbers offer specific evidence, but if you delve beyond what you find in accounts and records backed up by numerical evidence you will often find that, for instance in this example of Macedonia, a father is Greek, one of his sons is Serbian and another son is Bulgarian. Thus the father is included amongst the Greeks, one son amongst the Bulgarians and another son amongst the Serbians. And so the numbers themselves, which so greatly satisfy people today, fail to take account of the reality of one and the same family containing members of different nationalities, which would lead us to the actual truth. Numbers lead us in a direction which will best help Ahriman make all his figures add up as he prepares for his future incarnation in the third millennium.

Tomorrow we will speak further of this.

LECTURE 12

DORNACH, 2 NOVEMBER 1919

OUR reflections yesterday will have shown you that, in order to get insight into the real driving forces in human development and human nature, we must take full account of the powers of Lucifer, of Christ, and of Ahriman, and of their effect. These powers have certainly already been in play during the course of world evolution, and yet they were active in spheres that did not require human beings to have clear awareness of the way in which they worked. The very purpose of our fifth post-Atlantean epoch is that we increasingly acquire awareness of what works through us into earthly existence. It would actually already be necessary to reveal far, far more of the living mysteries of humanity if humanity had a greater inclination to absorb things in a more factual and objective way. But without certain insights of the kind indicated yesterday, humanity will make no progress initially either with the social realm or with inner life. Consider for a moment something that relates to our reflections on society, in which we have now been engaging for several months. They aim to show the need to separate cultural and spiritual life, as well as the life of rights, or the state, from merely economic life. Above all they aim to establish conditions across the world, or at least—and we cannot presently do more than this—to see that conditions across the world will be right if they establish an autonomous life of spirit, one that is independent of the other structures in society, unlike our present cultural and spiritual life, which is fully entangled with economic life on the one hand and the political life of the state on the other. Either modern, civilized humanity will have to adjust to this kind of autonomous life of culture and spirit, or modern civilization will decline and degenerate, leaving Asiatic cultures to develop something new for humanity in the future.

If you do not believe yet that things are as serious as I suggest, then you are in a sense furthering preparations for Ahriman's incarnation in the future. Today already one can discern in outward things, outward realities of human life, aspects that can inform us of this truth. Ahriman's incarnation will benefit very especially from a refusal to establish an autonomous, free life of spirit, instead leaving this entangled in economic circulation or in the life of the state. This is because ahrimanic powers have the greatest interest in maintaining this merger of spiritual life with economic life and the state. Ahrimanic powers regard a free life of spirit as a kind of darkness; and they will experience human interest in this free life of spirit as a burning fire, a soul fire, but nevertheless a powerfully blazing fire. Therefore, in order to find the right stance towards the incarnation of Ahriman in the near future, we are obliged to establish this free life of spirit. But nowadays there is still a strong tendency to conceal the realities we spoke of yesterday. The great majority of people conceal these things since they do not wish to contemplate the truth, the reality in things, preferring to delude themselves with words that are divorced from realities. Sometimes this endeavour to avoid approaching realities at all costs is one we might call honest and well-meaning.

Think for a moment of something like the letter by Romain Rolland just published,[59] in which the author states that we should no longer allow ourselves to be blinded by what the currently victorious powers used to say about justice, about legal representation and so on. He has been moved to make such statements in response to the treatment of Russia by the Entente powers. He says that irrespective of whether we are dealing with kingdoms or republics, these things said about law and justice are only phrases, are naturally concerned only with power.

We can say that an apparent engagement with realities such as this will invariably and repeatedly lead to blindness. Romain Rolland's blindness is as great as it always was, his illusions have not diminished. They would only diminish if such people got beyond mere phrases and recognized that all they desire signifies nothing unless they can come to truly understand that the old centralized state as such, irrespective of its particular constitution and structure—whether it is a democracy, republic, monarchy or what have you—is a path to Ahriman's incarnation unless it is given a threefold, tripartite form. All such things are therefore merely declamatory, even this recent 'world circular'[60] by Romain Rolland. People do not grasp realities, since they can only be comprehended if one recognizes how things must be deepened through spiritual perception. And here it is necessary to delve very deeply and thoroughly into the nature and essence of things.

I'm sure you know a text widely spoken in the world: 'In the beginning was the Word, and the Word was with God, and a God was the Word.' Try for a moment to determine whether people regard these words with all due gravity. They utter them, but just as a phrase. You can see this from the following. Most people place no importance on the fact that these lines are spoken in the imperfect tense:

> In the beginning *was* the Word
> And the Word *was* with God
> And a God *was* the Word.

Here 'Word' must at the same time have its older, ancient Greek meaning. It is not the word as people understand it today, merely a signifying sound, but the inward spirit. But the imperfect tense is used to refer to this Word too: 'In the beginning *was* the Word, and the Word *was* with God, and a God *was* the Word.' And so one has to say that since the Word *was* in the beginning, it no longer is. Otherwise the text would have to say, '*Now is* the Word.' Nor *is* the Word with God but *was* with God. And a God *was* the Word, and so no longer *is*. This is the way the text appears in the Gospel of St John itself, for what would otherwise be meant if it said, 'And the Word has become flesh, and has been dwelling among us'? The text relates, after all, to what lies in the further development of the Word. And by 'Word' is meant everything that we can gain through our intelligence as intellectual wisdom. We must be clear that everything we can acquire through what is represented here by the 'Word' is not what modern people should seek today and in the near future. If the text was to address something present now, it would really have to read: 'Let the human being seek the spirit revealed in the Word, for the spirit *is* with God, and the spirit *is* a God.'

Humanity has to move forward from the Word to the spirit, to perception and knowledge of the spirit. As I recall these first words of the Gospel of John, you can see how disinclined people are today to take these things really seriously, to really go beyond a merely arbitrary interpretation—such as is commonly given today to the most serious matters. We need to see that in our human nature, too, we must scrutinize what intelligence signifies and illumine it through what is revealed in spiritual vision—though spiritual vision itself is not always the essential thing so much as *understanding* of what has been spiritually perceived. I have repeatedly stressed that it is not only the clairvoyant who can understand the truth of what is clairvoyantly perceived, but every person, since people now certainly possess the maturity to comprehend the spiritual element in human nature: they need only resolve to exert themselves, and not rest too comfortably on their laurels. But for people to raise themselves to this fitting level they must accord due seriousness to things such as those with which we ended yesterday's reflections. Yesterday, citing a somewhat trivial example, I showed how easily numbers can deceive us. But surely people have a superstitious belief in numbers today. Anything that can be enumerated is accepted as scientific. Science is enamoured of weighing, measuring and counting. In the social sciences, statistics are greatly prized—likewise just a kind of weighing and counting. It will be very hard indeed for humanity to recognize that everything, absolutely everything that measure and number tell us of the outer world is illusory.

Look, what does 'measuring' mean? It means comparing against a standard. I can measure a line if I repeatedly compare it against a small rule. If you measure something, irrespective of whether it be lengths, surfaces or weights, no account is taken of qualities. The number three is always the same number, whether you use it to count sheep, people or politicians. No quality is indicated by the number, only quantity. But this means that everything we obtain in the form of number becomes mere smoke and mirrors. And we must recognize that at the moment we enter the world that can be weighed and measured, that is, the world of space and time as it is given to us, we enter also a world of illusion, one that is a mere mirage as long as we view it as a reality. This is really the ideal of contemporary thinking: to learn what all things in the temporal and spatial world signify, whereas in fact what these things signify is only their external aspect and we must go beyond time and space to delve further and deeper if we wish to arrive at truth and essence. Thus a future time will come where people will say, 'Yes, I can grasp the natural world around me with my intelligence, can do so as is, for instance, the ideal pursued by science. But this view I acquire is purely ahrimanic.' This doesn't mean we should reject science, that it ought not to exist. No. But we should remember that this science gives us only an ahrimanic mirage. Why is this? Why should we keep this science even though it offers us only smoke and mirrors? Because we are in a declining phase of earthly evolution; we are a being already in decline.

If you look back to the fourth of the five post-Atlantean epochs,

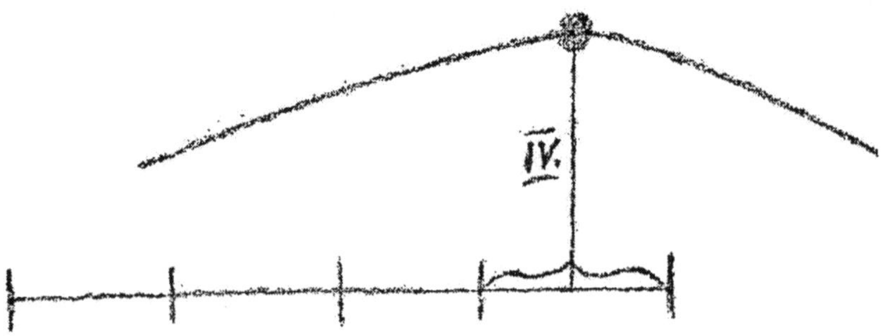

Board drawing 11

you find that people at the time had reached the highest relative point of knowledge and perception, whereas we are now already in decline. And in this state of relative decline—as I have explained before from various angles—our weakening corporeal nature would not cope with perceiving the world as the ancient Greeks still did.

'Outward history' says nothing of this of course! How would our worthy historians respond to such an idea today? They tell of the Greeks as if speaking of some region of the contemporary world, because they do not know that these Greeks looked upon nature with different eyes, that they listened out into the world with different ears than we possess. People today—and the historians will not tell you this—would continually get a headache or migraine if they saw and heard in their surroundings what the ancient Greeks saw and heard. The Greeks lived far more intensely in the external life of the sense world. In comparison we have already died away from such a living grasp of our outer surroundings. For us to cope with it, we have to be presented with a mere mirage of these outer surroundings. And that is indeed what is presented to us. What we do not merely see with our senses but what we dream in scientific ideas about our outer surroundings is most of all a mirage. Those who dream most about this outer world are the very ones who think they are most realistic in their thinking. Darwin or John Stuart Mill are real dreamers. The real dreamers are the ones who think they are most realistic.

But we cannot entirely rely on our interior life. There are many among you who can see from the developments that occurred in the Theosophical Society that merely pursuing interior experience—if done as many people today endeavour to—will not lead to anything that it should, since we must lead ourselves and not simply be led. Often, instead of reaching beyond ordinary life to higher vision or insight in freedom, through our own resolve, appeal is made to the unfree aspect of the human being. All kinds of hallucinatory capacities, capacities for illusion, are invoked instead.

But we ought to say this to ourselves: just as outward science becomes ahrimanic, so higher evolution of human interiority simply becomes luciferic if we mystically deepen this inner life that is innate in us. Anyone who, without any self-education—which is described in the book *Knowledge of the Higher Worlds*—undertakes to mystically deepen what already lies within him will find the luciferic awakening within him, and gaining particular ascendancy. And from this you will see that the luciferic element appears and arises today in anyone who even begins to brood on his interior experience. This element is actually terribly powerful today in contemporary humanity. It comes to expression in an egoism that most people do not even discern in themselves. Just consider how often we meet people who are satisfied with something they have done, who, as they may often say, have accomplished something that appears to them beyond reproof, according to their best knowledge and conscience. This is a purely luciferic perspective on things. You see, it doesn't at all matter in life whether we need to reprove ourselves or not, but rather that we perceive things objectively, that we comprehend and grasp them quite distinct from ourselves—that we comprehend the world and accomplish our actions in accordance with the objective course of realities. Most people today do not seek any objective penetration of the matter in hand, any discernment of how things should be done that is drawn from world-historical necessities.

For this reason, precisely on spiritual-scientific foundations, we must emphasize the objective nature of things: thus that Ahriman is preparing his incarnation, and how we need to relate to this fact as human beings! In such questions it really does not matter whether we need to reprove ourselves or not for the way in which we have done something. No, we must learn to discern objective phenomena. We must learn to perceive what acts in the world and, for the world's sake, conduct ourselves accordingly.

But all this tends to the conclusion that as modern people we can only properly judge and evaluate things if we recognize that we hover, really, between two extremes: between the ahrimanic on the one hand, which offers us an outward mirage, and the luciferic within, which infiltrates us with illusions, hallucinations and so on. Today people live out their ahrimanic inclinations in science and their luciferic ones in religion. And in the realm of art, they oscillate between the one and the other. In recent times some artists tended more towards the luciferic, others towards the ahrimanic. Those of a more luciferic bent became Expressionists, while those of a more ahrimanic inclination became Impressionists. And those who wish neither to follow the one nor the other school oscillate between them, with no proper judgement either of the luciferic or the ahrimanic, seeking to avoid both. Not Ahriman! I must and will not go there, for then I succumb to the ahrimanic. Or not the luciferic—that must not be! And such people seek to be 'very decent' and succumb neither to the ahrimanic nor the luciferic.

But that is not what it's about. Rather we should regard ahrimanic and luciferic impulses as two necessary scales. The scale beam, balancing both, is what we ourselves must be. That is the important thing.

How can we educate ourselves to do this? We can do so by imbuing ourselves very strongly with a luciferic element to counter what arises in us as ahrimanic quality. What ahrimanic element arises very strongly in us today? Knowledge of the outer world. The most ahrimanic element of all is our material perception of the outer world, for this is only a mirage. And if we can develop keen, fervent and enthusiastic interest in the mirage that arises from chemistry, physics, astronomy and so on, through our own luciferic interest we detach from Ahriman something that should belong to him.

It is precisely this that people do not want: it seems very boring to them. And many who flee outward, material knowledge misjudge their task and prepare the very best earthly conditions for Ahriman's incarnation. Likewise, what springs up inside people today has a very strong luciferic character. How can we educate ourselves properly in this respect? By taking our own ahrimanic element and drawing it into ourselves—that is, avoiding all illusions about our interiority, and regarding or observing ourselves as we otherwise regard the outer world. People today should really experience how needful they are of educating themselves in this way. Anyone with a certain capacity to observe these matters will frequently encounter the following fact of life.

Someone comes to you and relates something he feels indignant about in the behaviour of person A, person B, person C, and countless others. He describes very precisely how indignant he is about this, that and the other person. And he has no idea that everything he relates are his own qualities or flaws! People have no sense at all of this! This idiosyncrasy has never been as widespread as it is today. And those who think this does not apply to them are the ones who do it most of all. What is involved here is to approach one's own interiority with ahrimanic coldness, ahrimanic sobriety. This interiority of ours will still be hot enough, even if cooled down a little! There's no need to fear that it will grow too cool. And it is true to say that modern humanity needs to find the right stance towards the forthcoming incarnation of Ahriman, to become more objective about inner life, at the same time bringing much subjective interest to bear on the surrounding world—not fantasy, though, but attentiveness, devotion, and especially interest.

You see, it is of great benefit to Ahriman and the path he is taking in order to shape his incarnation as favourably as possible if your education or other circumstances in life lead you to regard outward life as tedious. Just think how many people nowadays regard one thing or another as boring. For instance, I have met countless people who find it very boring indeed to acquaint themselves with the workings of banks or the stock exchange, or single and double bookkeeping. It is never right to regard such things as utterly boring. To find something boring simply means that you haven't yet discovered the point where it comes to be of burning interest. Every dry accounts book can, if you discover the angle on it that makes it of keen interest, be just as interesting as the Maid of Orleans or Schiller or Shakespeare's *Hamlet*, or anything else, say the *Sistine Madonna* by Raphael. It is just a question of discovering the point where everything in life turns out to be fascinating.

You might consider this very paradoxical. But it isn't. What is paradoxical is people's relationship to the truth nowadays. It is a far,

far better stance to assume that *we ourselves* are flawed and unable to accomplish something than to ascribe this weakness to the world itself. Nothing better helps Ahriman prepare for his incarnation than for us to find something or other boring, to consider ourselves too good for something, to not want to have anything to do with whatever it is. We must always look for the point or angle that allows us to see the interest in something. Rather than subjectively rejecting or accepting things, it is important to objectively perceive the extent to which there is ahrimanic or luciferic quality in something, so that the balance beam sinks too low on one side or the other. Finding something interesting does not mean regarding it as right or justified, but only developing an inner strength to unite with the matter in hand and help send it in the right direction.

You may recall—it's a long time ago now—that a number of our friends bought some books on mathematics. A kind of 'theosophical sport' developed in which people were buying Lübsen's books on mathematics;[61] but after a while they put them back on their shelves and left them there, showing little sign of any emerging mathematical knowledge. Of course I'm not suggesting that you ought to revive such things straight away—I am not making any such demands. And yet taking up a subject that is of no interest to you, finding the point where you develop new insight into the world, is of huge importance. Something like this is certainly needed today. Such things should be taken seriously—things also such as those I wanted to impress on you in our reflections here: about the way in which Lucifer and Ahriman intervene in humanity's evolution, alongside the Christ impulse.

Now if luciferic wisdom had never existed, the Gnosis of the early centuries would not have enabled people to gain understanding of the Mystery of Golgotha. For as luciferic wisdom grew decadent, understanding of the Mystery of Golgotha also gradually declined. And today? Yes, where should we now seek this understanding? Those who can understand the nature of external, ahrimanic science realize that it cannot be found there. Take someone like Cardinal Newman,[62] who played an important part in religious life in the second half of the nineteenth century. When he was invested as a cardinal in Rome, he said he could foresee no salvation for humanity's religious development without the dawn of a new revelation. But he went no further than this. He showed no particular inclination to receive anything of the new life of spirit that can now penetrate humanity from worlds of spirit. He spoke only in the abstract!

Humanity needs a new revelation, and we can see this in all domains. Nowadays you can hear debates and discussions about our moral deterioration over the last four to five years. From this it is concluded that religious instruction should be intensified in schools. But to this we must repeatedly object that we have after all had religious instruction, and the modern era has been shaped precisely by its influence. If more of the old is to be introduced, the same confessions as before, we will just go round in circles. And before long we will be back where we were in 1914, simply reviving the old formulae and the old institutions. We ought to recognize instead that quite different yearnings now live in the human subconscious from what comes to expression on the surface.

When we founded the Waldorf School in Stuttgart,[63] we had to establish religious instruction by inviting priests from the various confessions to give it: the Catholic priest instructs the Catholics, the Protestant priest the Protestants. I don't even wish to speak of the problems we had with the priests themselves; that's quite another story. But I do want to say that a desire immediately arose for religious instruction at the school quite separate from these confessions. To start with I thought very few pupils would attend such lessons compared with those for Catholics and Protestants. But in Stuttgart, despite the fact that you can hear fierce invectives against the anthroposophic movement from almost every pulpit, a large number of children—at least five times more than we could have expected—registered for a kind of anthroposophic religious instruction that must be taught in two classes. Subjectively this is not necessarily at all welcome, for it could easily land us in deep water. But let's leave that to one side. I wished only to show that there is a yearning within people to move forwards but that they are still slumbering and do not see how powers are at work that suppress this longing. And then there is usually a lack of courage to really express this yearning outwardly, to bring it to the surface.

But consider what the effect might be of insight, say, into Ahriman's forthcoming human incarnation, and of how he is preparing this through things I described today and yesterday. We need to gain objective awareness of such matters so that we can adopt the right stance to everything occurring around us as preparation for the incarnation of Ahriman in the future. Only if you reflect thoroughly and maturely on what we have said about such ahrimanic currents in life will you be able to consider these things with the seriousness they deserve.

LECTURE 13

DORNACH, 9 NOVEMBER 1919

A lecture like the one I'm going to give in Basel tomorrow morning[64] naturally has to be comprehensible on its own terms for everyone. But people connected with the anthroposophic movement can have a more particular grasp of things. Today, therefore, assuming you have the necessary foundations already, I'd like to expound on certain matters that serve deepened insight into the sphere of truths that anthroposophy must speak to humanity. Let me recall again, firstly, that the forces at work in the human being are organized and oriented towards two poles. We best understand human nature, best develop a kind of human self-knowledge, if we take account of these two poles, that of the will and of the intelligence.

The human being is a being of will, and a being of intelligence. For the period between birth and death, the element of sensibility and feeling lies between these two poles. This feeling element is the bridge connecting intelligence and will. As you also know, these forces can more or less separate when a person arrives at what one calls the threshold to the world of spirit.

But what I wish to consider today especially is the relationship we have as intelligent human beings to the surrounding world on the one hand, to the world in general, and then the other relationship we have to the world by virtue of the fact that we are beings of will. Let us first reflect on the latter. You know that during our lifetime, between birth and death, we develop will-power as the impulse-giving energy of our actions, of everything we do. In its enactments through the human organism, this will-power is naturally very complex. But the nature of will within us bears a certain similarity with particular forces of nature. In fact the resemblance is sometimes so close as to be identical. And so we can speak of an intimate affinity of human will forces with nature forces.

But you also know from previous lectures that we are in a kind of sleeping state as regards everything concerning our will, even when we're awake. In our conscious mind we possess ideas of what we intend, but how this actually comes about—that a particular thought is expressed in a willed action—is beyond our ken. We do not know what the connection is between the thought 'I will move my arm' and the whole process that leads to this actually happening. This occurs entirely within the subconscious, and we can say that the actual will process is no more conscious for us than what occurs when we're asleep. But in asking how the human will is connected with the surrounding world, we must immediately engage with something that appears really somewhat paradoxical to the consciousness of today as it has developed over the last three, four or five centuries. People mostly think, as I have mentioned here in the past,[65] that the earth would have evolved in the same way if there were no people upon it. A modern natural scientist will describe the earth's development in terms, say, of geology and physical processes. And even if he does not expressly state this, underlying what he says is the view that from the beginning of the earth until its hypothetical end everything would unfold in the same way without a human population. Why do people schooled in modern science think in this way? It is because they believe that if, for example, something occurs in the mineral or plant realm of the earth on 9 November 1919 it was caused by whatever occurred in the mineral realm prior to this date. People think like this: here's the mineral kingdom where mineral phenomena occur [see drawing] and these phenomena are the effect of preceding causes. A mineral cause gives rise to a mineral effect.

Board drawing 12

Well, that's how people think. You can see that they think like this if you open any book on geology. You'll find a description of the present state of the earth characterized as an effect of the Ice Age or some other preceding epoch. But as causes such authors cite only occurrences or phenomena in the mineral kingdom itself, with no account taken of how human beings came to populate the earth. It is thought that even if the human being did not exist, everything apart from us would still have developed as it appears in external reality. But the human being has always also been present. You see, underlying this is something that does really point to the earth as a whole, a whole where nothing can occur in the earth's development without human beings also being among the active causes. Let me give you an example.

As you all know, our present epoch—if we regard it as including everything that has happened since the great Atlantean catastrophe—was preceded by another which we call the Atlantean. The continents of Europe and Africa in their present form did not exist at that time, and nor did the present form of America. In those days there was a primary continent on the earth, known as Atlantis, a region occupying the present area of the Atlantic Ocean. You also know that at one point in the development of Atlantis a particular kind of immorality became widespread across the civilized world of that time. People in those days were able to utilize natural forces to a much greater extent than was later the case. And over wide regions they exploited this capacity in an immoral manner. Looking back to these days, therefore, we can see it as an era of immorality. Then came the Atlantean catastrophe. A mainstream geologist will naturally attribute this catastrophe to mineral processes: one part of the ground sank lower, another was raised upwards. Someone whose thinking embraces modern science will not for a moment imagine that what human beings did in any way contributed to the causes. But it did. In fact, the Atlantean catastrophe was the effect of what human beings did upon the planet.

Besides merely external, mineral, natural causes of such great cataclysms that sweep over earthly existence, we must also seek causes that lie in human actions and activity. We human beings must be included as causative agents in the earth's existence. This is true not only of these great cataclysms but also of things that continually occur. The actual connection between events of the cosmos that impact on the earth, thus earthly or telluric events, and what occurs within us human beings remains hidden initially. And in this context, our whole science is really nothing other than a great and all-embracing illusion. You see, if you wish to study the true causes of phenomena, you must delve further than external causes in the mineral, plant or animal kingdom.

I would like to illustrate this as follows. Let us in a sense approach what we are considering today from the opposite perspective. Here is the earth's environment—which I will draw schematically [see drawing]—and this is the centre of the earth. If something occurs in the mineral, plant or animal kingdom, we can seek the cause of it. I'll hint at the cause by saying that these points here are where the causes lie [see drawing].

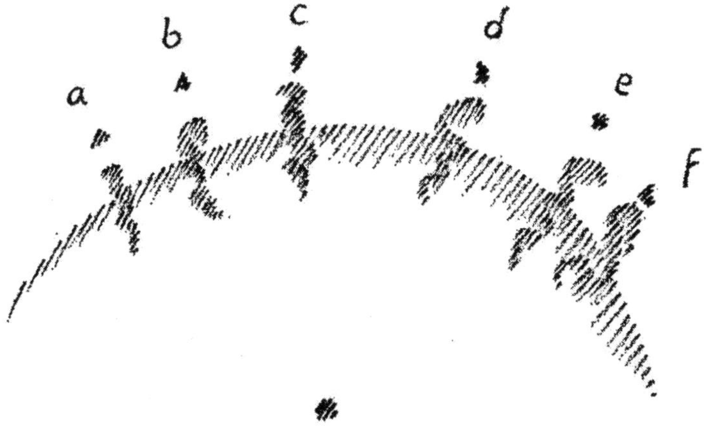

Board drawing 12

You can gain a sense of what I mean if you consider the following. If you go to Italy, to the region round Naples, you will find that the ground begins to smoke if you light a piece of paper. Simply lighting a piece of paper draws vapours from the earth. And then you can recognize that in the physical occurrence triggered by lighting a piece of paper lies something that draws up these vapours from below. In this case, by lighting the paper you are thinning the air. That is the physical process. Because a thinner mass of air is created, the vapours in the earth are drawn upwards. Otherwise they are suppressed by the ordinary air pressure, which is lowered by lighting the piece of paper. If I wanted only to describe purely mineral phenomena of this kind—these vapours rising from the earth—I could explain it thus. Here a piece of paper was lit—here and here, and so forth [see the points on the drawing]. This is just illustrated schematically, and shows that the cause of rising vapours does not lie below but above the earth. But now let these points a, b, c, d, e and f no longer represent lit pieces of paper but something different, of which we are speaking today. Imagine firstly that these points have no intrinsic meaning but rather that the whole system of points is significant. Do not picture lit pieces of paper any more, but something else that I do not yet wish to tell you, though I will in a moment. Something else exists here as an active cause above the surface of the earth. And these differently working causes are not isolated from each other but act together. And now imagine that instead of only six points, there are, say, one and a half billion points,[66] all working together and creating an overall effect. These one and a half billion points really do exist; for all of you have within you what one can call the centre of gravity of your own physical person. This centre of gravity is slightly higher in us when we're awake: it lies just beneath the diaphragm. When we're asleep it lies slightly lower, but it is still there. So there are one and a half billion centres of gravity across the globe, and these give rise to an overall effect, which is largely the cause of what occurs in the mineral, plant and animal kingdoms of the earth. Thus the actions of air, water and other mineral phenomena that you see around you can only be attributed to mineral causes if you pursue a mistaken science. In reality their cause lies in the human interior.

You see, this is a truth that hardly anyone has any inkling of today. Hardly anyone knows that processes occur in the mineral, plant and animal kingdoms whose true cause actually lies within human organisms. This is not the cause of all the effects, but of a great proportion of them. Human beings as they walk about upon the earth bear within them the real cause of what occurs. And so we cannot properly study mineralogy, botany or zoology without anthropology, without relating things to the human being. Science will tell you about chemical, physical, mechanical effects. But these have an intimate affinity with human will forces, which are in fact focused in our centre of gravity. If you wish to get at the truth when speaking of the earth, instead of speaking of some kind of abstract earth as geologists do, you have to include the human being as part of the earth. These truths are revealed after crossing the threshold. Everything that we can know on this side of the threshold belongs, really, to cognitive illusions and not to the realm of true knowledge and perception.

And now we must ask this: what connection is there for humanity today—which is what we are talking about here initially—between human will forces concentrated at our centre of gravity and external physical and chemical forces? In ordinary life this relationship comes to expression only in human metabolic processes. When we assimilate the substances of the external world, it is actually our will that digests and processes them. And if it were only our will at work, then what we assimilate from without would merely decompose. The human will has the power to dissolve and decompose all other substances and forces; and the connection between the human being and the rest of mineral, plant and animal nature is such today that our will is connected with the forces of dissolution of our planet, with the destructive forces of our planet.

It is true that we live from this destruction, and yet that is what it actually is! We could not live if we did not bring about this destruction. We must keep this in mind. And the wrongful magical effects you have heard speak of arise largely from certain people learning to use their will in an unjustified way. In doing so they do not keep destruction within the confines of human nature but abnormally extend it beyond human boundaries, making conscious use of the forces of destruction rooted in the will. This is of course something that should never be taught.

Through our will we are certainly connected with the forces of degeneration of our planet earth. And if, as modern people, we had nothing more than will forces, our earth would be destined for destruction through us ourselves, through humanity. And then we would face a future on earth that would present a truly unedifying prospect: the earth would gradually dissolve and be scattered abroad through space. This is our nature in respect of one of the two poles.

We are dual in nature. One part of our being is connected with the destructive forces of the planet, while the other, as mentioned, is the aspect of our intelligence. It is connected to the will via the bridge of sensibility and feeling. But this human intelligence relates very little to our earth as long as we are awake. During waking life we are not really able to establish a proper relationship with earth existence through our intelligence. What I indicated here for the will is very much something that, although unconscious, occurs through human beings in waking existence. If you go out for a walk and see an eroded cliff somewhere, and wonder about the real causes of this erosion, you have to look inward into your organic nature. This sounds very paradoxical to people today but it is so. And earth, as I said, would have a sad future if we did not have the other pole of our being, the upbuilding one. Just as the causes of all destruction lie in the human will, concentrated in turn at our centre of gravity, so the upbuilding forces lie in the sphere that we enter during sleep. During sleep our I and astral body are in a condition we usually describe figuratively by saying that they are outside the physical body. But in this respect we are very much a soul-spiritual being, developing forces that come into play during sleep. And while we sleep these forces connect us to everything that has an upbuilding, synthesizing effect on the planet earth, counteracting destructive forces with upbuilding ones. If you never walked about on the earth, the destructive forces that really issue from your will would never act within the mineral, plant and animal kingdoms on the earth. And if you never slept on earth, what continually restores and builds the earth up again would never issue from your intelligence. The forces that actually build up our planet earth also lie within human beings themselves. I am not saying they lie within the individual. Earlier I expressly said how these diverse causes are connected. But the forces of restoration and synthesis also lie within all humanity, at the pole of human intelligence—though not in waking intelligence. The intelligence of waking life is like a dead element intervening in earth evolution, whereas the human intelligence that acts unconsciously during sleep is what continually builds up planet earth. What I am trying to make clear is the error of seeking the destructive and upbuilding forces of our planet outside of the human being. They must be sought instead within us. If you take proper account of this, you will not regard what I will now say as incomprehensible.

When you look up at the stars you recognize that certain effects issue from them which human sense organs here on earth can perceive. But what you gaze up into when you look at the stars is not identical in nature with what you observe when you look at the mineral, plant and animal kingdoms on earth; rather it issues from the intelligence and will of beings whose life is connected with the stars. The stars only look like something physical because they are at a great distance. But they are not! They are constituted of what is occurring in the beings of will and intelligence there. I said to you on a previous occasion that astrophysicists present a very fine, very neat account of our sun. But if someone were to travel to the sun in some Jules Verne-type machine,[67] he would be astonished to discover nothing like our physical descriptions suggest he should. It is only here in our earthly existence that it appears so to us, as combined effect of what the sun reveals. In reality what we see here is the action of will and intelligence which appears to us as light at the distance we are from it. And if there were such a thing in this sense, a moon inhabitant observing the earth would not observe there the grasslands, the mineral expanses but—albeit also as light effects and similar—he would perceive what occurs around the centre of gravity of human bodies, and what occurs as the effect of our sleeping state, what happens when we're in the condition of sleep. That is really what would be seen from far off. The chairs we are sitting on here could not be seen from that distance, however perfect an instrument was used. But what happens around your centre of gravity and what would happen if all of you fell asleep—hopefully you don't all fall asleep on these occasions, only a few of you—is what would be perceived from outside the earth.

Thus in respect of the external cosmos, what happens through humankind here on earth is the visible thing, is the important thing, and not what we see here around us. The idea that everything which our external senses perceive is maya, a great illusion, mere phenomena, has become current today and is often reiterated. Such an abstract idea is of little value really. It only acquires value if we go into specific detail as we have just done here. There is no value in saying that the animal, plant and mineral kingdoms are maya. But it is worth recognizing that your outward perceptions are basically dependent on yourself and that—not at every moment but in overall terms as humanity—you yourself are interwoven with the tissue of cause and effect.

But even if a shocking truth such as this—for I think it might seem shocking—is expressed as a deeper truth of nature, it still does not yet acquire the aspect that is really of special significance for human life. Such a truth only becomes important if we draw a certain conclusion from it. We really are not just physical human beings here on earth, or just outwardly sense-perceptible human beings. Here on earth we are moral beings or immoral ones. What we do is determined by moral impulses.

And now reflect on the fact that our modern world-view casts the gravest doubt on such an idea, that science offers knowledge of earthly things which is entirely subsumed within purely external, natural causes and natural effects. And into this chain of purely natural causes and effects we are to place the human being too. That is what external, abstract science tells us. It reckons only with one dimension of earthly existence.

And then people become aware that moral impulses also dawn in human beings, but they cannot work out what connection there is between these moral impulses and what happens outside them in nature. This is the crux, the cross of modern philosophy: on the one hand philosophers learn from scientists that everything is embedded in natural causes and effects, while on the other hand it is apparent that human beings have moral impulses. For this reason Kant wrote two 'Critiques': his *Critique of Pure Reason*, which concerns how human beings relate to purely natural matters, and the *Critique of Practical Reason* in which he establishes his moral postulates, which, to put it metaphorically, hover in the air really, coming from somewhere or other and having no connection with natural causes. You see, as long as people believe that external natural phenomena can only be attributed to other such phenomena, as long as we thus succumb to maya, moral impulses can only be seen as something running parallel to, and unconnected with, the life of nature. Almost everything people say today suffers from this split and duality, or lives in its shadow. They are unable to reconcile earthly reality as such with moral impulses in humanity. But as soon as you know things such as those I briefly tried to outline today, you can see that your human nature is a unity and moral impulses live in you. Your moral impulses live in unified accord with your physical nature. But as a physical human being I am basically the cause—naturally along with the rest of humanity—of everything that also physically occurs. And then what human beings accomplish morally upon earth is seen as the real cause of what unfolds in the world.

As human beings on earth we have our natural history, our science, with accounts of physics, geology, botany and so on. These accounts initially satisfy people, confirming for them what their education has taught them. But let us imagine a Martian arriving on earth and observing things with his own predisposition. Having, after a while, learned a human language, he might read a human textbook on geology and begin to see what earthlings think about processes and occurrences on earth. And then he might very well object and say that this view does not include the most important thing of all. He will say that he has, for instance, seen lots of students hanging around in bars and drinking, indulging themselves, and that as they do this something is continually occurring: the human will interacts with the metabolism to produce occurrences that are missing from geology and physics textbooks. The Martian might well object that these books say nothing about the fact that earthly phenomena also depend on whether such students drink or not!

Someone not entirely persuaded by mundane ideas of the kind living in modern preconceptions would find this aspect lacking in accounts which human beings themselves write of earthly conditions. Our hypothetical Martian would have no doubt at all that the moral impulses active in all human deeds and human life are part and parcel of the life of the natural world. In modern preconceptions, the natural order has an extremely compelling quality, which may even seem unpleasantly intrusive to some—especially if they are materialistic thinkers. They believe that the natural world would be the same without human beings. They think therefore that whether I am a decent person or a rogue makes no particular difference to the world. It does not impact on the natural order. But this is not so: causative factors in the natural world do not lie outside human beings. The most important earthly occurrences are caused by factors that lie not outside but within humanity. And if global consciousness is to arise in people as a further development of merely earthly consciousness, humanity will have to recognize that it shapes the earth in its own image—not in short periods but over great spans of time. The best way of keeping humanity in comfortable slumber is to persuade people they have no part in the course of earth's development, so that human responsibility is confined and limited to the human individual alone, to an individual human person.

But in truth humanity is responsible for what the earth undergoes in cosmic ages. And one only feels oneself to be a real earthly human being by conceiving of the earth as the body of the whole of humanity dwelling upon it. This means having a feeling resembling that of an individual who recognizes that pursuit of his passions over a ten-year period has ruined his body; means recognizing that if earthly humanity lives in impulses of an impure moral nature, the body of the earth will become different from what it will do if we live in morally pure impulses. The mayfly, which lives for only a day, naturally has a different outlook from human beings. But human beings fail to recognize that what outwardly unfolds in the natural world is not dependent on merely natural causes. Far more important than enquiring into the modern shape of Europe, or studying the external mineral-botanical structure of the earth two millennia ago, is to ask this: how did people live here two millennia ago, or how did they live then anywhere within human civilization? The fate of the earth in two millennia will not depend on the nature of our present mineral world but on what we ourselves do or fail to do! With cosmic consciousness, human responsibility expands to become world responsibility. When we look up to the starry skies with the kind of awareness I have described to you, we feel a sense of responsibility towards the cosmic realms through which spirit swells and surges: we feel responsible to this realm for how we fashion the earth in accordance with it.

This is part and parcel of something I often reiterate: we must learn to look at things that are nowadays largely conveyed in the abstract instead as tangible realities. We gain little from adopting oriental terms such as maya, and saying that the outer world of the senses is illusion. We have to go deeper to reach the truth. Such abstractions do not get us very far, for in the way they have reached us they are nothing more than the relics of a primordial wisdom which itself did not live in abstractions but in detailed realities such as those that intuitive spiritual research must now draw forth again. Please do not believe that when you read about maya in oriental texts, and the reality of which it is only a reflection, that you can truly understand this. This is only a kind of summary of things that were known tangibly in primordial wisdom, and were then compiled and condensed in more general terms. We need to return to tangible realities. People often think they understand something of cosmic processes when they say things such as that 'the external sense world is maya'. We can only truly understand something by penetrating to detailed realities. The moment you realize that the mineral world is not simply the outcome of the mineral world of a different epoch but the result of processes that unfold within human beings themselves, then you recognize also what it means to see only maya in the outer world. And then you begin to see a far more intense reality in the human being than you ordinarily do. At that point a great sense of responsibility begins towards all existence.

If you try to comprehend these things inwardly—for they can only be perceived with inner vision, not with the ordinary external mode of intelligence based on the model of modern science—you will gradually begin to understand, too, that humanity is composed of free human beings. Nature does not actually contradict our freedom. This is because, as human beings, we *create* the natural world that so closely surrounds us. Nature only counters our freedom in partial phenomena. Its opposition to our freedom is no greater than when, to speak metaphorically, you extend a hand and another person takes hold of it and restrains it. Because someone else restrains one of your movements does not mean, of course, that you have no free will. As modern human beings we are also constrained in various ways by the fact that people in prehistoric times did something whose effects only come to expression today. But it was people who did this. What kind of people? Well not the kind we can easily reproach since it was we ourselves in previous lives who created the conditions in which we now live.

We must not limit ourselves to speaking only of recurring lives on earth but also conceive of the whole context in which effects in the outer world have been caused by ourselves in past lives. We must also remember, however, that we are not speaking individually here: all of us together on earth helped create the causes, as I have said before. No one, therefore, should exclude themselves from the picture, for all are part of what the whole of humanity brings about and what then comes to expression in the earth as the outwardly describable body of the ongoing life of humanity.

Thus I wanted to give you an idea of how the spiritual scientist must regard what is described in the accounts of external science. This really isn't much different from something I will depict in this series of forms:

Board drawing 13

Assume that some kind of being crawled out of the ground that had never lived in the human world, that it saw these shapes and—let us say it had a knowledge of arithmetic—described them as 'first shape', 'second shape', 'third shape'. The third is the effect of the second, the second the effect of the first. The first has the effect—triangle; the second has the effect—circle. This being that had crawled out of the ground would summarize cause and effect in this way. But this isn't so, for I drew one shape after another and in reality they are quite independent of each other. It would only appear so to this putative being whose preconception is that the one is the effect of the other. And this is roughly how the modern geologist describes the evolution of the earth: what emerges, say, in the Diluvial period, the Tertiary, the Alluvial and so forth. But these things do not dictate each other, just as little as this circle is the effect of the triangle and the triangle of the rectangle. They are independent of each other, just set alongside each other; and in precisely the same way the deeds of human beings on earth have brought about earth existence, albeit including what humanity accomplishes in sleep through the mysterious workings of intelligence—which likewise has effects when we are, as it were, outside the body.

So you can see that what is externally described by our supposed science is very largely mere illusion, maya. But simply speaking the word 'maya' is not enough. This critical verdict that the external world is only maya must be extended by recognizing where the true causes lie—causes that are, however, hidden. Exoteric human knowledge finds it very hard to reveal them. Outer knowledge cannot ascertain the degree to which humanity itself develops the conditions of earth existence, something we can only discern by progressing from outer to inner knowledge. As you can see from my book *Knowledge of the Higher Worlds*, it is possible to know what we do between falling asleep and awakening. We can investigate it through a mode of knowledge that delves down as far as the will. The way in which the will is connected with the outer world, you see, is hidden from people since the will process is hidden from human perception. The human being does not know what it signifies when he lifts his hand at any moment, when he enacts a process of will. He does not know that this will process perpetuates itself and signifies something for the whole of earth's continuance.

That is what I meant when I wrote the scene in *The Portal of Initiation*[68] in which I have Capesius and Strader do all kinds of things that then continue in cosmic occurrences, in thunder and lightning. Naturally this is pictorially presented, but such pictures signify a deeper truth. It is not mere fantasy but points to a real truth. For a fairly long time now in human evolution such truths have really only been uttered by true poets, whose imaginative capacities are always connected with supersensible occurrences.

People today have little understanding of this. They regard poetry, art altogether, as something invented, something set down alongside external reality. It is a great relief for them if they don't have to think of poetry as anything more meaningful than arbitrary invention. True poetry, true art, though, is a reflection of supersensible truth, albeit only a reflection. Even if the poet, if he has not freed himself from his merely materialistic education, may be unaware of the supersensible occurrences unfolding when his soul is tuned to the cosmos, he may still utter truths that are certainly supersensible in nature—even if compelled to do so through pictures drawn from sense existence.

Many such things are to be found in Part II of Goethe's *Faust*. There, as I have shown in specific instances,[69] the truths presented in images can certainly be related to supersensible processes. In relation to the history of art in recent eras we can even corroborate this. If you look at a painting from an era of art history not so far back in the past, you will find that the artist gives very secondary importance to the landscape. Only in the last three, four or five centuries does landscape really begin to figure in painting, and is accorded its own due. If you look further back in art history you find the landscape to be very much secondary to the human world, since in those days people were still mindful of the fact that the world of human beings was of far greater importance for objective realities than the landscape. The landscape is actually only an effect of the human world. Precisely in the rise of a predilection for landscape we find, in art, something that runs parallel to the rise of the materialistic outlook—which consists only in the belief that what is distinct and separate from the human being has its own intrinsic validity. But it does not. It has no distinct and separate validity! A Martian who came here would easily find meaning in Leonardo's *Last Supper*, but not in landscape paintings as such. He would see them quite differently anyway because of his different sense organs, and would also regard the whole configuration of earth differently. I only offer this as a metaphor to characterize what I'm getting at here.

You can see from this that the phrase about the outer world being maya can only be fully comprehended if we consider detailed realities. And to do so we have to include ourselves as human beings in the totality of earth existence. And then we must even accustom ourselves to think that there can be realities, outward realities, seeming realities, which are not in fact realities. If you have a rose in your room, it is a seeming reality only. A rose as it stands there before you cannot exist. It can only exist when joined to its roots on the rose bush, and when these in turn are joined with the earth. Equally, what the geologist describes as earth cannot exist as such. To true discernment, it is just as much an untrue reality as the rose is.

Spiritual science seeks never to make do with untrue reality but always to seek what must be added to it to create a whole—a whole, true reality. The unreal meaning of modern civilization expresses itself in the fact that people regard everything that manifests outwardly as a reality. But reality can only exist in something intrinsically whole. To regard the earth itself as distinct from the human beings who dwell there is no more a reality than a rose that has been cut from the rose bush. Look, these things have to be pondered and assimilated—they must not remain theoretical only but must become part of our sensibility and outlook. We must feel ourselves to be a part of the whole earth. And it is important that we keep telling ourselves that this finger here that has grown on my hand only remains a reality while it belongs to my organism. If I cut it off, it is no longer its true reality. Nor is the human being a true reality if sundered from the earth. Nor is the earth a true reality if sundered from humankind. To think, as scientists do today, that earth would evolve in the same way if humanity did not exist is an unreal thought. That it would not evolve like this I explained to you a little while ago from a different angle,[70] when I showed that the bodies people shed at death form an ingredient of the evolving earth that is as necessary as the ferment in a loaf; and that if no further human bodies became one with the earth the whole physical process of earth's evolution would also be different from what it is when these bodies—irrespective of whether they are buried or cremated—are consigned to the earth.

Today I wanted to describe, more precisely for once, the connection existing between the poles of human will and intelligence and the surrounding cosmos.

LECTURE 14

DORNACH, 14 NOVEMBER 1919

FROM the last few lectures you will have seen how we come to a kind of illusory idea about the external world and how in fact what is usually seen as the natural world is inwardly dependent on humanity itself. We can only acquire a true outlook on the world by seeing the earth, the world altogether, in its totality—in other words by recognizing that the human being belongs intrinsically to it and that our reciprocal relationship with the world must invariably be taken into account. Otherwise we always arrive at an abstraction without essence, a merely abstract understanding of the mineral and at most also of the plant and animal kingdoms, although the latter two no longer properly figure in our modern view of nature. In speaking of the natural world today, people are really only considering the mineral world, to which is appended this brief tale called history, as a quite different kind of truth. This outlook, which does not really encompass the human being, is one that we must slowly begin to depart from in our time. We have seen from many different perspectives why we should depart from the world-view that has emerged, by a kind of necessity, over the last three to four centuries. Today I will only mention that human beings in their outward knowledge, their outward perceptions, are increasingly becoming dependent on their physical body and its imperatives unless they seek to contribute to their own development by bringing forth a higher knowledge that requires their active will. In future, either humanity will succumb to the kind of world-view acquired by, one can say, staying as one is by birth, gaining no other ideas and concepts than those into which one grows naturally through birth and ordinary education as it usually is today, or else people will depart from their belief that anything worth knowing is innate in human nature as a given, that reality can be judged by these standards, instead creating a true human evolution as prefigured in spiritual science. That would be the other path, and one that humanity will have to pursue if the earth is not to decline and degenerate. In a sense we can also regard what I have just said in geographical terms, in which case it acquires a special meaning for the present time.

If we go far enough back in earthly evolution we find that the human being is not rooted in terrestrial existence as such. As you know, and as I have described in my *Occult Science, An Outline*, the human being underwent a long process of evolution prior to earthly existence. You know that humanity was then withdrawn again into a purely spiritual existence and from this descended in turn to earth existence. Now it is the case, in fact, that the human being took with him in this descent into earth existence a widespread primordial wisdom, a kind of inherited wisdom if you like—a wisdom which was by nature single and unified for all humanity. You can find more details about this in my lecture series *The Mission of the Folk Souls*, given in Kristiania [Oslo].[71] So this inherited wisdom was a unified endowment. In speaking of 'knowledge' here I do not now mean only what is called so in science, but everything that we can assimilate into our soul world as vision of our surroundings and our life.

And now this primordial wisdom became more specific and localized, differing depending on the diverse regions of the earth. If you survey the cultures of the diverse peoples of the earth—and you can do this all the better if you draw on various aspects of our spiritual science that relate to this—you can discover that in different nations and races knowledge was different from time immemorial. You can distinguish in this way between Indian, Chinese, Japanese and European culture; and within European culture, in turn, there are different, specific nuances, and then also American culture and so forth.

And if you ask how the original inherited, primordial wisdom increasingly diversified in this way, you will find this was due to the inner disposition and nature of each race. But essentially we always find adaptations of these inner conditions in different peoples to the outer conditions of the earth. And we get at least a picture of diversification if we try to find the connection between what is, say, Indian culture and the climatic and geographical character of the Indian sub-continent. Likewise we gain an idea of the specific nature of Russian culture if we consider how the Russian is connected with his region of the earth. But now we can also say that in relation to these geographical conditions, as in many other respects, modern humanity is currently in a kind of crisis. This dependency of the human being on his region gradually grew to the greatest conceivable proportions in the nineteenth century, although it is also true to say that people emancipated themselves from their regions in their minds; and yet this meant they became paradoxically all the more dependent on them. We can see this if we compare, say, how an ancient Greek related to ancient Greece, and how a modern Englishman or German relates to his regions. The Greeks still had much of the primordial wisdom in their culture, in their education. They were perhaps physically more strongly dependent on their Greek territory than modern people are dependent on their territory today. But this stronger dependency was relieved, assuaged, by the inner primordial wisdom with which they were filled. Humanity gradually lost sight of this primordial knowledge. We can show quite clearly how direct comprehension of certain primordial wisdoms faded around the mid-fifteenth century and how even traditional vestiges of it slowly dried up in the nineteenth century. Rather like plants in greenhouses, the primordial wisdoms were still preserved artificially in all kinds of secret societies, which sometimes use them for very bad purposes. These secret societies preserved the original wisdom in the nineteenth century—it was somewhat different in the eighteenth century—in a way comparable to hothouse plants. It is an apt metaphor: for the Freemason symbols in use today are related to the primordial wisdom from which they originate precisely as hothouse plants relate to those growing freely in nature. Actually the Freemason symbols are less connected with their origins than are artificially bred plants with their natural habitats.

Precisely by losing their inner immersion in primordial wisdom, though, human beings become fully dependent on their geographical regions. If they were not to regain a freely developed store of spiritual truths, people across the globe would become entirely differentiated according to these territories and regions.

Here, in fact, we can distinguish three types that we have already distinguished in other ways. We can say that if spiritual-scientific impulses do not become widespread in the world, from the West only commercial and economic truths would spread and become dominant, from which in turn various other truths can spring. But economic thinking, economic and commercial ideas would hold sway. And from the East would spread essentially spiritual truths. Asia would increasingly become confined to spiritual truths, albeit very decadent ones. And central Europe would tend to cultivate the intellectual realm. The intellect would become particularly dominant here, connected with some of the tradition of ancient times, and with both economic and commercial truths borne over from the West and spiritual truths borne over from the East. But people living within these three main regions of the earth would increasingly become specifically oriented to each tendency. In our world today there is certainly a general trend towards dominance of such specialization. I beg you to take this very, very seriously: if spiritual science did not make inroads into the world, the East would gradually become quite incapable of running its own economy, of developing economic thinking. The East would only be able to engage in production, that is, to directly cultivate the soil, to create and process natural produce, by means of tools supplied by the West. And all economic activities governed by human reason would develop in the West. From this perspective, the recent catastrophe of the Great War is nothing other than the beginning of the tendency towards commercial penetration of the East by the West—that is, towards making the East into a region in which people labour, while the West becomes a region of commercial and economic activity drawing on what the East produces from nature through labour. Here we do not need to set a precise boundary between East and West since this will be variable.

If the currently prevailing tendency were to continue, and if it were not imbued by spirit, there is no doubt—just speaking hypothetically—that the whole of the East would succumb to commercial exploitation by the West. And this course of evolution would be regarded as inevitable for humanity on earth, would be seen as entirely just and inevitable. There is no other way of preventing half of humankind becoming slaves and the other half exploiters of this slavery than once again to imbue the earth with a spirituality that all must work together to achieve.

Such ideas are easily rejected nowadays. People are all too inclined to brush them aside simply because it will make their outward lives uncomfortable to face actual reality. People think that even if commercial exploitation of the East occurs, it will take so long that they will no longer be there to see it. Those with children may be more concerned for the sake of their offspring, but they prefer to bury their head in the sand a little with the idea that better times will surely come, and suchlike. A love of ease means that very few people indeed concern themselves in their inmost being with the fact that shaping humanity's future in a way worthy of human dignity will only be achieved by spreading not only commerce but spirit through the world. We can say that the cultural life of humanity has acquired its present configuration from three directions; and it is extraordinarily interesting to contemplate these three aspects of earthly culture for a moment, especially in relation to the task we have set ourselves in these lectures.

You see, if we survey the earth from the East towards the West, we must say this: Everything humanity possesses as a certain foundation of ethical and moral truths comes from the Orient. The form in which the Orient once developed its ethical principles alongside a general world-view, the form of a general cosmology and so on, has been lost. But what has remained as a residue of oriental thinking and feeling is a certain ethical stance. With this in mind, try reading the talks given by Rabindranath Tagore, collected under the title *Nationalism*.[72] You will see that they scarcely contain anything of the wise teachings that once lived in human souls in the East. But they are extraordinarily interesting; and if you read these talks by Tagore you will find that none of it, the whole ethos of the talks, could have been spoken without the underlying, albeit no longer conscious, primordial wisdom of Asia. These talks are filled—and this is even their chief feature—with a moral pathos, an ethical will, an austere moral critique directed at the whole individual mechanism of the West, and its still worse political mechanism. The ethical truths that reverberate from the East when people such as Tagore speak are imbued through and through with a wisdom drawn from the stars. If you set aside all prejudice and examine with an open mind everything that has developed as culture and education here in central Europe and the West, you are compelled to acknowledge that everything of this kind living here, whether uttered by philosophers or non-philosophers, by the simplest people or the most educated, all ethical and moral views now deeply instinctive in people in the central and western regions of the world originally filtered through from Asia, from the Orient. The Orient is, really, the true home of ethics, of ethos.

If we look towards the West whose culture has, one can say, unfurled before historical eyes, we see how a more rational, intellectual approach to world phenomena comes into play, and is related to the utilitarian principle. There is a great contrast, of which humanity ought to be aware, between the pathos living in the speeches of Tagore and in everything developed in the West as the utilitarian principle.

If we speak radically we will have to say that an outlook such as that of John Stuart Mill[73] or Bergson[74] in philosophy, or Adam Smith[75] in economics, is something entirely alien to an Asian mind, even if he tries to understand it. He can regard it as an interesting fact that human beings say such things, but he will never be tempted to draw forth from within him such things as these, with their focus on outward human utility. The Asian fundamentally despises the nature of European and American thinking because it always presents him with a utilitarian standpoint which can only be governed by the intellect, by the rational mind. And thus it is that modes of thinking connected with the idea of utility have chiefly arisen in the West.

Earlier I pointed out that primordial wisdom diversified across the globe in the different peoples of the earth. And so now we can distinguish the major types: the ethical type in the East, in the Orient, the intellectual utilitarian type in the Occident, the West. And between them the third type keeps trying to squeeze through, to emerge: the aesthetic type as I will call it. The aesthetic type is as inherent to central Europe as the ethical type is to the Orient and the utilitarian, intellectual type to the Occident.

We need only recall one phenomenon to offer outward proof, also, of how the aesthetic type of human being seeks to emerge in central Europe specifically. At the same time as the French Revolution was raging in the West, bringing both devastating results and fruitful outcomes, and the East was wrapped in spiritual dreams, we find Schiller, for example, writing his *Letters on the Aesthetic Education of Man*.[76] These relate directly to the French Revolution but they seek to solve the problem thrown up politically by the French Revolution in purely humanistic, human terms. They seek to establish the human being as free in a purely inward sense. And it is interesting that the whole mode of reflection in Schiller's 'Aesthetic Letters' is founded, firstly, on rejecting the intellectualism of a purely utilitarian perspective, but secondly also on dismissing a merely ethical standpoint. You see, the ethical standpoint was one which had also been rationalized and intellectualized at a certain point. Everything in the world passes through diverse metamorphoses and then appears in a different form. Thus the ethical standpoint of the Orient is certainly not at all intellectual, and yet one can comprehend it in intellectual terms, can intellectualize or 'Kantianize' it. Kant first formulated the following fine statement:[77]

> Duty! You great and lofty name, comprehending within you nothing arbitrary, nothing self-ingratiating, but demanding subjection . . .

He means subjection to ethical values. But Schiller by contrast says:

> Gladly I serve my friend, but, forgive me, through my own inclination;
> And often I'm troubled to think that therefore I am lacking in all virtue.[78]

As a true central European, Schiller could not accept this Kantian intellectualization of ethics. For him a person was not wholly human if he must first subject himself to duty to fulfil his duty. He thought full humanity meant feeling an inner inclination to do what is ethically worthwhile. And so he rejected the ethical rigour of Kant. But he equally dismissed the purely intellectual principle of authority and saw in the conjuring forth of beauty, and its enjoyment, and thus in the human being's aesthetic conduct, the highest free expression of human nature. One can say that he wrote his 'Aesthetic Letters' as a description of the person of Goethe. Schiller started from a sense of envy and inner antipathy towards Goethe, and had to wrestle with himself before he succeeded in acknowledging him. You may say that there was a time in Schiller's life when any talk of Goethe tasted bitter to him. But then they became acquainted, and not only developed mutual respect but learned to immerse themselves in each other's being. And then, as a spiritual biography, a spiritual characterization of Goethe, Schiller wrote his *Letters on the Aesthetic Education of Man*. Everything contained in these 'Letters' could never have been written if Goethe had not modelled for Schiller what they convey.

At the beginning of their friendship, on 23 August 1794, Schiller wrote the letter to Goethe which I have often cited: 'For a long while now, albeit from some way off, I have observed the progress of your mind.' And now he describes Goethe as the mind, or spirit, who is in reality a resurrected Greek;[79] and so we see how he connects here with ancient Greece and the first dawning of the aesthetic spirit of central Europe.

And in Goethe we see someone working his way from the most intellectual element through to an acknowledgement of truth, which is encompassed as much through art as through science. If you trace how Goethe studied the ethics of Spinoza with Herder, then travelled to Italy and in letters home wrote of how, in works of art he regarded as emerging from a Greek spirit, he saw 'necessity', saw 'God',[80] we can say that the intellectualism of Spinoza becomes aesthetic experience on his Italian journey through sight of these works of art. And Goethe bears witness to the fact that the ancient Greeks, in creating their works of art, proceeded by the same laws as nature employs—laws which he believes he is slowly discovering.[81] In other words, Goethe does not think that when one creates a work of art one is creating something fantastical, and that only science is strictly true. No. Goethe thought that true art contains the deeper truth of nature's essence. Thus his outlook was aesthetic. And we can put it like this: Occident, intellectual, utilitarian; the central regions of the world, aesthetic; the Orient, ethics and morality. And it is certainly correct to say that wherever ethical truths have arisen, whether in the East, the centre or in the West, they originated in the East. And wherever utilitarian truths emerge, in the centre or in the East, they actually originated in the West. Beauty, aesthetics, originate from the centre. Everywhere we can trace in this way the source of these three elements in human life, sometimes in very minute detail. Look, if karma has determined that someone should found anthroposophy in central Europe, then something of Goethe's belief—that ultimately the same element as lives in art is also the element of truth—must live within this anthroposophy; the same element that comes to expression in painting, in sculpture, even in architecture also inevitably lives in the thought edifice of truth. Indeed one must, as I tried to do in the first chapter of my *Philosophy of Freedom*—which has become the last chapter in the new edition[82]—say that the philosopher, the human being who founds a world-view must be an 'artist' in concepts.

Such an idea is generally dismissed but there I had to accept and acknowledge it. All this springs from a unified spirit.

In consequence all ideas one expresses acquire such hues and complexions. But then people write books—such as the recently published pamphlet by Aimée Blech[83]—containing all sorts of malicious, intentionally malicious slander. She writes, for instance, that what I present as anthroposophy contains some fine or beautiful things, but it is at odds with the clarity of the French spirit! Certainly it opposes intellectualism, a prosaic, rhetorical formulation of concepts. Such people prefer to be presented with coarsely palpable ideas copied from the material world, since these can be grasped in more clearly defined outline. Yes, we can pursue these things in detail. I could present to you the small details of matters that would illustrate what I have now painted with a larger brush. But the detailed instance I have cited is sufficient, and is extraordinarily interesting.

It is important to recognize that ethics and art and intellectualism are not simply all produced in the West. No indeed. Art is drawn from the world's central regions, ethics from the Orient, and to these is added the intellectual or utilitarian element. Similarly, a kind of aesthetic element is cultivated in the centre, and everything that was incorporated into this aesthetic element especially in the nineteenth century came over from the West. It would be interesting to write a history of biology from this perspective. If you read Goethe's ideas on metamorphosis, you can find a magnificent theory of evolution there, but the West will always regard it as aesthetically contaminated. In the nineteenth century, when the whole globe became dependent on the West, the western element of Darwinism came to pervade evolutionary ideas. It introduced into them the utilitarian perspective, ideas of expediency. Utility is completely absent from Goethe's teachings since he is imbued with aestheticism. In future, people should not refuse to accept anything from each other but embrace it all, in the same way that—as I described earlier—they are economically differentiated. If they refuse to do so, globally we would find a certain ethos spreading across Asia, such as that embodied in the fiery words of Rabindranath Tagore, while in central Europe, somewhat differently, a certain principle of 'beyond good and evil' would become current, a kind of vogueish, dandified Nietzschean outlook, an aestheticizing of everything, even moral ideas. Especially towards the end of the nineteenth century, we saw the victorious rise of aestheticism there. And meanwhile the merely utilitarian perspective would be unstoppable in the West: intellectual cleverness in the utilitarian outlook, an echo of the spiritual element in ideas of utility. The only possible remedy is for human beings to be pervaded by a truly spiritual element, though this will of course require them to accord full seriousness to this spiritual element, will necessitate developing the will to see things as they appear today to anyone who really tries to keep an open mind. This catastrophe of the war has drawn some very remarkable things to the surface—including phenomena that are in part very uncomfortable but on the other hand instructive. Let me describe one such phenomenon.

You see, in modern German literature, hardly a week goes by—you can barely keep up with it—without someone or other expounding (I was about to say 'evacuating') on their views of the war and political events. We have read what has been thought by the heads—I say expressly 'heads' rather than minds—of people like Jagow,[84] Bethmann,[85] Tirpitz[86] and Ludendorff.[87] Michaelis, as far as I am aware, has spared us his thoughts so far.[88] On the one hand it is unpleasant to read all this stuff. And yet it is also extremely interesting! It is extremely interesting from the following perspective. You see, we can find that books such as the one by Bethmann, or the one by Tirpitz, approach matters from completely opposite viewpoints. But what does the viewpoint matter here?! It is sometimes just to do with how the Good Lord has belaboured them for a while—Bethmann has been subject to his probing eye, and Tirpitz to the heel of his boot, and afterwards they have different viewpoints. So we need not worry about the viewpoint. This is of much less importance than observing the spirit that lives in such writings.

We can first of all do the following. I myself undertook the experiment. After I'd allowed the very turbid gravy of these texts, this Bethmann and Tirpitz gravy, to work their effect upon me, I tried to read a series of essays by Herman Grimm—essays that are very dear to me, which non-Germans, however, would consider chauvinistically German. But that again is just a point of view, with which I am not concerned now. What I am considering here is the spirit living in a text. At first view we can ask how the spirit, the mode of thinking, the inner constituents of this Bethmann-Tirpitz gravy relate to what lives in the, if you like, political observations of Herman Grimm.[89] And it has to be said that Goethe was alive for Herman Grimm, a living presence for him, and had not lived in vain. But the same cannot be said about Tirpitz or Bethmann: for them, Goethe was not present. I'm not saying they haven't read him. It might have been wiser for them not to read him, for he simply did not exist for them. What you read in these books strikes me initially as if written by a medieval foot soldier, and to possess their kind of logic. Ludendorff's logic is particularly interesting. This is the man who performed the great 'service' of helping get Lenin transported through Germany to Russia in his sealed train,[90] so we can see him as the real 'importer' of Bolshevism into Russia. He does not have the effrontery to deny this completely in his book, although he has effrontery enough in other ways. He says this: it was a military necessity to get Lenin to Russia; but the political leaders should have averted the grave consequences of this, and failed to do so. That is the logic of these gentlemen! And yet I certainly do not want to suggest that Clemenceau possessed superior logic.[91] Please do not think I am partisan here in any way. The logic of Lloyd George[92] and Wilson[93] was no better either, though in their case this was not so glaringly obvious.

Well, this is what one first discovers. But then it continues, and you find, if you look for a historical comparison, that you have to go a fairly long way back. A curious similarity exists between the mode of thinking practised by Tirpitz and Ludendorff and that of cultural authorities in Rome in the first and second pre-Christian centuries. If you try to uncover an intimate commonality of soul here, it is as if the mode of thinking of ancient, pre-Christian Rome surfaced again in these people and as if everything since, including Christianity—even if these gentlemen seem to speak of Christ and suchlike—never occurred.

You see, it is often thought that saying the luciferic element has remained behind residually in humanity refers only to non-mundane matters. But in the world itself this principle of residual presence exists very emphatically. One can say that the pre-Caesarean grandees of ancient Rome have reappeared in such people. And everything else that has happened in Europe since does not really exist for them.

People ought to recognize this fully—it ought to be observed. Only then can we establish for ourselves a free perspective adequate for evaluating the modern era. Great demands today are placed upon the human capacity for judgement. All this must be said when speaking of the need to penetrate these times of ours with spiritual impulses. From a superficial perspective it is easy to say this. Yes of course we must introduce spiritual impulses into our era! But it is not so simple to actually do this. You need only consider if, wherever spiritual impulses have made some headway, they have also produced desirable fruits. At the end of the day the following has to be said: if you think of certain pamphlets that have been written by adherents [of anthroposophy] of many years standing, even pamphlets in which the spiritual science figuring here is 'properly' conveyed to the world, these things are nevertheless turned on their heads. These are 'plants' that have grown from the soil where efforts have been made to cultivate spirit and communicate it to humankind. But it would be naive to think that we have got beyond a stage where supposed adherents of our movement turn upside down the spiritual truths that have been communicated. This is still going on! It is not nearly as easy as one might think to count on spiritual truths being disseminated amongst humanity. You see, the nature of humanity today has a tendency to differentiate itself into the three types I characterized, the ethical, the aesthetic and the intellectual, but then to further diversify within each of these.

Now spiritual truths will, by their nature, not be assimilated fully by people intrinsically specialized and differentiated in this way. It is quite impossible for people differentiated in these ways, and in others too, to take up spiritual truths 'cleanly'. Remember that people everywhere today are tending to encapsulate themselves within national chauvinisms. Indeed, if you wish to absorb generally human and spiritual truths but still retain your nationalist chauvinism you will turn them into their opposite. It is actually impossible today to communicate things that it would, from a certain perspective, be desirable to communicate, and this is due to the differentiation I am speaking of. And so we have to awaken people's interest by approaching them from perspectives that have already formed and exist. We have to relate to what already exists, but at the same time to recognize that human beings today are tending to distance themselves from ancient, inherited wisdom, and have nothing to replace it with but regional, territorial differences across the globe. And so it will not work to disseminate spiritual wisdoms amongst humanity without at the same time spreading a certain ethos. Many people have read the book *Knowledge of the Higher Worlds*. These books are being widely read at present. And those who read them find that the first advice they offer is ethical in nature—and that in ethical terms this attracts the readers' full approval. Yes, the first advice they encounter must be ethical in nature, and it must offer an essence of the best ethos of earthly culture. But on the other hand it is also necessary to cultivate a certain artistic element. Within the anthroposophic movement this led to very great difficulties since there was a certain disinclination for artistic things. People strove instead for an abstract, neutral symbolism. And still today there are movements that regard themselves as 'theosophical' which reject all art. It was good destiny, good karma for our movement, therefore, that we also embarked on artistic efforts here in Dornach, and were able to elaborate them from the abstract, symbolic element. If it had been up to some, we might have been looking now at many black crosses everywhere, bearing seven rose-like splodges on them, as profound symbols of our building! Naturally we had to resist this symbolic character, had to seek to create out of the artistic element.

We must therefore connect with the best tradition—if impulses can be called tradition—of human culture. And above all we must consider that these things are profound and serious truths, and that they sound like this: Whoever seeks true knowledge must cultivate a sense of truth. When we speak radically of this we touch on something that many find extremely objectionable, for rigorous contemplation of truth is highly uncomfortable for many people today. In life they try to prettify it. But untruth, even if untrue only through sentimentality, does not accord with real dedication to the truths which, for instance, seek to enter the world through anthroposophy.

In this respect the churches have sinned greatly: the various confessions have bred a state of affairs irreconcilable with a full and pure sense of truth. Certain types of piety have been introduced into the world which flatter human egoism more than they accord with the human sense for truth. And this is why it is so necessary to attend to cultivating inner truthfulness, something highlighted in many places in anthroposophic writings. Life itself today demands much untruth of people, and there are two clear tendencies, really, which produce in humankind a reluctance to accept the truth of reality. Today there is a tendency to characterize things according to personal predilection rather than as reality itself dictates. Nowadays—and in another context I have been compelled to refer to this in public often recently—people are acclaimed as practical or pragmatic when they adopt a certain intransigent routine and work in their field with a degree of ruthlessness, rejecting everything that does not serve their view of regimented endeavour. From this standpoint people are distinguished either as 'practical' or as 'dreamers'. The dire consequences of these things became apparent during the nineteenth century, and into our own time, with a degree of world-historical untruthfulness. Until the catastrophe of this world war broke out, this great trial that came upon us, it was actually difficult to characterize these matters in a forthright way. But I am about to publish a collection of essays I wrote in the eighties and nineties of the last century, and they show how efforts had to be made at the time to cast a chink of light at least on certain truths.[94] One of these essays, entitled 'Bismarck, the Successful Politician',[95] sought to show that the success of this individual was based on the fact that he never really saw any further than a few steps in front of his nose. Back then there was no point in publishing such things since scarcely anyone could accept them. Now, though, there is more of a basis for saying these things, since many lessons can be learned from the catastrophic war. Most people, of course, fail to learn from events. They have a certain store of views, which they do not change. They cannot grasp at all what it means to learn from reality.

Whenever I take people on a tour of our building here, I tell them that if I were to design such a building a second time I would do it differently. I would certainly never do it again in the same way. This is not to find any fault with the building; but I myself would never reproduce it again exactly, since one must always learn from what has been done and from the reality before you. This morning, to my dismay I read of Field-Marshal Hindenburg's comment[96] that if he were to wage this war again he would do so exactly as he did previously.

People read such things but overlook the need to learn the bitter lessons of the war and thus gain understanding of the times we live in. Whatever messages we receive from the world, and I mean also through reading, we should examine accordingly and recognize that revising our views of important matters is necessary, indispensable. Up until the outbreak of war there was a seeming outward justification in regarding Bismarck as a pragmatic man. Herman Grimm considered him a 'tower' of practicality.[97] But the catastrophic war has shown him to be a fantasist: founding the empire, was of course, a fantasy.

I'm trying to make clear that life itself can and must reveal human illusions, also in the moral and historical realm. Last Sunday[98] I showed that it is illusory to regard the natural world as distinct from humanity, as scientists assume, and that we must recognize how humanity participates in what occurs in the natural context. Thus the scientific view of nature can be a tissue of illusions. Today I was trying to show how we must allow our views to be corrected by the facts of the history and the realities of life, since, for long periods, things often only reveal their outward and seeming nature. Today we often find that individuals regarded as eminently practical are in fact fantasists, and we must accustom ourselves to revising the way we see things. There is plenty of opportunity to do so today, and likewise a great need for it. Our outlook will only truly accord with the anthroposophic movement if we see that we must revise our judgements, sometimes in the most important matters. Judgements about nature can usually be revised in the light of spiritual science itself. Judgements about life can only be revised if we really develop in ourselves the outlook and ethos we need for the anthroposophic movement.[99]

Lecture 15

DORNACH, 15 NOVEMBER 1919

Yesterday I drew your attention to the kind of primordial knowledge, the *ur*-wisdom that possessed the human soul, and how, into our own time, this slowly dried up, was exhausted, until people across the civilized world came to feel ever more reliant for their knowledge and insight on what they can draw from physical existence. By knowledge and insight I do not just mean 'science' or academic knowledge but what lives as consciousness in people's ordinary lives.

Standing on the foundation of spiritual science, we must of course first ask how this primordial wisdom arose for humanity. And now I must highlight from new perspectives things we have often discussed in the past from a different angle.

Let us look back to the time when the human being began to become, we can say, a citizen of the earth, descending with his being of spirit and soul to the actual earth, mantling himself with the forces of the earth to become an earthly being in the earthly sphere. If the human being had descended to the earth only with the preconditions implicit in his own nature, humanity would inevitably have evolved in a quite different way from how it did in reality through the various cultural epochs. People at that time would have had to begin with a particular relationship to the world around them. They would have had to acquire a knowledge of the earth through instincts not precisely clairvoyant but clairvoyant in some degree. For a long time they would have remained inept, childlike beings. By our era, however, they would have worked their way through to a certain soul and bodily nature with human qualities but would not have reached anything like the spiritual or mental heights that they have. We must thank the beings we have always referred to as luciferic[100] for the fact that human beings have been able to evolve other than through many phases of childhood: these luciferic beings interwove themselves with earth evolution to bring this about. Now we also know that a Lucifer individuality himself incarnated in Asia at a particular point in pre-Christian times, and was the originating source of pagan *ur*-wisdom, in particular of the kind that we can still discern by studying historical facts. In what we might call the play of humanity's evolution, the luciferic beings, however, were always present.

Now I want to ask you very seriously—although I'm aware how little notice is taken, really, of such pleas—not to be smug or philistine when thinking of the being of Lucifer. A great many of those who feel part of the anthroposophic movement tend to repudiate Lucifer. I have often spoken of this tendency. They say, 'That's luciferic, for heaven's sake, have nothing to do with it!' But all these things have to be viewed and judged from the most varied angles. We must recognize and squarely acknowledge that in fact all the primordial pagan wisdom of humanity arose from a luciferic source. But we also need to study how this took place. And the further back we go in humanity's evolution, the more we find certain people whose reincarnations had equipped them, made them mature enough, to acquaint themselves with the wisdoms possessed by luciferic beings. We speak, for instance, of the Seven Holy Rishis in India. Those initiated into these things in India always drew on the wisdom of the Seven Holy Rishis when they uttered their wisdom, knowing that the true teachers of the Rishis were luciferic beings. What the luciferic beings brought with them into earth evolution, with which, as I said, they interwove themselves, was first and foremost always the whole thought world, the intellectual world of thought, the rational world in the best sense, the world of wisdom pervading human culture. If we go back to the origins of humanity we always find the sources of this pagan wisdom in luciferic beings.

We can ask how such a thing can be possible. And here we must be quite clear that the human being would have remained childlike without receiving continual instruction through the mysteries from all kinds of luciferic beings. The essential thing is that those who needed the knowledge, the wisdom required for the education and development of humanity, this inherited, primordial wisdom, were not shy, like a modern philistine, of receiving this wisdom from the luciferic element, but they accepted everything a person must incur if he receives such instruction from the spheres of spirit from luciferic beings. Above all the human being had to take on—we might call it an obligation, although such words of course can never precisely express what is meant—this luciferic wisdom, which is of course cosmic wisdom [to be used as good wisdom in the service of earth evolution].[101] The difference between good wisdom and luciferic wisdom consists in the fact that the good wisdom is in other hands, while luciferic wisdom, whose content is the same, is in luciferic hands. The content is entirely the same. That is the important thing. It is not true to say that there is a wisdom that one can neatly pocket in the inner chamber of the soul to become a good person by means of it. Wisdom is whole and entire in the world, and the difference is only that it can, for instance, be in the hands of wise people who handle it well, or in the hands of angeloi, archangeloi and so forth, or in the hands of Lucifer. In ancient times, wisdom needed for humanity's progress could not be gained anywhere else; and so the initiates of those days had to receive it from luciferic hands, and had to undertake not to succumb to the other aspirations of these luciferic beings.

It was Lucifer's intention to pass wisdom to humanity in order to ensure that instead of undertaking the path of earthly evolution, human beings would pass through evolution in a super-earthly sphere, in a sphere removed from the earth. And so if I were to draw this schematically, I would say that if this is the surface of the earth here [drawing, white] the human being ought to take this path [red] when he arrives on earth at this point.

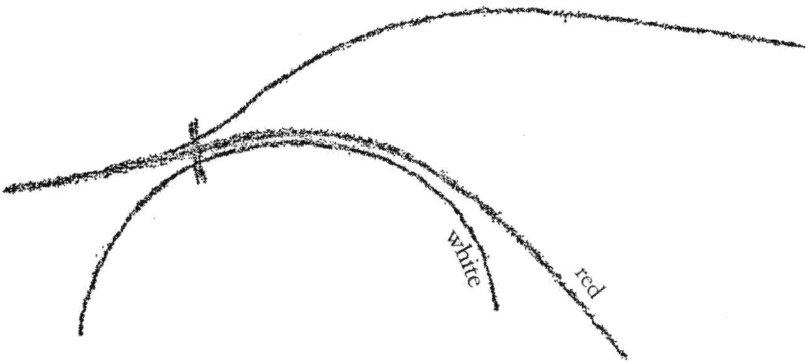

Board drawing 17

The luciferic beings instil their wisdom into the human being, but by doing so they seek to divert him from the earth so that he does not pass through earth evolution. Lucifer wants to leave the earth to its fate, unpopulated by humankind; he wants to win over humanity to a distinct realm alien to the Christ realm.

The wise initiates of ancient times, who received the primordial wisdom from Lucifer's hands, therefore had to undertake not to submit to Lucifer but, receiving his wisdom, to use it in the service of earth's evolution. And this is largely what was also accomplished in the mysteries of pre-Christian times. And if you ask what humanity really received in these pre-Christian mysteries, through the influence of the luciferic beings who first, thus still in the post-Atlantean period, inspired certain individuals, the Indian Rishis, and then also sent their grand ambassador to the earth as I indicated,[102] you find that it is everything which human beings have developed as capacities of speech and thinking. Speaking and thinking, you see, are originally very much luciferic in nature, except that the wise initiates of primordial times were able to inveigle these arts away from Lucifer. If you wish to flee Lucifer, you'll have to resolve to be silent in future and to refrain from thinking!

These things belong to the initiation science that humanity must gradually learn, even though centuries of philistine education in the civilized world make people draw back fearfully from such truths. For a very long time people have been indoctrinated with this caricature of Lucifer and Ahriman, identical with the medieval concept of the devil. They have been allowed to grow up in an atmosphere of philistinism so that still today they regard these wisdoms only with horror, though they are intimately connected with humanity's evolution. You see, it is awfully pleasant for people to think they are keeping themselves safe from the devil, and dedicating themselves to Christ in childlike simplicity. Then, they think, they will be blessed, and their soul will be saved. But the subterranean depths of human life are not so straightforward. And it is very important for the future of human evolution that these things we have been speaking of now should not be kept from people. It is important to know that the art of speech and the art of thinking were only able to enter this earthly evolution because humankind received them through the mediation of Lucifer. You can still detect the luciferic element in your thinking today. Ahriman has meanwhile long since seized hold of the languages that adapted and diversified according to different regions: Ahriman caused this differentiation so that original, unified language was brought down into diverse, earthly language. Whereas Lucifer always has a tendency to unite and create uniformity, the ahrimanic principle is pervaded by the tendency for differentiation. What would thinking be like if it were not luciferic?

Well, if thinking were not luciferic, most people in the world would think like a figure whose thinking was least luciferic of all: Goethe. Goethe is one of those whose thinking was least luciferic, and who in certain respects was intent on looking the luciferic powers squarely in the face. But this necessitates adhering as far as possible to specific, tangible details. The moment you generalize, standardize and unify, you are approaching luciferic thinking. You would only be less susceptible to luciferic thinking if you were to regard every person, every single animal, every separate plant, each different stone on its own, distinct terms, focusing your thinking only on each distinct object rather than comprehending them in terms of species and collective types, not generalizing in any way, not unifying them in general concepts. But if you were to begin doing so already as a child, you'd be kept down in the nursery class! So that isn't possible.

Instead we have to recognize that generalized thinking, which was especially current in pagan peoples, will gradually fade altogether. People are now no longer predisposed to make much use of such unifying simplification on the earth. And this is due to the fact that our God-created human nature has gradually developed a greater affinity with the earth, with earthly things, as we evolved. Through this developing affinity with the earth we are now already by our very nature less related to the luciferic element that seeks to divert us away from the earth.

But it would be a poor outlook if human beings were only to relinquish the luciferic element without anything else replacing it. It would be very bad indeed, for it would mean that they would come to identify entirely with the earth, that is, with the particular territory or region where they are born. Each culture would become entirely differentiated and distinct. We can see this tendency already emerging, developing especially since the beginning of the nineteenth century. But today, still more since the catastrophic world war, we see an increasing tendency to fragment into ever smaller and smaller groups. Nationalism, national chauvinism is increasingly becoming prominent: people dividing into ever smaller and smaller groups until at last such a group could consist of only a single individual. Then perhaps this individual might go on dividing, into a left and a right side, and end up in a war with himself, the right side battling with the left. Human evolution is already showing much potential for this, and a counterbalance is needed. We can only counter this tendency with a new wisdom, rather like the primordial wisdom that imbued pagan culture but now developing through, and accomplished by, free human will—a new wisdom that can inform earthly culture. This new wisdom must again be initiation wisdom and must exceed all that can only be encompassed in isolated fashion in each separate individual.

And here we arrive at something that must not be withheld from people today. If, as they develop into the future, they were to do nothing to achieve a new wisdom for themselves, things would occur in the subconscious depths of human nature which I have to some degree already described to you: that is, the ahrimanization of all human culture. The culture of humanity would be ahrimanized; and it would then prove easy for this incarnated Ahriman of whom I spoke[103] to pervade earthly culture with his own being. And for this reason we must work to hinder all the currents that support and promote ahrimanic culture.

And what would happen if, for instance, people stayed as they are well on the way to becoming—if, as we recently discussed, they did not grasp, comprehend and thus lead in the right direction the currents that Ahriman is drawing toward him? In this case, as soon as Ahriman incarnated in the western world at a particular moment, human culture would become entirely ahrimanized. And what would Ahriman bring? Employing the most grandiose arts, Ahriman would bring to the human being all that we understand here as clairvoyant knowledge, which so far otherwise has only been gained by the greatest effort and exertion. Just imagine how infinitely comforting this would be. People would not have to do anything themselves. They could go on living their materialistic lives, could eat and drink—or at least could eat as much as remains after the catastrophic war—and would not need to concern themselves with any spiritual striving or mental exertion. The ahrimanic streams would take their 'pleasant' course. When, at the due moment, Ahriman is incarnated in the western world, he would found a great secret school where the most grandiose arts of magic would be practised; and from here all humanity would be showered with everything that can otherwise only be gained through great exertion.

It would be philistine to think that Ahriman, when he comes, will be a kind of mischief-maker[104] who plays all kinds of tricks on human beings. No indeed. All those comfort-lovers who reject spiritual science today would succumb to his magic, for, through his magic arts, he would be able to turn large numbers of people into clairvoyants. But these great clairvoyant gifts would be entirely diverse: what one person sees will be different from what another person does. Confusion would reign, and though people received a foundation of clairvoyant wisdom, they would inevitably fall into conflict through the very different nature of their perceptions. But ultimately people would be very content with their visions, since each person would be able to see into the world of spirit. And this in turn would mean that all earthly culture would fall prey to Ahriman! Humanity would succumb to Ahriman simply because it had not acquired by its own exertions what Ahriman would then endow it with. It would be the very worst advice imaginable to tell people that they should just stay as they are, that Ahriman will make you all clairvoyant if you desire it. And you will want it, for Ahriman will possess great power! But the consequence of this would be the empire of Ahriman established on earth, the whole earth being ahrimanized so that what human culture had achieved hitherto would in a sense be destroyed. What modern humanity today basically already unconsciously utterly desires would be fulfilled.

And so this is the important thing: the future wisdom, which is clairvoyant in nature, must be wrested from Ahriman again. We can say that this book of wisdom is only one, not two wisdoms. It is only a question of whether Ahriman holds the book or Christ. Christ cannot have it unless humanity fights for it. And humanity can only fight for it by recognizing that by the time Ahriman appears on earth it must have acquired this content of spiritual science by its own exertions.

This, you see, is the cosmic work of spiritual science. It consists of preventing the knowledge of the future from becoming ahrimanic, or from remaining so. Excluding from one's religious practice anything of the nature of knowledge, continually and repeatedly emphasizing instead that simple faith is entirely sufficient, is a good way of cooperating with Ahriman. If you go no further than this 'simple faith' you are condemning yourself to dullness and torpidity of soul, and then the wisdom that should in a sense be wrested from Ahriman cannot penetrate you. So it is not a matter of humanity simply receiving the wisdom of the future but of humanity working to acquire it, and of those who do this undertaking to save the culture of the earth, saving earthly culture for Christ just as the ancient Rishis and initiates undertook not to succumb to Lucifer's aim of alienating humanity from the earth.

Now what is the essential aspect of these things for human feeling? The essential thing is that for the wisdom of the future, too, we have to struggle in a way similar to the initiates of very ancient times who mediated to human beings the capacity for speech and for thinking, necessarily achieved by opposition to Lucifer. Just as these initiates of primordial wisdom had to wrest from Lucifer what became human reason, so insight into the inner nature of things as it will be in future must be wrested from the ahrimanic powers. These things are strongly at play between the lines of life, and are already playing into life today.

Recently I read a piece written by a friend of the anthroposophic movement shortly before his death.[105] He was wounded in the war, and lay in a military hospital for a long time. During the various operations he underwent he gained glimpses of the world of spirit. But the last lines he left contain a remarkable passage in which he describes what he experienced shortly before death. Among his last experiences was one in which everything spread around him in the atmosphere turned, as he put it, into 'granite': very dense and stony. It is as if heavy granite is pressing on his soul. We have to understand such an expression; and we can understand it if we know that we need to battle for the wisdom of the future, which the ahrimanic powers will not so easily allow to be wrested from them. One ought not to imagine that wisdom will simply be granted us in voluptuous visions. True wisdom must, as I said recently in a public[106] lecture, be 'acquired in suffering'. And this suffering of a dying man I have described to you is, really, a very good picture of it. You see, in struggling for the wisdom of the future one of the most common experiences is precisely this: that the world around you presses in upon you, as if the air were suddenly to turn to granite. It is possible to understand the nature of such experiences. We need only consider that the ahrimanic powers are endeavouring to render the earth entirely rigid. They would be victorious if they succeeded in completely rigidifying earth, water, air and so forth; and then the earth could not evolve back to the warmth condition from which it originally evolved at the stage of Old Saturn. The intention is that it should attain this warmth condition again at the time of Vulcan, and the endeavour of ahrimanic powers is to prevent this happening. We are on a knife edge, which could begin to be decided in the present era if human souls failed to find enthusiasm for the spiritual content of spiritual science. Then human souls, in their laxness and laziness and love of ease, would give the first impetus for the earth to rigidify. If you consider that the real aim of ahrimanic powers lies in this rigidification, then it will scarcely surprise you that this contraction, constriction of life, this granite-like pressure, is one of the experiences that will have to be undergone in the battle for the wisdom of the future.

We must realize that people can prepare themselves in the present to see into the world of spirit by first using their healthy common sense to comprehend what spiritual science seeks to bring them. The effort brought to such study, governed by the faculty of healthy human reason, can already be part of the struggle that will lead them into receiving visions from the world of spirit. And there are various things to overcome in the process. For people today this effort is initially so arduous because, in seeking to understand spiritual science, they must battle against the granite nature of their own skulls. If their skulls were not tough as granite, spiritual science would find far wider acceptance today. Much more prudent than all philistine execration of ahrimanic powers would be to battle against Ahriman in this way. This struggle cannot be philistine in fact, but must involve an honest, authentic study of spiritual-scientific content. And then human beings would gradually gain spiritual vision, awareness and feeling of what would otherwise come about physically on earth: of rigidification, of granitization.

And this is why people today are disinclined to approach spiritual science: it is out of cowardice. They are unaware of this, but it is so: fear and cowardice of what lurks in wait, of what they will have to endure in their endeavours. Time and time again you hear it said that people go to anthroposophic meetings to seek elevation. And by this they often mean a revelling in inner voluptuousness. This cannot be on offer, for it would lull people into dull slumber, and distance them from the light that they need. The essential thing is that as the near future approaches, from this present time onwards, people must not be kept in the dark as to the real, driving forces of human evolution. People must recognize that human beings live in a kind of equilibrium between luciferic and ahrimanic powers, and that the Christ being has really become their companion in a sense: a confederate firstly leading them out of the battle with Lucifer and then into the battle with Ahriman.

Human evolution altogether must be seen in the light of these realities. Someone who characterizes the mysteries of the world as spiritual science must do is sometimes greatly ridiculed. In my book *Theosophy*, for instance, I inevitably had to describe things in terms of their sevenfold nature and was ridiculed for it. Tomorrow I will speak of another thing that elicited ridicule. But people do not think it ridiculous to divide the colours of the rainbow into seven or the octave into seven intervals: prime, second, third and so forth, with the octave as the recapitulation of the prime. In the physical realm people accept such categories, but dismiss them utterly when it comes to spiritual truths. And what we must work hard to comprehend again in this way was once intrinsic to primordial pagan wisdom. In the school of Pythagoras, which was a mystery school in fact, we see a last gleam of this original pagan wisdom. You can read in every school book about Pythagoras but will not discover there any comprehension of why Pythagoras constructed the world order on number. In fact it was because original wisdom founded everything on number. But the last ember of insight into the wisdom of number still glowed when Pythagoras founded his school. Other aspects of primordial wisdom survived longer—some of it even into the sixteenth and seventeenth centuries. For instance, up to the fifteenth and sixteenth centuries one can still find some rational accounts of physical aspects of reality that relate to higher worlds. And then, if I can put it like this, humanity's *ur*-intellect gradually fades away altogether.

Imagine we had lurking in some corner here a real proponent of modern education, who thought you anthroposophists here were being fooled with complete nonsense. Our era, he might say, boasts such glorious achievements! What on earth does it mean to say that original wisdom has dried up? In recent centuries we have achieved many great things, things of great grandeur. Even if 1914 marks the end of it, until then at least culture developed glorious achievements... But if you look without preconceptions at what we have acquired and developed in most recent times, you will find this: certainly, people have compiled all kinds of scientific, descriptive and historical accounts. Compilation, the gathering of 'facts' has indeed become fashionable. They have undertaken experiments too, and have described these. But ask yourselves whether anything produced in recent times contains any new ideas or concepts. Certain isolated minds like Goethe have produced new ideas and concepts, but Goethe was not understood. If you closely examine science or even recent historical research, you will find that the ideas at work there are not new. Yes, Darwin undertook his voyages, and described many things that he saw, then compiled and formulated them as an idea. But if you examine the minutest details of the idea of evolution, you will find it exists already in the writings of the Greek thinker Anaxagoras. And the most important ideas in modern science were already present in pre-Christian times in the works of Aristotle. These ideas are a store of primordial wisdom, drawn from a luciferic source. But this source of original wisdom must gradually dry up, and new wisdom, in the form of insights into the world of spirit, must be won by great effort. For this to happen, human beings need a degree of willingness to accept things that are working directly towards truly new ideas. In particular modern humanity needs new ideas in relation to the soul. Scientific ideas about the psyche today are basically mere words. When modern academics today speak of the will, of thinking, of feeling, this is really nothing but a kaleidoscopic scattering of words: a kind of squeezing out of words, of word-sounds, signifying little. People are not in the least concerned to give serious consideration to truly new enquiries.

In this respect one can have some really odd experiences. A while back I was invited to give a talk to a Schopenhauer Society in

Dresden.[107] A Schopenhauer Society, that sounds very interesting, I thought. And so I tried to characterize the contrast between sleeping and waking, between waking up and falling asleep, in psychological terms. As I recently described this to you, too,[108] I was trying to explain how the 'zero point' is present initially only at the moment of waking up or falling asleep: how sleep is not just a cessation of waking life but relates to it as debts to assets.

If you were to look through modern psychology to learn something about this, you would not even find the beginning of an attempt to broach these wide-ranging matters. After my talk, in a supposed discussion, various people stood up to speak, educated people. One of them drew the following conclusion. He said that nothing they had heard could be considered part of serious scientific enquiry, and that serious science should concern itself with other matters. What I had said apparently had nothing to do with necessary research, with things they wanted to know, for close scrutiny would show them not to be new truths at all, but matters they had long known about. In other words, what they did not wish to know, and what was in no way part of their science, must be things long known about!

Now of course real contradictions do exist, but contradictions of this kind exist only in the heads of modern academics. If someone says that certain things cannot be known and do not form the subject of human knowledge—all well and good. But if he says at the same time that these things have long been known and are therefore of no interest, this is a crass contradiction! Conflating two judgements like this is something modern academics often habitually do.

But such thinking is responsible for something intrinsic to our era. Thanks to the divine powers and thanks also—if you will forgive me—to Lucifer and Ahriman, an individual is not, ultimately, completely idiotic. And yet there is a huge gulf between this truth and discussing such matters in public. A person may comprehend something of these things, and may sometimes form a view of them that is by no means wide of the mark. But to move on from this point to speaking of it publicly in an appropriate way is a very long road indeed. While many gladly immerse themselves in spiritual science, engaging in it within the confines of a more sect-like kind of society, when they are in the public domain again, and ought to present matters about which the world produces its documents and its testimonies, the whole thing vanishes in smoke; and then they become good citizens of the land of philistinism again. But this in turn decisively supports the progress of Ahriman.

NOTES

Sources: These lectures, given unscripted to members of the Anthroposophical Society, were recorded in shorthand by the professional stenographer Helene Finckh who, from 1917 onwards, took down most of Rudolf Steiner's lectures and afterwards transcribed them. The present edition is based on these typescripts. The original shorthand transcripts are extant and were reviewed for the purposes of this edition.

The board drawings: The original board drawings and captions done by Steiner during the lectures are extant since the boards were covered in sheets of black paper, which were subsequently preserved. They are available in miniature in a separate edition as accompaniment to the lectures. In this edition we retained the drawings based on Steiner's that were made by Hedwig Frey. Caption numbers refer in each instance to the corresponding original board drawings.

The lectures of 10 November (public lecture in Basel) and 19 November (Dornach) contained in the edition entitled *Menschliche Verantwortlichkeit—Weltverantwortlichkeit—Menscheitskultur* (Number 4 in the series *Die geistigen Hintergründe der sozialen Frage*, Dornach 1951) appeared in the complete works (GA) as numbers 72 and 255.

In relation to lectures 1–3 and 7–15, the publisher adopted numerous references provided for the first edition by C.S. Picht.

For works by Rudolf Steiner forming part of the complete works (GA) the bibliographic number is provided. See also the list of works at the end of the book.

Before beginning the first lecture of 3 October, Rudolf Steiner spoke some words in memory of Anna Ziegler, which are reprinted in GA 261.

1. Berthold Auerbach 1812–82, author of *Schwarzwälder Dorfgeschichten* (10 vols, Stuttgart and Berlin 1911).
2. Gerhart Hauptmann, 1862–1946. His famous work *The Weavers*, a play about the 1840s, first appeared in Silesian dialect in 1891, and in a translation into high German in 1892.
3. Nikolaus Copernicus, 1473–1543, 'De revolutionibus orbium coelestium libri VI', Nuremberg 1543. For more on the laws of Copernicus, especially the third, see Rudolf Steiner, GA 323, lecture 2. The passage in question runs as follows:

   Now the remarkable thing is that Copernicus bases his system of the cosmos on three main principles. The first is that the earth revolves around its own north–south axis in 24 hours. The second principle upon which Copernicus founds his view of the heavens is that the earth orbits round the sun, and that therefore a revolution of the earth round the sun exists, and that of course the earth also revolves in the process. This revolution does not however occur around the north–south axis, which always points to the North Pole, but around the ecliptic axis which forms an angle with the actual earth axis. And so in a sense the earth spins around its north–south axis during the 24-hour day, and then also, as it performs roughly 365 such revolutions in the year, another revolution occurs, an annual revolution, distinct from the orbit around the sun. If the earth keeps revolving in this way, as well as orbiting round the sun, this is the same kind of revolution that the moon makes around the earth, always turning the same face towards us. The earth does this too as it orbits round the sun, but not around the same axis it revolves around in its daily axis spin. Thus in this annual 'day', in addition to the daily revolutions lasting only 24 hours, it spins around a different axis.

The third principle that Copernicus formulates is that besides the revolution of the earth around the north–south axis and a second around the ecliptic there is a third also, which can be described as a retrograde motion of the north–south axis around the ecliptic axis itself. In consequence, the revolution around the ecliptic axis is in a sense cancelled again. Therefore the earth axis always points to the North Pole (the Pole Star). As the earth orbits the sun, it would otherwise inevitably describe an ellipse around the ecliptic pole, but through its own revolution in the opposite direction—each time the earth progresses a little further, the earth axis revolves back—it continually points to the North Pole. In the third principle of Copernicus, this alignment to the North Pole occurs because the earth axis itself, through its intrinsic revolution, a kind of inclination, continually cancels the other revolution. And therefore in the course of the year this latter has no significance because it is continually cancelled.

In modern astronomy, founded on the ideas of Copernicus, the two first principles are held to be valid but the third is ignored. This third principle is waved aside with, you might say, a light hand, by saying that the stars are so far away that the earth's axis, remaining parallel, always points to the same place. The north–south axis is thus said to always remain parallel to itself in this orbit round the sun. This is not what Copernicus stated. He assumed that the earth's axis continually revolved. In other words, modern astronomy does not share the perspective of the Copernican system but instead, because it was easier to do so, people accepted the two first principles of Copernicus and left out the third. They deceived themselves that there was no need to accept the principle that the axis of the earth must keep moving in order to keep pointing in the same direction, by stating that this point was so far away that the axis still points in the same direction even when this axis moves forward. Anyone can see this is illusory. Thus today we have a Copernican system that leaves out a very important element of Copernicanism.

4. Friedrich Wilhelm Bessel, 1784–1846, *Tabulae reductionem observationum*, Königsberg 1830. His correction methods for determining star locations have provided the basis for all such calculations up to the most recent times.

5. Weekly journal for politics, literature and art. Published by Friedrich Naumann, Berlin 1919, no. 34 (21.8), pp. 457f.: Erich Schairer, 'Ein falscher Prophet'.
6. Hope or belief in a 'thousand-year reich', associated with the Last Judgement and resurrection of the dead.
7. *Die Erziehung des Kindes vom Gesichtspunkt der Geisteswissenschaft*. This was first published in 1907, with numerous further editions, most recently Dornach 1985.
8. See Matthew 6:24; Luke 16:9,11. Mammon (meaning 'treasure' in Aramaic) is wealth personified as an actual spiritual entity.
9. The Eighth Ecumenical Council of Constantinople, in 869, under Pope Hadrian II, reversed the decree of Photius to state that the human being has a single rational and perceiving soul—'unam animam rationabilem et intellectualem'. Thus a distinct spiritual principle in the human being was no longer acknowledged. Henceforth the spirit was seen only as a property of the soul.
10. Erich Ludendorff, 1865–1937. Although he was nominally subordinate to General Field Marshall Hindenburg, in the last years of the war Ludendorff possessed almost unlimited power in both the military and the civil domain.
11. For instance, in GA 146.
12. Vladimir Ilyich Uljanov Lenin, 1870–1924.
13. Leon Trotsky, 1879–1940.
14. Rabindranath Tagore, 1861–1941. Rudolf Steiner quoted on various occasions from his book *Nationalism*. See also page 196.
15. The so-called 'self-determination of peoples' came to expression in Woodrow Wilson's 'Fourteen Points' and in the political organization of Europe created by the Versailles Treaty of 1919.
16. Giordano Bruno, 1548–1600.
17. Eduard von Hartmann, 1842–1906.
18. A copy of *The Philosophy of Freedom* containing Hartmann's notes and remarks on the book is held by the Archive of Rudolf Steiner's literary estate in Dornach.
19. Helena Petrovna Blavatsky, 1831–91.
20. Max Müller, 1823–1900, orientalist and philologist.
21. No reference to this has so far been found in comments or works by Max Müller.
22. Lujo Brentano, 1844–1931. 'Der Unternehmer', special issue of 'Das gelbe Blatt', no. 16, Stuttgart 1919, pp. 230ff.
23. It has not been possible to ascertain who this was.
24. In February 1919 in Bern.
25. *Vorwärts*, nos 232–8 of 4–11 October 1919: Christian Schibli, 'Die Sozialisierung'.
26. In Aristotle, the *psyche dianoetike* is the rational soul intrinsic to the human being, in contrast to the *psyche aisthetike* (sentient soul) of animals and the psyche treptike (*nutrient soul*) of plants.
27. Thomas Cromwell, 1485–1540. The chancellor of Henry VIII. He was beheaded.

28. James I, 1566–1625, King of England from 1603. See Rudolf Steiner, GA 185.
29. 'The Evolution of Humanity and Spiritual Science' (1 February 1911), printed in the newsletter *Was in der Anthroposophischen Gesellschaft vorgeht*, 1945, no. 5.
30. *Vom lebendigen Gotte*, 1919, by Bo Yin Ra, a pseudonym for Joseph Anton Schneiderfranken (1876–1943).
31. The first Goetheanum, which was burned down at New Year 1922/23.
32. Immanuel Kant, *Kritik der reinen Vernunft*, Riga 1781; *Kritik der praktischen Vernunft*, Riga 1788.
33. See lecture 5 in this volume (11 October).
34. Louis Claude, Marquis de Saint-Martin, 1743–1803. A French occultist, known as 'le philosophe inconnu'.
35. Friedrich Nietzsche, *Die Philosophie im tragischen Zeitalter der Griechen* (published posthumously).
36. The seven sages were: Bios, Cheilon, Cleobulos, Periandios, Pittakos, Solon, Thales. See Paul Deussen, *Die Philosophie der Griechen*, second edition 1919, p. 3.
37. This account is probably taken from Laurenz Müllner, 'Die Bedeutung Galileis für die Philosophie' (inaugural speech, Vienna 1894). Müllner there quotes from a text by Galileo: 'The anatomist, having shown how the main stem of nerves, issuing from the brain, passes along the neck, extends through the spine to branch throughout the whole body, and how only a very fine thread, of the thickness of yarn, reaches the heart, he turned to a nobleman who was known to him as a peripatetic, and for whose sake he had uncovered and revealed all this with the greatest care, to ask whether he was now satisfied, and was persuaded that the nerves have their source in the brain and not in the heart. At this our philosopher, having stood there for a while in thought, replied: You have shown this all to me so clearly and visibly that—if it did not contradict the text of Aristotle, who clearly states that the nerves originate in the heart—one would be compelled to admit that you are right.'
38. Corinthians 3:19: 'For the wisdom of this world is foolishness with God.'
39. *Der Versuch als Vermittler von Objekt und Subjekt*, 1792.
40. The German Monist Association was founded on 11 January 1906, with Ernst Haeckel as its honorary president.
41. Ernst Boldt, 'Rudolf Steiners diplomatischer Appell an den Instinkt der Mittelmässigkeit. Ein Beitrag zum "Fall Steiner" ' in *Prana*, Book 4, Summer 1919, Theosophisches Verlagshaus, Leipzig.
42. In Rudolf Steiner, GA 16.
43. Rudolf Steiner, *Die Grundfrage der Erkenntnistheorie mit besonderer Rücksicht auf Fichte's Wissenschaftslehre. Prolegomena zur Verständigung des philosophierenden Bewusstseins mit sich selbst*. Inaugural dissertation submitted for the award of doctorate from the Faculty of Philosophy at Rostock University (1891). In expanded book form, this was published as *Truth and Science* (1892), GA 3.
44. For instance in lecture 5 of GA 137.
45. In the preceding lecture.

46. The new 'substantially enlarged and expanded' edition was published in 1918.
47. See lecture 6 in this volume (12 October).
48. Johann Tetzel, a Dominican, *c.* 1465–1519. He was commissioned to run the trade in indulgences in Germany, as sub-commissioner for the Pope's agents in this business.
49. The Siennese banker Agostino Chigi (*c.* 1465–1520) was the official banker for Pope Leo X.
50. GA 104.
51. This tale is not contained in the printed version of this cycle.
52. In lecture 4 of this volume (10 October).
53. In lecture 9 of this volume (19 October).
54. In lecture 8 of this volume (18 October).
55. The 'Socialist Workers' Party' was founded in 1875, at the Gotha Congress.
56. In lecture 7 of this volume (17 October).
57. See the detailed account in the lecture on 27 October 1919 in Zurich, lecture 9 in GA 193.
58. The editor inserted the phrase in brackets.
59. Romain Rolland, 1866–1944. 'Pour nos frères de Russie', 23 October 1919 (in *L'Humanité*, 26 October 1919), reprinted in Romain Rolland, *Quinze ans de Combat*, Paris 1935.
60. In the spring and summer of 1919, Romain Rolland disseminated a 'Déclaration d'Indépendance de l'Esprit' followed by a commentary entitled 'Pour l'Union des Travailleurs des Mains et de l'Esprit', both reprinted in *Quinze ans de Combat* (see above). On p. 57 of the latter book, in an article of March 1922, Rolland also comments on Steiner's book *Towards Social Renewal*, and on his ideas of threefolding.
61. Heinrich Borchert Lübsen, 1801–64. Author of books on mathematics, which Rudolf Steiner recommended because of their clarity of presentation.
62. Cardinal Newman, 1801–90. The comment by Newman in the form cited here figures in C.G. Harrison, *The Transcendental Universe*, on p. 14 of the 1897 translation into German.
63. The first Waldorf school was founded in the spring of 1919.
64. 'The Spirit as Guide through the Sensory and Supersensible World', a public lecture on 10 November 1919 (in *Die geistigen Hintergründe der sozialen Frage IV: Menschliche Verantwortlichkeit, Weltverantwortlichkeit, Menschheitskultur*, Dornach 1951, pp. 70ff.; the lecture is due to be published in GA 72).
65. In lecture 3 of this volume (5 October).
66. A figure that approximates to the population of the whole world at the time.
67. Jules Verne, *From the Earth to the Moon*, published in English in 1867. Original French edition 1865.
68. Rudolf Steiner's first Mystery Play, GA 14. He is speaking here of Scene 4.
69. In GA 272 and 273.
70. In lecture 3 of this volume (5 October).
71. GA 121.
72. First published by Macmillan in 1917.
73. John Stuart Mill, 1806–73.
74. Henri Bergson, 1859–1945.

75. Adam Smith, 1723–90.
76. First published in 1795.
77. In the *Kritik der praktischen Vernunft*, Riga 1788, Part I, Vol. I., Section 3: 'Von den Triebfedern der reinen praktischen Vernunft'.
78. In 'Gewissensskrupel' (Distiches).
79. Schiller wrote: 'Now ... since your Greek spirit has been cast into this Nordic creation ...'
80. Goethe, *Italian Journey*, Rome, 6 September 1787: 'These lofty works of art have at the same time been produced as the loftiest works of nature, by human beings pursuing true and natural laws. Everything arbitrary and fantasized here falls away: here is necessity, here is God.'
81. *Italian Journey*, Rome, 28 January 1787: 'I have the suspicion that they proceeded according to the same laws as nature does, which I am seeking to uncover.'
82. GA 4. The new edition appeared in 1918.
83. Aimée Blech (president of the Theosophical Society in Paris): *Annie Besant. Un abrégé de sa vie*, Paris 1918, pp. 59–64. The passage in question runs: 'Dr Steiner was a significant personality, both as an intellectual and psychic. He swiftly acquired certain occult capacities. His intellectual development, his remarkable philosophical capabilities, his gift for speaking and his magnetic powers, of which he made good use, soon drew the fanatical reverence of his German members. His great activity and his trips throughout Germany led to a continual and rapid increase in member numbers. He germanized theosophy, if one may put it like that, and transformed it by adding his own ideas to it, the results of his own research. To French minds, who seek precision and clarity, it appeared rather a nebulous form of theosophy, but suited to the Germans who, as Dr Steiner himself said, are proud of their philosophical antecedents and would not gladly have accepted a theosophy originating in India and England.' The 'malicious slander' appears, among other places, in the next passage, which relates to the exclusion of the anthroposophists from the Theosophical Society: 'It is certain that the separation from Steiner was a blessing. This occultist was, among other things, also a dangerous pan-Germanist. If he had become the president of the Theosophical Society his scope for action would have been greatly enhanced, and he could have exerted an influence in almost all the countries of the globe. He would have gained the authority to pursue his pan-Germanistic policies without any hindrance, which he would also very likely have done.'
84. Gottlieb von Jagow, *Ursachen und Ausbruch des Weltkriegs*, Berlin 1919.
85. Theobald von Bethmann Hollweg (German Chancellor from 1909–17): *Betrachtungen zum Weltkrieg*, Part I: 'Vor dem Kriege', Part 2: Während des Krieges', Berlin 1919–21.
86. Alfred von Tirpitz, *Erinnerungen*, Leipzig 1919.
87. Erich Ludendorff, *Meine Kriegserinnerungen 1914–1918*, Berlin 1919.
88. Georg Michaelis (German Chancellor from July to October 1917). His memoir, *Für Staat und Volk. Eine Lebensgeschichte*, did not appear until 1922.
89. Essays by Herman Grimm: *Essays 1–4*, Gütersloh 1884–90; *Fragmente*, 2 vols, Berlin and Stuttgart 1902.

90. 'By sending Lenin to Russia, our government had taken upon itself a special responsibility. In military terms the journey was justified, for Russia must fall. But our government had to ensure that we did not fall also ...' Ludendorff, op. cit., pp. 407f.
91. Clemenceau, 1841–1929, French Prime Minister, who played a leading role in the Versailles peace negotiations.
92. David Lloyd George, 1863–1945. Minister from 1905, Prime Minister from 1916 to 1922.
93. Woodrow Wilson, 1856–1924. See note 15.
94. The essays were not published at the time, although the selection referred to by Steiner was ready for publication. They first appeared from 1939 in what are now the GAs 29, 30, 31 and 32.
95. See *Das Magazin für Literatur*, Berlin 1898, no. 32 (13 August) pp. 745–50 (in GA 31): 'Bismarck owes his success to the fact that he was never ahead of his time in any way, even by a year or two ... Goethe characterized the problematic nature of certain figures by saying that they are "by nature unfit for any situation, and yet no situation satisfies them". If one transforms this sentence into its opposite, one finds an apt characterization of Bismarck: he was a man fit for any situation, and satisfied with any' (p. 264).
96. Hindenburg: Paul von Beneckendorff, 1847–1934, Chief of the German Army 1916–18. See Hindenburg's comment in the *Hamburger Nachrichten* of 13 November 1919, reprinted in the supplement to the *Schwäbischer Merkur*, no. 526, 14 November 1919, Stuttgart: 'In all that I was forced to experience, this has been a little comfort to me: if I look back over the whole campaign, then no one can say that a single decision, if I had to make it again, would be any different from what it was, given the *same conditions* and the *same knowledge* of our situation and that of the enemy.'
97. In *Fragmente II*, Berlin and Stuttgart 1902, p. 43.
98. See lecture 13 in this volume (9 November).
99. After the lecture ended, Rudolf Steiner then announced some eurythmy performances and further lectures, and dealt with some 'complaints' from members about the irregular starting times for the lectures due to the eurythmy performances.
100. See lecture 11 of this volume (1 November).
101. Incomplete transcript. Words in square brackets added by the editor.
102. In lecture 11 of this volume (1 November).
103. In lectures 11 and 12 of this volume (1 and 2 November).
104. Steiner uses the term 'Krampus'—equivalent to the mischievous Knecht Ruprecht who traditionally accompanies the figure of St Nicholas.
105. This was a poem written by Karl Thylmann (1888–1916) in his last days. See Karl Thylmann, *Gesamtwerk* vol. I, 'Narkose', Stuttgart 1968.The lines in question run:

    ... Wadding all my flesh
    The air is granite.
    Thus is death! The air grows starry granite.
    The air is starry, flickering granite.

106. 'The Spirit as Guide through the Sensory and Supersensible World', Basel 10 November 1919, see note 64.
107. 'The Philosophical Justification for Anthroposophy', a public lecture given on 20 September 1919 (no extant transcript).
108. In lecture 4 of this volume (23 October).

RUDOLF STEINER'S COLLECTED WORKS

The German Edition of Rudolf Steiner's Collected Works (the *Gesamtausgabe* [GA] published by Rudolf Steiner Verlag, Dornach, Switzerland) presently runs to 354 titles, organized either by type of work (written or spoken), chronology, audience (public or other), or subject (education, art, etc.). For ease of comparison, the Collected Works in English [CW] follows the German organization exactly. A complete listing of the CWs follows with literal translations of the German titles. Other than in the case of the books published in his lifetime, titles were rarely given by Rudolf Steiner himself, and were often provided by the editors of the German editions. The titles in English are not necessarily the same as the German; and, indeed, over the past seventy-five years have frequently been different, with the same book sometimes appearing under different titles.

For ease of identification and to avoid confusion, we suggest that readers looking for a title should do so by CW number. Because the work of creating the Collected Works of Rudolf Steiner is an ongoing process, with new titles being published every year, we have not indicated in this listing which books are presently available. To find out what titles in the Collected Works are currently in print, please check our website at www.rudolfsteinerpress.com (or www.steinerbooks.org for US readers).

Written Work

CW 1	Goethe: Natural-Scientific Writings, Introduction, with Footnotes and Explanations in the text by Rudolf Steiner
CW 2	Outlines of an Epistemology of the Goethean World View, with Special Consideration of Schiller
CW 3	Truth and Science
CW 4	The Philosophy of Freedom
CW 4a	Documents to 'The Philosophy of Freedom'
CW 5	Friedrich Nietzsche, A Fighter against His Time
CW 6	Goethe's Worldview
CW 6a	Now in CW 30
CW 7	Mysticism at the Dawn of Modern Spiritual Life and Its Relationship with Modern Worldviews
CW 8	Christianity as Mystical Fact and the Mysteries of Antiquity
CW 9	Theosophy: An Introduction into Supersensible World Knowledge and Human Purpose
CW 10	How Does One Attain Knowledge of Higher Worlds?
CW 11	From the Akasha-Chronicle

CW 12	Levels of Higher Knowledge
CW 13	Occult Science in Outline
CW 14	Four Mystery Dramas
CW 15	The Spiritual Guidance of the Individual and Humanity
CW 16	A Way to Human Self-Knowledge: Eight Meditations
CW 17	The Threshold of the Spiritual World. Aphoristic Comments
CW 18	The Riddles of Philosophy in Their History, Presented as an Outline
CW 19	Contained in CW 24
CW 20	The Riddles of the Human Being: Articulated and Unarticulated in the Thinking, Views and Opinions of a Series of German and Austrian Personalities
CW 21	The Riddles of the Soul
CW 22	Goethe's Spiritual Nature And Its Revelation In 'Faust' and through the 'Fairy Tale of the Snake and the Lily'
CW 23	The Central Points of the Social Question in the Necessities of Life in the Present and the Future
CW 24	Essays Concerning the Threefold Division of the Social Organism and the Period 1915–1921
CW 25	Cosmology, Religion and Philosophy
CW 26	Anthroposophical Leading Thoughts
CW 27	Fundamentals for Expansion of the Art of Healing according to Spiritual-Scientific Insights
CW 28	The Course of My Life
CW 29	Collected Essays on Dramaturgy, 1889–1900
CW 30	Methodical Foundations of Anthroposophy: Collected Essays on Philosophy, Natural Science, Aesthetics and Psychology, 1884–1901
CW 31	Collected Essays on Culture and Current Events, 1887–1901
CW 32	Collected Essays on Literature, 1884–1902
CW 33	Biographies and Biographical Sketches, 1894–1905
CW 34	Lucifer-Gnosis: Foundational Essays on Anthroposophy and Reports from the Periodicals 'Lucifer' and 'Lucifer-Gnosis,' 1903–1908
CW 35	Philosophy and Anthroposophy: Collected Essays, 1904–1923
CW 36	The Goetheanum-Idea in the Middle of the Cultural Crisis of the Present: Collected Essays from the Periodical 'Das Goetheanum,' 1921–1925
CW 37	Now in CWs 260a and 251
CW 38	Letters, Vol. 1: 1881–1890
CW 39	Letters, Vol. 2: 1890–1925
CW 40	Truth-Wrought Words
CW 40a	Sayings, Poems and Mantras; Supplementary Volume
CW 42	Now in CWs 264–266
CW 43	Stage Adaptations
CW 44	On the Four Mystery Dramas. Sketches, Fragments and Paralipomena on the Four Mystery Dramas
CW 45	Anthroposophy: A Fragment from the Year 1910

Public Lectures

CW 51	On Philosophy, History and Literature
CW 52	Spiritual Teachings Concerning the Soul and Observation of the World
CW 53	The Origin and Goal of the Human Being
CW 54	The Riddles of the World and Anthroposophy
CW 55	Knowledge of the Supersensible in Our Times and Its Meaning for Life Today
CW 56	Knowledge of the Soul and of the Spirit
CW 57	Where and How Does One Find the Spirit?
CW 58	The Metamorphoses of the Soul Life. Paths of Soul Experiences: Part One
CW 59	The Metamorphoses of the Soul Life. Paths of Soul Experiences: Part Two
CW 60	The Answers of Spiritual Science to the Biggest Questions of Existence
CW 61	Human History in the Light of Spiritual Research
CW 62	Results of Spiritual Research
CW 63	Spiritual Science as a Treasure for Life
CW 64	Out of Destiny-Burdened Times
CW 65	Out of Central European Spiritual Life
CW 66	Spirit and Matter, Life and Death
CW 67	The Eternal in the Human Soul. Immortality and Freedom
CW 68	Public lectures in various cities, 1906–1918
CW 69	Public lectures in various cities, 1906–1918
CW 70	Public lectures in various cities, 1906–1918
CW 71	Public lectures in various cities, 1906–1918
CW 72	Freedom—Immortality—Social Life
CW 73	The Supplementing of the Modern Sciences through Anthroposophy
CW 73a	Specialized Fields of Knowledge and Anthroposophy
CW 74	The Philosophy of Thomas Aquinas
CW 75	Public lectures in various cities, 1906–1918
CW 76	The Fructifying Effect of Anthroposophy on Specialized Fields
CW 77a	The Task of Anthroposophy in Relation to Science and Life: The Darmstadt College Course
CW 77b	Art and Anthroposophy. The Goetheanum-Impulse
CW 78	Anthroposophy, Its Roots of Knowledge and Fruits for Life
CW 79	The Reality of the Higher Worlds
CW 80	Public lectures in various cities, 1922
CW 81	Renewal-Impulses for Culture and Science—Berlin College Course
CW 82	So that the Human Being Can Become a Complete Human Being
CW 83	Western and Eastern World-Contrast. Paths to Understanding It through Anthroposophy
CW 84	What Did the Goetheanum Intend and What Should Anthroposophy Do?

Lectures to the Members of the Anthroposophical Society

CW 88	Concerning the Astral World and Devachan
CW 89	Consciousness—Life—Form. Fundamental Principles of a Spiritual-Scientific Cosmology
CW 90	Participant Notes from the Lectures during the Years 1903–1905
CW 91	Participant Notes from the Lectures during the Years 1903–1905
CW 92	The Occult Truths of Ancient Myths and Sagas
CW 93	The Temple Legend and the Golden Legend
CW 93a	Fundamentals of Esotericism
CW 94	Cosmogony. Popular Occultism. The Gospel of John. The Theosophy in the Gospel of John
CW 95	At the Gates of Theosophy
CW 96	Origin-Impulses of Spiritual Science. Christian Esotericism in the Light of New Spirit-Knowledge
CW 97	The Christian Mystery
CW 98	Nature Beings and Spirit Beings—Their Effects in Our Visible World
CW 99	The Theosophy of the Rosicrucians
CW 100	Human Development and Christ-Knowledge
CW 101	Myths and Legends. Occult Signs and Symbols
CW 102	The Working into Human Beings by Spiritual Beings
CW 103	The Gospel of John
CW 104	The Apocalypse of John
CW 104a	From the Picture-Script of the Apocalypse of John
CW 105	Universe, Earth, the Human Being: Their Being and Development, as well as Their Reflection in the Connection between Egyptian Mythology and Modern Culture
CW 106	Egyptian Myths and Mysteries in Relation to the Active Spiritual Forces of the Present
CW 107	Spiritual-Scientific Knowledge of the Human Being
CW 108	Answering the Questions of Life and the World through Anthroposophy
CW 109	The Principle of Spiritual Economy in Connection with the Question of Reincarnation. An Aspect of the Spiritual Guidance of Humanity
CW 110	The Spiritual Hierarchies and Their Reflection in the Physical World. Zodiac, Planets and Cosmos
CW 111	Contained in CW 109
CW 112	The Gospel of John in Relation to the Three Other Gospels, Especially the Gospel of Luke
CW 113	The Orient in the Light of the Occident. The Children of Lucifer and the Brothers of Christ
CW 114	The Gospel of Luke
CW 115	Anthroposophy—Psychosophy—Pneumatosophy
CW 116	The Christ-Impulse and the Development of 'I'-Consciousness
CW 117	The Deeper Secrets of the Development of Humanity in Light of the Gospels

CW 118 The Event of the Christ-Appearance in the Etheric World
CW 119 Macrocosm and Microcosm. The Large World and the Small World. Soul-Questions, Life-Questions, Spirit-Questions
CW 120 The Revelation of Karma
CW 121 The Mission of Individual Folk-Souls in Connection with Germanic-Nordic Mythology
CW 122 The Secrets of the Biblical Creation-Story. The Six-Day Work in the First Book of Moses
CW 123 The Gospel of Matthew
CW 124 Excursus in the Area of the Gospel of Mark
CW 125 Paths and Goals of the Spiritual Human Being. Life Questions in the Light of Spiritual Science
CW 126 Occult History. Esoteric Observations of the Karmic Relationships of Personalities and Events of World History
CW 127 The Mission of the New Spiritual Revelation. The Christ-Event as the Middle-Point of Earth Evolution
CW 128 An Occult Physiology
CW 129 Wonders of the World, Trials of the Soul, and Revelations of the Spirit
CW 130 Esoteric Christianity and the Spiritual Guidance of Humanity
CW 131 From Jesus to Christ
CW 132 Evolution from the View Point of the Truth
CW 133 The Earthly and the Cosmic Human Being
CW 134 The World of the Senses and the World of the Spirit
CW 135 Reincarnation and Karma and their Meaning for the Culture of the Present
CW 136 The Spiritual Beings in Celestial Bodies and the Realms of Nature
CW 137 The Human Being in the Light of Occultism, Theosophy and Philosophy
CW 138 On Initiation. On Eternity and the Passing Moment. On the Light of the Spirit and the Darkness of Life
CW 139 The Gospel of Mark
CW 140 Occult Investigation into the Life between Death and New Birth. The Living Interaction between Life and Death
CW 141 Life between Death and New Birth in Relationship to Cosmic Facts
CW 142 The Bhagavad Gita and the Letters of Paul
CW 143 Experiences of the Supersensible. Three Paths of the Soul to Christ
CW 144 The Mysteries of the East and of Christianity
CW 145 What Significance Does Occult Development of the Human Being Have for the Sheaths—Physical Body, Etheric Body, Astral Body, and Self?
CW 146 The Occult Foundations of the Bhagavad Gita
CW 147 The Secrets of the Threshold
CW 148 Out of Research in the Akasha: The Fifth Gospel
CW 149 Christ and the Spiritual World. Concerning the Search for the Holy Grail

CW 150	The World of the Spirit and Its Extension into Physical Existence; The Influence of the Dead in the World of the Living
CW 151	Human Thought and Cosmic Thought
CW 152	Preliminary Stages to the Mystery of Golgotha
CW 153	The Inner Being of the Human Being and Life Between Death and New Birth
CW 154	How does One Gain an Understanding of the Spiritual World? The Flowing in of Spiritual Impulses from out of the World of the Deceased
CW 155	Christ and the Human Soul. Concerning the Meaning of Life. Theosophical Morality. Anthroposophy and Christianity
CW 156	Occult Reading and Occult Hearing
CW 157	Human Destinies and the Destiny of Peoples
CW 157a	The Formation of Destiny and the Life after Death
CW 158	The Connection Between the Human Being and the Elemental World. Kalevala—Olaf Åsteson—The Russian People—The World as the Result of the Influences of Equilibrium
CW 159	The Mystery of Death. The Nature and Significance of Middle Europe and the European Folk Spirits
CW 160	In CW 159
CW 161	Paths of Spiritual Knowledge and the Renewal of the Artistic Worldview
CW 162	Questions of Art and Life in Light of Spiritual Science
CW 163	Coincidence, Necessity and Providence. Imaginative Knowledge and the Processes after Death
CW 164	The Value of Thinking for a Knowledge That Satisfies the Human Being. The Relationship of Spiritual Science to Natural Science
CW 165	The Spiritual Unification of Humanity through the Christ-Impulse
CW 166	Necessity and Freedom in the Events of the World and in Human Action
CW 167	The Present and the Past in the Human Spirit
CW 168	The Connection between the Living and the Dead
CW 169	World-being and Selfhood
CW 170	The Riddle of the Human Being. The Spiritual Background of Human History. Cosmic and Human History, Vol. 1
CW 171	Inner Development-Impulses of Humanity. Goethe and the Crisis of the 19th Century. Cosmic and Human History, Vol. 2
CW 172	The Karma of the Vocation of the Human Being in Connection with Goethe's Life. Cosmic and Human History, Vol. 3
CW 173	Contemporary-Historical Considerations: The Karma of Untruthfulness, Part One. Cosmic and Human History, Vol. 4
CW 174	Contemporary-Historical Considerations: The Karma of Untruthfulness, Part Two. Cosmic and Human History, Vol. 5
CW 174a	Middle Europe between East and West. Cosmic and Human History, Vol. 6
CW 174b	The Spiritual Background of the First World War. Cosmic and Human History, Vol. 7

CW 175	Building Stones for an Understanding of the Mystery of Golgotha. Cosmic and Human Metamorphoses
CW 176	Truths of Evolution of the Individual and Humanity. The Karma of Materialism
CW 177	The Spiritual Background of the Outer World. The Fall of the Spirits of Darkness. Spiritual Beings and Their Effects, Vol. 1
CW 178	Individual Spiritual Beings and their Influence in the Soul of the Human Being. Spiritual Beings and their Effects, Vol. 2
CW 179	Spiritual Beings and Their Effects. Historical Necessity and Freedom. The Influences on Destiny from out of the World of the Dead. Spiritual Beings and Their Effects, Vol. 3
CW 180	Mystery Truths and Christmas Impulses. Ancient Myths and their Meaning. Spiritual Beings and Their Effects, Vol. 4
CW 181	Earthly Death and Cosmic Life. Anthroposophical Gifts for Life. Necessities of Consciousness for the Present and the Future.
CW 182	Death as Transformation of Life
CW 183	The Science of the Development of the Human Being
CW 184	The Polarity of Duration and Development in Human Life. The Cosmic Pre-History of Humanity
CW 185	Historical Symptomology
CW 185a	Historical-Developmental Foundations for Forming a Social Judgement
CW 186	The Fundamental Social Demands of Our Time—In Changed Situations
CW 187	How Can Humanity Find the Christ Again? The Threefold Shadow-Existence of our Time and the New Christ-Light
CW 188	Goetheanism, a Transformation-Impulse and Resurrection-Thought. Science of the Human Being and Science of Sociology
CW 189	The Social Question as a Question of Consciousness. The Spiritual Background of the Social Question, Vol. 1
CW 190	Impulses of the Past and the Future in Social Occurrences. The Spiritual Background of the Social Question, Vol. 2
CW 191	Social Understanding from Spiritual-Scientific Cognition. The Spiritual Background of the Social Question, Vol. 3
CW 192	Spiritual-Scientific Treatment of Social and Pedagogical Questions
CW 193	The Inner Aspect of the Social Riddle. Luciferic Past and Ahrimanic Future
CW 194	The Mission of Michael. The Revelation of the Actual Mysteries of the Human Being
CW 195	Cosmic New Year and the New Year Idea
CW 196	Spiritual and Social Transformations in the Development of Humanity
CW 197	Polarities in the Development of Humanity: West and East Materialism and Mysticism Knowledge and Belief
CW 198	Healing Factors for the Social Organism
CW 199	Spiritual Science as Knowledge of the Foundational Impulses of Social Formation

CW 200 The New Spirituality and the Christ-Experience of the 20th Century
CW 201 The Correspondences Between Microcosm and Macrocosm. The Human Being—A Hieroglyph of the Universe. The Human Being in Relationship with the Cosmos: 1
CW 202 The Bridge between the World-Spirituality and the Physical Aspect of the Human Being. The Search for the New Isis, the Divine Sophia. The Human Being in Relationship with the Cosmos: 2
CW 203 The Responsibility of Human Beings for the Development of the World through their Spiritual Connection with the Planet Earth and the World of the Stars. The Human Being in Relationship with the Cosmos: 3
CW 204 Perspectives of the Development of Humanity. The Materialistic Knowledge-Impulse and the Task of Anthroposophy. The Human Being in Relationship with the Cosmos: 4
CW 205 Human Development, World-Soul, and World-Spirit. Part One: The Human Being as a Being of Body and Soul in Relationship to the World. The Human Being in Relationship with the Cosmos: 5
CW 206 Human Development, World-Soul, and World-Spirit. Part Two: The Human Being as a Spiritual Being in the Process of Historical Development. The Human Being in Relationship with the Cosmos: 6
CW 207 Anthroposophy as Cosmosophy. Part One: Characteristic Features of the Human Being in the Earthly and the Cosmic Realms. The Human Being in Relationship with the Cosmos: 7
CW 208 Anthroposophy as Cosmosophy. Part Two: The Forming of the Human Being as the Result of Cosmic Influence. The Human Being in Relationship with the Cosmos: 8
CW 209 Nordic and Central European Spiritual Impulses. The Festival of the Appearance of Christ. The Human Being in Relationship with the Cosmos: 9
CW 210 Old and New Methods of Initiation. Drama and Poetry in the Change of Consciousness in the Modern Age
CW 211 The Sun Mystery and the Mystery of Death and Resurrection. Exoteric and Esoteric Christianity
CW 212 Human Soul Life and Spiritual Striving in Connection with World and Earth Development
CW 213 Human Questions and World Answers
CW 214 The Mystery of the Trinity: The Human Being in Relationship with the Spiritual World in the Course of Time
CW 215 Philosophy, Cosmology, and Religion in Anthroposophy
CW 216 The Fundamental Impulses of the World-Historical Development of Humanity
CW 217 Spiritually Active Forces in the Coexistence of the Older and Younger Generations. Pedagogical Course for Youth

CW 217a	Youth's Cognitive Task
CW 218	Spiritual Connections in the Forming of the Human Organism
CW 219	The Relationship of the World of the Stars to the Human Being, and of the Human Being to the World of the Stars. The Spiritual Communion of Humanity
CW 220	Living Knowledge of Nature. Intellectual Fall and Spiritual Redemption
CW 221	Earth-Knowing and Heaven-Insight
CW 222	The Imparting of Impulses to World-Historical Events through Spiritual Powers
CW 223	The Cycle of the Year as Breathing Process of the Earth and the Four Great Festival-Seasons. Anthroposophy and the Human Heart (Gemüt)
CW 224	The Human Soul and its Connection with Divine-Spiritual Individualities. The Internalization of the Festivals of the Year
CW 225	Three Perspectives of Anthroposophy. Cultural Phenomena observed from a Spiritual-Scientific Perspective
CW 226	Human Being, Human Destiny, and World Development
CW 227	Initiation-Knowledge
CW 228	Science of Initiation and Knowledge of the Stars. The Human Being in the Past, the Present, and the Future from the Viewpoint of the Development of Consciousness
CW 229	The Experiencing of the Course of the Year in Four Cosmic Imaginations
CW 230	The Human Being as Harmony of the Creative, Building, and Formative World-Word
CW 231	The Supersensible Human Being, Understood Anthroposophically
CW 232	The Forming of the Mysteries
CW 233	World History Illuminated by Anthroposophy and as the Foundation for Knowledge of the Human Spirit
CW 233a	Mystery Sites of the Middle Ages: Rosicrucianism and the Modern Initiation-Principle. The Festival of Easter as Part of the History of the Mysteries of Humanity
CW 234	Anthroposophy. A Summary after 21 Years
CW 235	Esoteric Observations of Karmic Relationships in 6 Volumes, Vol. 1
CW 236	Esoteric Observations of Karmic Relationships in 6 Volumes, Vol. 2
CW 237	Esoteric Observations of Karmic Relationships in 6 Volumes, Vol. 3: The Karmic Relationships of the Anthroposophical Movement
CW 238	Esoteric Observations of Karmic Relationships in 6 Volumes, Vol. 4: The Spiritual Life of the Present in Relationship to the Anthroposophical Movement
CW 239	Esoteric Observations of Karmic Relationships in 6 Volumes, Vol. 5

CW 240	Esoteric Observations of Karmic Relationships in 6 Volumes, Vol. 6
CW 243	The Consciousness of the Initiate
CW 245	Instructions for an Esoteric Schooling
CW 250	The Building-Up of the Anthroposophical Society. From the Beginning to the Outbreak of the First World War
CW 251	The History of the Goetheanum Building-Association
CW 252	Life in the Anthroposophical Society from the First World War to the Burning of the First Goetheanum
CW 253	The Problems of Living Together in the Anthroposophical Society. On the Dornach Crisis of 1915. With Highlights on Swedenborg's Clairvoyance, the Views of Freudian Psychoanalysts, and the Concept of Love in Relation to Mysticism
CW 254	The Occult Movement in the 19th Century and Its Relationship to World Culture. Significant Points from the Exoteric Cultural Life around the Middle of the 19th Century
CW 255	Rudolf Steiner during the First World War
CW 255a	Anthroposophy and the Reformation of Society. On the History of the Threefold Movement
CW 255b	Anthroposophy and Its Opponents, 1919–1921
CW 256	How Can the Anthroposophical Movement Be Financed?
CW 256a	Futurum, Inc. / International Laboratories, Inc.
CW 256b	The Coming Day, Inc.
CW 257	Anthroposophical Community-Building
CW 258	The History of and Conditions for the Anthroposophical Movement in Relationship to the Anthroposophical Society. A Stimulus to Self-Contemplation
CW 259	The Year of Destiny 1923 in the History of the Anthroposophical Society. From the Burning of the Goetheanum to the Christmas Conference
CW 260	The Christmas Conference for the Founding of the General Anthroposophical Society
CW 260a	The Constitution of the General Anthroposophical Society and the School for Spiritual Science. The Rebuilding of the Goetheanum
CW 261	Our Dead. Addresses, Words of Remembrance, and Meditative Verses, 1906–1924
CW 262	Rudolf Steiner and Marie Steiner-von Sivers: Correspondence and Documents, 1901–1925
CW 263/1	Rudolf Steiner and Edith Maryon: Correspondence: Letters, Verses, Sketches, 1912–1924
CW 264	On the History and the Contents of the First Section of the Esoteric School from 1904 to 1914. Letters, Newsletters, Documents, Lectures
CW 265	On the History and from the Contents of the Ritual-Knowledge Section of the Esoteric School from 1904 to 1914. Documents, and Lectures from the Years 1906 to 1914, as well as on New Approaches to Ritual-Knowledge Work in the Years 1921–1924

CW 266/1 From the Contents of the Esoteric Lessons. Volume 1: 1904–1909. Notes from Memory of Participants. Meditation texts from the notes of Rudolf Steiner
CW 266/2 From the Contents of the Esoteric Lessons. Volume 2: 1910–1912. Notes from Memory of Participants
CW 266/3 From the Contents of the Esoteric Lessons. Volume 3: 1913, 1914 and 1920–1923. Notes from Memory of Participants. Meditation texts from the notes of Rudolf Steiner
CW 267 Soul-Exercises: Vol. 1: Exercises with Word and Image Meditations for the Methodological Development of Higher Powers of Knowledge, 1904–1924
CW 268 Soul-Exercises: Vol. 2: Mantric Verses, 1903–1925
CW 269 Ritual Texts for the Celebration of the Free Christian Religious Instruction. The Collected Verses for Teachers and Students of the Waldorf School
CW 270 Esoteric Instructions for the First Class of the School for Spiritual Science at the Goetheanum 1924, 4 Volumes
CW 271 Art and Knowledge of Art. Foundations of a New Aesthetic
CW 272 Spiritual-Scientific Commentary on Goethe's 'Faust' in Two Volumes. Vol. 1: Faust, the Striving Human Being
CW 273 Spiritual-Scientific Commentary on Goethe's 'Faust' in Two Volumes. Vol. 2: The Faust-Problem
CW 274 Addresses for the Christmas Plays from the Old Folk Traditions
CW 275 Art in the Light of Mystery-Wisdom
CW 276 The Artistic in Its Mission in the World. The Genius of Language. The World of Self-Revealing Radiant Appearances—Anthroposophy and Art. Anthroposophy and Poetry
CW 277 Eurythmy. The Revelation of the Speaking Soul
CW 277a The Origin and Development of Eurythmy
CW 278 Eurythmy as Visible Song
CW 279 Eurythmy as Visible Speech
CW 280 The Method and Nature of Speech Formation
CW 281 The Art of Recitation and Declamation
CW 282 Speech Formation and Dramatic Art
CW 283 The Nature of Things Musical and the Experience of Tone in the Human Being
CW 284/285 Images of Occult Seals and Pillars. The Munich Congress of Whitsun 1907 and Its Consequences
CW 286 Paths to a New Style of Architecture. 'And the Building Becomes Human'
CW 287 The Building at Dornach as a Symbol of Historical Becoming and an Artistic Transformation Impulse
CW 288 Style-Forms in the Living Organic
CW 289 The Building-Idea of the Goetheanum: Lectures with Slides from the Years 1920–1921
CW 290 The Building-Idea of the Goetheanum: Lectures with Slides from the Years 1920–1921

CW 291	The Nature of Colours
CW 291a	Knowledge of Colours. Supplementary Volume to 'The Nature of Colours'
CW 292	Art History as Image of Inner Spiritual Impulses
CW 293	General Knowledge of the Human Being as the Foundation of Pedagogy
CW 294	The Art of Education, Methodology and Didactics
CW 295	The Art of Education: Seminar Discussions and Lectures on Lesson Planning
CW 296	The Question of Education as a Social Question
CW 297	The Idea and Practice of the Waldorf School
CW 297a	Education for Life: Self-Education and the Practice of Pedagogy
CW 298	Rudolf Steiner in the Waldorf School
CW 299	Spiritual-Scientific Observations on Speech
CW 300a	Conferences with the Teachers of the Free Waldorf School in Stuttgart, 1919 to 1924, in 3 Volumes, Vol. 1
CW 300b	Conferences with the Teachers of the Free Waldorf School in Stuttgart, 1919 to 1924, in 3 Volumes, Vol. 2
CW 300c	Conferences with the Teachers of the Free Waldorf School in Stuttgart, 1919 to 1924, in 3 Volumes, Vol. 3
CW 301	The Renewal of Pedagogical-Didactical Art through Spiritual Science
CW 302	Knowledge of the Human Being and the Forming of Class Lessons
CW 302a	Education and Teaching from a Knowledge of the Human Being
CW 303	The Healthy Development of the Human Being
CW 304	Methods of Education and Teaching Based on Anthroposophy
CW 304a	Anthroposophical Knowledge of the Human Being and Pedagogy
CW 305	The Soul-Spiritual Foundational Forces of the Art of Education. Spiritual Values in Education and Social Life
CW 306	Pedagogical Praxis from the Viewpoint of a Spiritual-Scientific Knowledge of the Human Being. The Education of the Child and Young Human Beings
CW 307	The Spiritual Life of the Present and Education
CW 308	The Method of Teaching and the Life-Requirements for Teaching
CW 309	Anthroposophical Pedagogy and Its Prerequisites
CW 310	The Pedagogical Value of a Knowledge of the Human Being and the Cultural Value of Pedagogy
CW 311	The Art of Education from an Understanding of the Being of Humanity
CW 312	Spiritual Science and Medicine
CW 313	Spiritual-Scientific Viewpoints on Therapy
CW 314	Physiology and Therapy Based on Spiritual Science
CW 315	Curative Eurythmy
CW 316	Meditative Observations and Instructions for a Deepening of the Art of Healing
CW 317	The Curative Education Course

CW 318 The Working Together of Doctors and Pastors
CW 319 Anthroposophical Knowledge of the Human Being and Medicine
CW 320 Spiritual-Scientific Impulses for the Development of Physics 1: The First Natural-Scientific Course: Light, Colour, Tone, Mass, Electricity, Magnetism
CW 321 Spiritual-Scientific Impulses for the Development of Physics 2: The Second Natural-Scientific Course: Warmth at the Border of Positive and Negative Materiality
CW 322 The Borders of the Knowledge of Nature
CW 323 The Relationship of the various Natural-Scientific Fields to Astronomy
CW 324 Nature Observation, Mathematics, and Scientific Experimentation and Results from the Viewpoint of Anthroposophy
CW 324a The Fourth Dimension in Mathematics and Reality
CW 325 Natural Science and the World-Historical Development of Humanity since Ancient Times
CW 326 The Moment of the Coming Into Being of Natural Science in World History and Its Development Since Then
CW 327 Spiritual-Scientific Foundations for Success in Farming. The Agricultural Course
CW 328 The Social Question
CW 329 The Liberation of the Human Being as the Foundation for a New Social Form
CW 330 The Renewal of the Social Organism
CW 331 Work-Council and Socialization
CW 332 The Alliance for Threefolding and the Total Reform of Society. The Council on Culture and the Liberation of the Spiritual Life
CW 332a The Social Future
CW 333 Freedom of Thought and Social Forces
CW 334 From the Unified State to the Threefold Social Organism
CW 335 The Crisis of the Present and the Path to Healthy Thinking
CW 336 The Great Questions of the Times and Anthroposophical Spiritual Knowledge
CW 337a Social Ideas, Social Reality, Social Practice, Vol. 1: Question-and-Answer Evenings and Study Evenings of the Alliance for the Threefold Social Organism in Stuttgart, 1919–1920
CW 337b Social Ideas, Social Realities, Social Practice, Vol. 2: Discussion Evenings of the Swiss Alliance for the Threefold Social Organism
CW 338 How Does One Work on Behalf of the Impulse for the Threefold Social Organism?
CW 339 Anthroposophy, Threefold Social Organism, and the Art of Public Speaking
CW 340 The National-Economics Course. The Tasks of a New Science of Economics, Volume 1
CW 341 The National-Economics Seminar. The Tasks of a New Science of Economics, Volume 2

CW 342	Lectures and Courses on Christian Religious Work, Vol. 1: Anthroposophical Foundations for a Renewed Christian Religious Working
CW 343	Lectures and Courses on Christian Religious Work, Vol. 2: Spiritual Knowledge—Religious Feeling—Cultic Doing
CW 344	Lectures and Courses on Christian Religious Work, Vol. 3: Lectures at the Founding of the Christian Community
CW 345	Lectures and Courses on Christian Religious Work, Vol. 4: Concerning the Nature of the Working Word
CW 346	Lectures and Courses on Christian Religious Work, Vol. 5: The Apocalypse and the Work of the Priest
CW 347	The Knowledge of the Nature of the Human Being According to Body, Soul and Spirit. On Earlier Conditions of the Earth
CW 348	On Health and Illness. Foundations of a Spiritual-Scientific Doctrine of the Senses
CW 349	On the Life of the Human Being and of the Earth. On the Nature of Christianity
CW 350	Rhythms in the Cosmos and in the Human Being. How Does One Come To See the Spiritual World?
CW 351	The Human Being and the World. The Influence of the Spirit in Nature. On the Nature of Bees
CW 352	Nature and the Human Being Observed Spiritual-Scientifically
CW 353	The History of Humanity and the World-Views of the Folk Cultures
CW 354	The Creation of the World and the Human Being. Life on Earth and the Influence of the Stars

SIGNIFICANT EVENTS IN THE LIFE OF RUDOLF STEINER

1829: June 23: birth of Johann Steiner (1829–1910)—Rudolf Steiner's father—in Geras, Lower Austria.

1834: May 8: birth of Franciska Blie (1834–1918)—Rudolf Steiner's mother—in Horn, Lower Austria. 'My father and mother were both children of the glorious Lower Austrian forest district north of the Danube.'

1860: May 16: marriage of Johann Steiner and Franciska Blie.

1861: February 25: birth of *Rudolf Joseph Lorenz Steiner* in Kraljevec, Croatia, near the border with Hungary, where Johann Steiner works as a telegrapher for the South Austria Railroad. Rudolf Steiner is baptized two days later, February 27, the date usually given as his birthday.

1862: Summer: the family moves to Mödling, Lower Austria.

1863: The family moves to Pottschach, Lower Austria, near the Styrian border, where Johann Steiner becomes stationmaster. 'The view stretched to the mountains ... majestic peaks in the distance and the sweet charm of nature in the immediate surroundings.'

1864: November 15: birth of Rudolf Steiner's sister, Leopoldine (d. November 1, 1927). She will become a seamstress and live with her parents for the rest of her life.

1866: July 28: birth of Rudolf Steiner's deaf-mute brother, Gustav (d. May 1, 1941).

1867: Rudolf Steiner enters the village school. Following a disagreement between his father and the schoolmaster, whose wife falsely accused the boy of causing a commotion, Rudolf Steiner is taken out of school and taught at home.

1868: A critical experience. Unknown to the family, an aunt dies in a distant town. Sitting in the station waiting room, Rudolf Steiner sees her 'form,' which speaks to him, asking for help. 'Beginning with this experience, a new soul life began in the boy, one in which not only the outer trees and mountains spoke to him, but also the worlds that lay behind them. From this moment on, the boy began to live with the spirits of nature ...'

1869: The family moves to the peaceful, rural village of Neudörfl, near Wiener-Neustadt in present-day Austria. Rudolf Steiner attends the village school. Because of the 'unorthodoxy' of his writing and spelling, he has to do 'extra lessons.'

1870: Through a book lent to him by his tutor, he discovers geometry: 'To grasp something purely in the spirit brought me inner happiness. I know that I first learned happiness through geometry.' The same tutor allows him to draw, while other students still struggle with their reading and writing. 'An artistic element' thus enters his education.

1871: Though his parents are not religious, Rudolf Steiner becomes a 'church child,' a favourite of the priest, who was 'an exceptional character.' 'Up to the age of ten or eleven, among those I came to know, he was far and away the most significant.' Among other things, he introduces Steiner to Copernican, heliocentric cosmology. As an altar boy, Rudolf Steiner serves at Masses, funerals, and Corpus Christi processions. At year's end, after an incident in which he escapes a thrashing, his father forbids him to go to church.

1872: Rudolf Steiner transfers to grammar school in Wiener-Neustadt, a five-mile walk from home, which must be done in all weathers.

1873–75: Through his teachers and on his own, Rudolf Steiner has many wonderful experiences with science and mathematics. Outside school, he teaches himself analytic geometry, trigonometry, differential equations, and calculus.

1876: Rudolf Steiner begins tutoring other students. He learns bookbinding from his father. He also teaches himself stenography.

1877: Rudolf Steiner discovers Kant's *Critique of Pure Reason*, which he reads and rereads. He also discovers and reads von Rotteck's *World History*.

1878: He studies extensively in contemporary psychology and philosophy.

1879: Rudolf Steiner graduates from high school with honours. His father is transferred to Inzersdorf, near Vienna. He uses his first visit to Vienna 'to purchase a great number of philosophy books'—Kant, Fichte, Schelling, and Hegel, as well as numerous histories of philosophy. His aim: to find a path from the 'I' to nature.

October 1879–1883: Rudolf Steiner attends the Technical College in Vienna—to study mathematics, chemistry, physics, mineralogy, botany, zoology, biology, geology, and mechanics—with a scholarship. He also attends lectures in history and literature, while avidly reading philosophy on his own. His two favourite professors are Karl Julius Schröer (German language and literature) and Edmund Reitlinger (physics). He also audits lectures by Robert Zimmermann on aesthetics and Franz Brentano on philosophy. During this year he begins his friendship with Moritz Zitter (1861–1921), who will help support him financially when he is in Berlin.

1880: Rudolf Steiner attends lectures on Schiller and Goethe by Karl Julius Schröer, who becomes his mentor. Also 'through a remarkable combination of circumstances,' he meets Felix Koguzki, a 'herb gatherer' and healer, who could 'see deeply into the secrets of nature.' Rudolf Steiner will meet and study with this 'emissary of the Master' throughout his time in Vienna.

1881: January: '... I didn't sleep a wink. I was busy with philosophical problems until about 12:30 a.m. Then, finally, I threw myself down on my couch. All my striving during the previous year had been to research whether the following statement by Schelling was true or not: *Within everyone dwells a secret, marvelous capacity to draw back from the stream of time—out of the self clothed in all that comes to us from outside—into our innermost being and there, in the immutable form of the Eternal, to look into ourselves*. I believe, and I am still quite certain of it, that I discovered this capacity in myself; I had long had an inkling of it. Now the whole of idealist philosophy stood before me in modified form. What's a sleepless night compared to that!'

Rudolf Steiner begins communicating with leading thinkers of the day, who send him books in return, which he reads eagerly.

July: 'I am not one of those who dives into the day like an animal in human form. I pursue a quite specific goal, an idealistic aim—knowledge of the truth! This cannot be done offhandedly. It requires the greatest striving in the world, free of all egotism, and equally of all resignation.'

August: Steiner puts down on paper for the first time thoughts for a 'Philosophy of Freedom.' 'The striving for the absolute: this human yearning is freedom.' He also seeks to outline a 'peasant philosophy,' describing what the worldview of a 'peasant'—one who lives close to the earth and the old ways—really is.

1881–1882: Felix Koguzki, the herb gatherer, reveals himself to be the envoy of another, higher initiatory personality, who instructs Rudolf Steiner to penetrate Fichte's philosophy and to master modern scientific thinking as a preparation for right entry into the spirit. This 'Master' also teaches him the double (evolutionary and involutionary) nature of time.

1882: Through the offices of Karl Julius Schröer, Rudolf Steiner is asked by Joseph Kürschner to edit Goethe's scientific works for the *Deutschen National-Literatur* edition. He writes 'A Possible Critique of Atomistic Concepts' and sends it to Friedrich Theodor Vischer.

1883: Rudolf Steiner completes his college studies and begins work on the Goethe project.

1884: First volume of Goethe's *Scientific Writings* (CW 1) appears (March). He lectures on Goethe and Lessing, and Goethe's approach to science. In July, he enters the household of Ladislaus and Pauline Specht as tutor to the four Specht boys. He will live there until 1890. At this time, he meets Josef Breuer (1842–1925), the co-author with Sigmund Freud of *Studies in Hysteria*, who is the Specht family doctor.

1885: While continuing to edit Goethe's writings, Rudolf Steiner reads deeply in contemporary philosophy (Eduard von Hartmann, Johannes Volkelt, and Richard Wahle, among others).

1886: May: Rudolf Steiner sends Kürschner the manuscript of *Outlines of Goethe's Theory of Knowledge* (CW 2), which appears in October, and which he sends out widely. He also meets the poet Marie Eugenie Delle Grazie and writes 'Nature and Our Ideals' for her. He attends her salon, where he meets many priests, theologians, and philosophers, who will become his friends. Meanwhile, the director of the Goethe Archive in Weimar requests his collaboration with the *Sophien* edition of Goethe's works, particularly the writings on colour.

1887: At the beginning of the year, Rudolf Steiner is very sick. As the year progresses and his health improves, he becomes increasingly 'a man of letters,' lecturing, writing essays, and taking part in Austrian cultural life. In August–September, the second volume of Goethe's *Scientific Writings* appears.

1888: January–July: Rudolf Steiner assumes editorship of the 'German Weekly' (*Deutsche Wochenschrift*). He begins lecturing more intensively, giving, for example, a lecture titled 'Goethe as Father of a New Aesthetics.' He meets and becomes soul friends with Friedrich Eckstein (1861–1939), a vegetarian, philosopher of symbolism, alchemist, and musician, who will introduce him to various spiritual currents (including Theosophy) and with whom he will meditate and interpret esoteric and alchemical texts.

1889: Rudolf Steiner first reads Nietzsche (*Beyond Good and Evil*). He encounters Theosophy again and learns of Madame Blavatsky in the Theosophical circle around Marie Lang (1858–1934). Here he also meets well-known figures of Austrian life, as well as esoteric figures like the occultist Franz Hartmann and Karl Leinigen-Billigen (translator of C.G. Harrison's *The Transcendental Universe*). During this period, Steiner first reads A.P. Sinnett's *Esoteric Buddhism* and Mabel Collins's *Light on the Path*. He also begins travelling, visiting Budapest, Weimar, and Berlin (where he meets philosopher Eduard von Hartmann).

1890: Rudolf Steiner finishes volume 3 of Goethe's scientific writings. He begins his doctoral dissertation, which will become *Truth and Science* (CW 3). He also meets the poet and feminist Rosa Mayreder (1858–1938), with whom he can exchange his most intimate thoughts. In September, Rudolf Steiner moves to Weimar to work in the Goethe-Schiller Archive.

1891: Volume 3 of the Kürschner edition of Goethe appears. Meanwhile, Rudolf Steiner edits Goethe's studies in mineralogy and scientific writings for the *Sophien* edition. He meets Ludwig Laistner of the Cotta Publishing Company, who asks for a book on the basic question of metaphysics. From this will result, ultimately, *The Philosophy of Freedom* (CW 4), which will be published not by Cotta but by Emil Felber. In October, Rudolf Steiner takes the oral exam for a doctorate in philosophy, mathematics, and mechanics at Rostock University, receiving his doctorate on the twenty-sixth. In November, he gives his first lecture on Goethe's 'Fairy Tale' in Vienna.

1892: Rudolf Steiner continues work at the Goethe-Schiller Archive and on his *Philosophy of Freedom*. *Truth and Science*, his doctoral dissertation, is published. Steiner undertakes to write introductions to books on Schopenhauer and Jean Paul for Cotta. At year's end, he finds lodging with Anna Eunike, née Schulz (1853–1911), a widow with four daughters and a son. He also develops a friendship with Otto Erich Hartleben (1864–1905) with whom he shares literary interests.

1893: Rudolf Steiner begins his habit of producing many reviews and articles. In March, he gives a lecture titled 'Hypnotism, with Reference to Spiritism.' In September, volume 4 of the Kürschner edition is completed. In November, *The Philosophy of Freedom* appears. This year, too, he meets John Henry Mackay (1864–1933), the anarchist, and Max Stirner, a scholar and biographer.

1894: Rudolf Steiner meets Elisabeth Förster Nietzsche, the philosopher's sister, and begins to read Nietzsche in earnest, beginning with the as yet unpublished *Antichrist*. He also meets Ernst Haeckel (1834–1919). In the fall, he begins to write *Nietzsche, A Fighter against His Time* (CW 5).

1895: May, *Nietzsche, A Fighter against His Time* appears.

1896: January 22: Rudolf Steiner sees Friedrich Nietzsche for the first and only time. Moves between the Nietzsche and the Goethe-Schiller Archives, where he completes his work before year's end. He falls out with Elisabeth Förster Nietzsche, thus ending his association with the Nietzsche Archive.

1897: Rudolf Steiner finishes the manuscript of *Goethe's Worldview* (CW 6). He moves to Berlin with Anna Eunike and begins editorship of the *Magazin für Literatur*. From now on, Steiner will write countless reviews, literary and philosophical articles, and so on. He begins lecturing at the 'Free Literary Society.' In September, he attends the Zionist Congress in Basel. He sides with Dreyfus in the Dreyfus affair.

1898: Rudolf Steiner is very active as an editor in the political, artistic, and theatrical life of Berlin. He becomes friendly with John Henry Mackay and poet Ludwig Jacobowski (1868–1900). He joins Jacobowski's circle of writers, artists, and scientists—'The Coming Ones' (*Die Kommenden*)—and contributes lectures to the group until 1903. He also lectures at the 'League for College Pedagogy.' He writes an article for Goethe's sesquicentennial, 'Goethe's Secret Revelation,' on the 'Fairy Tale of the Green Snake and the Beautiful Lily.'

1898–99: 'This was a trying time for my soul as I looked at Christianity. . . . I was able to progress only by contemplating, by means of spiritual perception, the evolution of Christianity. . . . Conscious knowledge of real Christianity began to dawn in me around the turn of the century. This seed continued to develop. My soul trial occurred shortly before the beginning of the twentieth century. It was decisive for my soul's development that I stood spiritually before the Mystery of Golgotha in a deep and solemn celebration of knowledge.'

1899: Rudolf Steiner begins teaching and giving lectures and lecture cycles at the Workers' College, founded by Wilhelm Liebknecht (1826–1900). He will continue to do so until 1904. Writes: *Literature and Spiritual Life in the Nineteenth Century; Individualism in Philosophy*; *Haeckel and His Opponents; Poetry in the Present;* and begins what will become (fifteen years later) *The Riddles of Philosophy* (CW 18). He also meets many artists and writers, including Käthe Kollwitz, Stefan Zweig, and Rainer Maria Rilke. On October 31, he marries Anna Eunike.

1900: 'I thought that the turn of the century must bring humanity a new light. It seemed to me that the separation of human thinking and willing from the spirit had peaked. A turn or reversal of direction in human evolution seemed to me a necessity.' Rudolf Steiner finishes *World and Life Views in the Nineteenth Century* (the second part of what will become *The Riddles of Philosophy*) and dedicates it to Ernst Haeckel. It is published in March. He continues lecturing at *Die Kommenden*, whose leadership he assumes after the death of Jacobowski. Also, he gives the Gutenberg Jubilee lecture before 7,000 typesetters and printers. In September, Rudolf Steiner is invited by Count and Countess Brockdorff to lecture in the Theosophical Library. His first lecture is on Nietzsche. His second lecture is titled 'Goethe's Secret Revelation.' October 6, he begins a lecture cycle on the mystics that will become *Mystics after Modernism* (CW 7). November-December: 'Marie von Sivers appears in the audience....' Also in November, Steiner gives his first lecture at the Giordano Bruno Bund (where he will continue to lecture until May, 1905). He speaks on Bruno and modern Rome, focusing on the importance of the philosophy of Thomas Aquinas as monism.

1901: In continual financial straits, Rudolf Steiner's early friends Moritz Zitter and Rosa Mayreder help support him. In October, he begins the lecture cycle *Christianity as Mystical Fact* (CW 8) at the Theosophical Library. In November, he gives his first 'Theosophical lecture' on Goethe's 'Fairy Tale' in Hamburg at the invitation of Wilhelm Hubbe-Schleiden. He also attends a gathering to celebrate the founding of the Theosophical Society at Count and Countess Brockdorff's. He gives a lecture cycle, 'From Buddha to Christ,' for the circle of the *Kommenden*. November 17, Marie von Sivers asks Rudolf Steiner if Theosophy needs a Western-Christian spiritual movement (to complement Theosophy's Eastern emphasis). 'The question was posed. Now, following spiritual laws, I could begin to give an answer....' In December, Rudolf Steiner writes his first article for a Theosophical publication. At year's end, the Brockdorffs and possibly Wilhelm Hubbe-Schleiden ask Rudolf Steiner to join the Theosophical Society and undertake the leadership of the German section. Rudolf Steiner agrees, on the condition that Marie von Sivers (then in Italy) work with him.

1902: Beginning in January, Rudolf Steiner attends the opening of the Workers' School in Spandau with Rosa Luxemberg (1870–1919). January 17, Rudolf Steiner joins the Theosophical Society. In April, he is asked to become general secretary of the German Section of the Theosophical Society, and works on preparations for its founding. In July, he visits London for a Theosophical congress. He meets Bertram Keightly, G.R.S. Mead, A.P. Sinnett, and Annie Besant, among others. In September, *Christianity as Mystical Fact* appears. In October, Rudolf Steiner gives his first public lecture on Theosophy ('Monism and Theosophy') to about three hundred people at the Giordano Bruno Bund. On October 19–21, the German Section of the Theosophical Society has its first meeting; Rudolf Steiner is the general secretary, and Annie Besant attends. Steiner lectures on practical karma studies. On October 23, Annie Besant inducts Rudolf Steiner into the Esoteric School of the Theosophical Society. On October 25, Steiner begins a weekly series of lectures: 'The Field of Theosophy.' During this year, Rudolf Steiner also first meets Ita Wegman (1876–1943), who will become his close collaborator in his final years.

1903: Rudolf Steiner holds about 300 lectures and seminars. In May, the first issue of the periodical *Luzifer* appears. In June, Rudolf Steiner visits

London for the first meeting of the Federation of the European Sections of the Theosophical Society, where he meets Colonel Olcott. He begins to write *Theosophy* (CW 9).

1904: Rudolf Steiner continues lecturing at the Workers' College and elsewhere (about 90 lectures), while lecturing intensively all over Germany among Theosophists (about 140 lectures). In February, he meets Carl Unger (1878–1929), who will become a member of the board of the Anthroposophical Society (1913). In March, he meets Michael Bauer (1871–1929), a Christian mystic, who will also be on the board. In May, *Theosophy* appears, with the dedication: 'To the spirit of Giordano Bruno.' Rudolf Steiner and Marie von Sivers visit London for meetings with Annie Besant. June: Rudolf Steiner and Marie von Sivers attend the meeting of the Federation of European Sections of the Theosophical Society in Amsterdam. In July, Steiner begins the articles in *Luzifer-Gnosis* that will become *How to Know Higher Worlds* (CW 10) and *Cosmic Memory* (CW 11). In September, Annie Besant visits Germany. In December, Steiner lectures on Freemasonry. He mentions the High Grade Masonry derived from John Yarker and represented by Theodore Reuss and Karl Kellner as a blank slate 'into which a good image could be placed.'

1905: This year, Steiner ends his non-Theosophical lecturing activity. Supported by Marie von Sivers, his Theosophical lecturing—both in public and in the Theosophical Society—increases significantly: 'The German Theosophical Movement is of exceptional importance.' Steiner recommends reading, among others, Fichte, Jacob Boehme, and Angelus Silesius. He begins to introduce Christian themes into Theosophy. He also begins to work with doctors (Felix Peipers and Ludwig Noll). In July, he is in London for the Federation of European Sections, where he attends a lecture by Annie Besant: 'I have seldom seen Mrs. Besant speak in so inward and heartfelt a manner. . . .' 'Through Mrs. Besant I have found the way to H.P. Blavatsky.' September to October, he gives a course of thirty-one lectures for a small group of esoteric students. In October, the annual meeting of the German Section of the Theosophical Society, which still remains very small, takes place. Rudolf Steiner reports membership has risen from 121 to 377 members. In November, seeking to establish esoteric 'continuity,' Rudolf Steiner and Marie von Sivers participate in a 'Memphis-Misraim' Masonic ceremony. They pay forty-five marks for membership. 'Yesterday, you saw how little remains of former esoteric institutions.' 'We are dealing only with a "framework"... for the present, nothing lies behind it. The occult powers have completely withdrawn.'

1906: Expansion of Theosophical work. Rudolf Steiner gives about 245 lectures, only 44 of which take place in Berlin. Cycles are given in Paris, Leipzig, Stuttgart, and Munich. Esoteric work also intensifies. Rudolf Steiner begins writing *An Outline of Esoteric Science* (CW 13). In January, Rudolf Steiner receives permission (a patent) from the Great Orient of the Scottish A & A Thirty-Three Degree Rite of the Order of the Ancient

Freemasons of the Memphis-Misraim Rite to direct a chapter under the name 'Mystica Aeterna.' This will become the 'Cognitive-Ritual Section' (also called 'Misraim Service') of the Esoteric School. (See: *Freemasonry and Ritual Work: The Misraim Service*, CW 265). During this time, Steiner also meets Albert Schweitzer. In May, he is in Paris, where he visits Edouard Schuré. Many Russians attend his lectures (including Konstantin Balmont, Dimitri Mereszkovski, Zinaida Hippius, and Maximilian Woloshin). He attends the General Meeting of the European Federation of the Theosophical Society, at which Col. Olcott is present for the last time. He spends the year's end in Venice and Rome, where he writes and works on his translation of H.P. Blavatsky's *Key to Theosophy*.

1907: Further expansion of the German Theosophical Movement according to the Rosicrucian directive to 'introduce spirit into the world'—in education, in social questions, in art, and in science. In February, Col. Olcott dies in Adyar. Before he dies, Olcott indicates that 'the Masters' wish Annie Besant to succeed him: much politicking ensues. Rudolf Steiner supports Besant's candidacy. April-May: preparations for the Congress of the Federation of European Sections of the Theosophical Society—the great, watershed Whitsun 'Munich Congress,' attended by Annie Besant and others. Steiner decides to separate Eastern and Western (Christian-Rosicrucian) esoteric schools. He takes his esoteric school out of the Theosophical Society (Besant and Rudolf Steiner are 'in harmony' on this). Steiner makes his first lecture tours to Austria and Hungary. That summer, he is in Italy. In September, he visits Edouard Schuré, who will write the introduction to the French edition of *Christianity as Mystical Fact* in Barr, Alsace. Rudolf Steiner writes the autobiographical statement known as the 'Barr Document.' In *Luzifer-Gnosis*, 'The Education of the Child' appears.

1908: The movement grows (membership: 1,150). Lecturing expands. Steiner makes his first extended lecture tour to Holland and Scandinavia, as well as visits to Naples and Sicily. Themes: St. John's Gospel, the Apocalypse, Egypt, science, philosophy, and logic. *Luzifer-Gnosis* ceases publication. In Berlin, Marie von Sivers (with Johanna Mücke (1864–1949) forms the *Philosophisch-Theosophisch* (after 1915 *Philosophisch-Anthroposophisch*) *Verlag* to publish Steiner's work. Steiner gives lecture cycles titled *The Gospel of St. John* (CW 103) and *The Apocalypse* (104).

1909: *An Outline of Esoteric Science* appears. Lecturing and travel continues. Rudolf Steiner's spiritual research expands to include the polarity of Lucifer and Ahriman; the work of great individualities in history; the Maitreya Buddha and the Bodhisattvas; spiritual economy (CW 109); the work of the spiritual hierarchies in heaven and on earth (CW 110). He also deepens and intensifies his research into the Gospels, giving lectures on the Gospel of St. Luke (CW 114) with the first mention of two Jesus children. Meets and becomes friends with Christian Morgenstern (1871–1914). In April, he lays the foundation stone for the Malsch model—the building that will lead to the first Goetheanum. In May, the International Congress of the Federation of European Sections of the

Theosophical Society takes place in Budapest. Rudolf Steiner receives the Subba Row medal for *How to Know Higher Worlds*. During this time, Charles W. Leadbeater discovers Jiddu Krishnamurti (1895–1986) and proclaims him the future 'world teacher,' the bearer of the Maitreya Buddha and the 'reappearing Christ.' In October, Steiner delivers seminal lectures on 'anthroposophy,' which he will try, unsuccessfully, to rework over the next years into the unfinished work, *Anthroposophy (A Fragment)* (CW 45).

1910: New themes: *The Reappearance of Christ in the Etheric* (CW 118); *The Fifth Gospel; The Mission of Folk Souls* (CW 121); *Occult History* (CW 126); the evolving development of etheric cognitive capacities. Rudolf Steiner continues his Gospel research with *The Gospel of St. Matthew* (CW 123). In January, his father dies. In April, he takes a month-long trip to Italy, including Rome, Monte Cassino, and Sicily. He also visits Scandinavia again. July–August, he writes the first mystery drama, *The Portal of Initiation* (CW 14). In November, he gives 'psychosophy' lectures. In December, he submits 'On the Psychological Foundations and Epistemological Framework of Theosophy' to the International Philosophical Congress in Bologna.

1911: The crisis in the Theosophical Society deepens. In January, 'The Order of the Rising Sun,' which will soon become 'The Order of the Star in the East,' is founded for the coming world teacher, Krishnamurti. At the same time, Marie von Sivers, Rudolf Steiner's co-worker, falls ill. Fewer lectures are given, but important new ground is broken. In Prague, in March, Steiner meets Franz Kafka (1883–1924) and Hugo Bergmann (1883-1975). In April, he delivers his paper to the Philosophical Congress. He writes the second mystery drama, *The Soul's Probation* (CW 14). Also, while Marie von Sivers is convalescing, Rudolf Steiner begins work on *Calendar 1912/1913*, which will contain the 'Calendar of the Soul' meditations. On March 19, Anna (Eunike) Steiner dies. In September, Rudolf Steiner visits Einsiedeln, birthplace of Paracelsus. In December, Friedrich Rittelmeyer, future founder of the Christian Community, meets Rudolf Steiner. The *Johannes-Bauverein*, the 'building committee,' which would lead to the first Goetheanum (first planned for Munich), is also founded, and a preliminary committee for the founding of an independent association is created that, in the following year, will become the Anthroposophical Society. Important lecture cycles include *Occult Physiology* (CW 128); *Wonders of the World* (CW 129); *From Jesus to Christ* (CW 131). Other themes: esoteric Christianity; Christian Rosenkreutz; the spiritual guidance of humanity; the sense world and the world of the spirit.

1912: Despite the ongoing, now increasing crisis in the Theosophical Society, much is accomplished: *Calendar 1912/1913* is published; eurythmy is created; both the third mystery drama, *The Guardian of the Threshold* (CW 14) and *A Way of Self-Knowledge* (CW 16) are written. New (or renewed) themes included life between death and rebirth and karma and reincarnation. Other lecture cycles: *Spiritual Beings in the Heavenly Bodies and in the Kingdoms of Nature* (CW 136); *The Human Being in the Light of Occultism, Theosophy, and Philosophy* (CW 137); *The Gospel of St. Mark* (CW 139); and *The Bhagavad Gita and the Epistles of Paul* (CW 142). On May 8, Rudolf Steiner celebrates White Lotus Day, H.P. Blavatsky's death day, which he had faithfully observed for the past decade, for the last time. In August, Rudolf Steiner suggests the 'independent association' be called the 'Anthroposophical Society.' In September, the first eurythmy course takes place. In October, Rudolf Steiner declines recognition of a Theosophical Society lodge dedicated to the Star of the East and decides to expel all Theosophical Society members belonging to the order. Also, with Marie von Sivers, he first visits Dornach, near Basel, Switzerland, and they stand on the hill where the Goetheanum will be built. In November, a Theosophical Society lodge is opened by direct mandate from Adyar (Annie Besant). In December, a meeting of the German section occurs at which it is decided that belonging to the Order of the Star of the East is incompatible with membership in the Theosophical Society. December 28: informal founding of the Anthroposophical Society in Berlin.

1913: Expulsion of the German section from the Theosophical Society. February 2–3: Foundation meeting of the Anthroposophical Society. Board members include: Marie von Sivers, Michael Bauer, and Carl Unger. September 20: Laying of the foundation stone for the *Johannes Bau* (Goetheanum) in Dornach. Building begins immediately. The third mystery drama, *The Soul's Awakening* (CW 14), is completed. Also: *The Threshold of the Spiritual World* (CW 147). Lecture cycles include: *The Bhagavad Gita and the Epistles of Paul* and *The Esoteric Meaning of the Bhagavad Gita* (CW 146), which the Russian philosopher Nikolai Berdyaev attends; *The Mysteries of the East and of Christianity* (CW 144); *The Effects of Esoteric Development* (CW 145); and *The Fifth Gospel* (CW 148). In May, Rudolf Steiner is in London and Paris, where anthroposophical work continues.

1914: Building continues on the *Johannes Bau* (Goetheanum) in Dornach, with artists and co-workers from seventeen nations. The general assembly of the Anthroposophical Society takes place. In May, Rudolf Steiner visits Paris, as well as Chartres Cathedral. June 28: assassination in Sarajevo ('Now the catastrophe has happened!'). August 1: War is declared. Rudolf Steiner returns to Germany from Dornach—he will travel back and forth. He writes the last chapter of *The Riddles of Philosophy*. Lecture cycles include: *Human and Cosmic Thought* (CW 151); *Inner Being of Humanity between Death and a New Birth* (CW 153); *Occult Reading and Occult Hearing* (CW 156). December 24: marriage of Rudolf Steiner and Marie von Sivers.

1915: Building continues. Life after death becomes a major theme, also art. Writes: *Thoughts during a Time of War* (CW 24). Lectures include: *The Secret of Death* (CW 159); *The Uniting of Humanity through the Christ Impulse* (CW 165).

1916: Rudolf Steiner begins work with Edith Maryon (1872–1924) on the sculpture 'The Representative of Humanity' ('The Group'—Christ, Lucifer, and Ahriman). He also works with the alchemist Alexander von Bernus on the quarterly *Das Reich*. He writes *The Riddle of Humanity* (CW 20). Lectures include: *Necessity and Freedom in World History and Human Action* (CW 166); *Past and Present in the Human Spirit* (CW 167); *The Karma of Vocation* (CW 172); *The Karma of Untruthfulness* (CW 173).

1917: Russian Revolution. The U.S. enters the war. Building continues. Rudolf Steiner delineates the idea of the 'threefold nature of the human being' (in a public lecture March 15) and the 'threefold nature of the social organism' (hammered out in May-June with the help of Otto von Lerchenfeld and Ludwig Polzer-Hoditz in the form of two documents titled *Memoranda*, which were distributed in high places). August–September: Rudolf Steiner writes *The Riddles of the Soul* (CW 20). Also: commentary on 'The Chymical Wedding of Christian Rosenkreutz' for Alexander Bernus (*Das Reich*). Lectures include: *The Karma of Materialism* (CW 176); *The Spiritual Background of the Outer World: The Fall of the Spirits of Darkness* (CW 177).

1918: March 18: peace treaty of Brest-Litovsk—'Now everything will truly enter chaos! What is needed is cultural renewal.' June: Rudolf Steiner visits Karlstein (Grail) Castle outside Prague. Lecture cycle: *From Symptom to Reality in Modern History* (CW 185). In mid-November, Emil Molt, of the Waldorf-Astoria Cigarette Company, has the idea of founding a school for his workers' children.

1919: Focus on the threefold social organism: tireless travel, countless lectures, meetings, and publications. At the same time, a new public stage of Anthroposophy emerges as cultural renewal begins. The coming years will see initiatives in pedagogy, medicine, pharmacology, and agriculture. January 27: threefold meeting: ' We must first of all, with the money we have, found free schools that can bring people what they need.' February: first public eurythmy performance in Zurich. Also: 'Appeal to the German People' (CW 24), circulated March 6 as a newspaper insert. In April, *Towards Social Renewal* (CW 23) appears—'perhaps the most widely read of all books on politics appearing since the war.' Rudolf Steiner is asked to undertake the 'direction and leadership' of the school founded by the Waldorf-Astoria Company. Rudolf Steiner begins to talk about the 'renewal' of education. May 30: a building is selected and purchased for the future Waldorf School. August–September, Rudolf Steiner gives a lecture course for Waldorf teachers, *The Foundations of Human Experience (Study of Man)* (CW 293). September 7: Opening of the first Waldorf School. December (into January): first science course, the *Light Course* (CW 320).

1920: The Waldorf School flourishes. New threefold initiatives. Founding of limited companies *Der Kommende Tag* and *Futurum A.G.* to infuse spiritual values into the economic realm. Rudolf Steiner also focuses on the sciences. Lectures: *Introducing Anthroposophical Medicine* (CW 312); *The Warmth Course* (CW 321); *The Boundaries of Natural Science* (CW 322); *The Redemption of Thinking* (CW 74). February: Johannes Werner

Klein—later a co-founder of the Christian Community—asks Rudolf Steiner about the possibility of a 'religious renewal,' a 'Johannine church.' In March, Rudolf Steiner gives the first course for doctors and medical students. In April, a divinity student asks Rudolf Steiner a second time about the possibility of religious renewal. September 27–October 16: anthroposophical 'university course.' December: lectures titled *The Search for the New Isis* (CW 202).

1921: Rudolf Steiner continues his intensive work on cultural renewal, including the uphill battle for the threefold social order. 'University' arts, scientific, theological, and medical courses include: *The Astronomy Course* (CW 323); *Observation, Mathematics, and Scientific Experiment* (CW 324); the *Second Medical Course* (CW 313); *Colour*. In June and September-October, Rudolf Steiner also gives the first two 'priests' courses' (CW 342 and 343). The 'youth movement' gains momentum. Magazines are founded: *Die Drei* (January), and—under the editorship of Albert Steffen (1884–1963)—the weekly, *Das Goetheanum* (August). In February–March, Rudolf Steiner takes his first trip outside Germany since the war (Holland). On April 7, Steiner receives a letter regarding 'religious renewal,' and May 22–23, he agrees to address the question in a practical way. In June, the Klinical-Therapeutic Institute opens in Arlesheim under the direction of Dr. Ita Wegman. In August, the Chemical-Pharmaceutical Laboratory opens in Arlesheim (Oskar Schmiedel and Ita Wegman are directors). The Clinical Therapeutic Institute is inaugurated in Stuttgart (Dr. Ludwig Noll is director); also the Research Laboratory in Dornach (Ehrenfried Pfeiffer and Günther Wachsmuth are directors). In November–December, Rudolf Steiner visits Norway.

1922: The first half of the year involves very active public lecturing (thousands attend); in the second half, Rudolf Steiner begins to withdraw and turn toward the Society—'The Society is asleep.' It is 'too weak' to do what is asked of it. The businesses—*Der Kommende Tag* and *Futurum A.G.*—fail. In January, with the help of an agent, Steiner undertakes a twelve-city German lecture tour, accompanied by eurythmy performances. In two weeks he speaks to more than 2,000 people. In April, he gives a 'university course' in The Hague. He also visits England. In June, he is in Vienna for the East–West Congress. In August–September, he is back in England for the Oxford Conference on Education. Returning to Dornach, he gives the lectures *Philosophy, Cosmology, and Religion* (CW 215), and gives the third priests' course (CW 344). On September 16, The Christian Community is founded. In October–November, Steiner is in Holland and England. He also speaks to the youth: *The Youth Course* (CW 217). In December, Steiner gives lectures titled *The Origins of Natural Science* (CW 326), and *Humanity and the World of Stars: The Spiritual Communion of Humanity* (CW 219). December 31: Fire at the Goetheanum, which is destroyed.

1923: Despite the fire, Rudolf Steiner continues his work unabated. A very hard year. Internal dispersion, dissension, and apathy abound. There is conflict—between old and new visions—within the Society. A wake-up call is needed, and Rudolf Steiner responds with renewed lecturing vitality. His focus: the spiritual context of human life; initiation science; the course of the year; and community building. As a foundation for an artistic school, he creates a series of pastel sketches. Lecture cycles: *The Anthroposophical Movement; Initiation Science* (CW 227) (in England at the Penmaenmawr Summer School); *The Four Seasons and the Archangels* (CW 229); *Harmony of the Creative Word* (CW 230); *The Supersensible Human* (CW 231), given in Holland for the founding of the Dutch society. On November 10, in response to the failed Hitler-Ludendorff putsch in Munich, Steiner closes his Berlin residence and moves the *Philosophisch-Anthroposophisch Verlag* (Press) to Dornach. On December 9, Steiner begins the serialization of his *Autobiography: The Course of My Life* (CW 28) in *Das Goetheanum*. It will continue to appear weekly, without a break, until his death. Late December–early January: Rudolf Steiner re-founds the Anthroposophical Society (about 12,000 members internationally) and takes over its leadership. The new board members are: Marie Steiner, Ita Wegman, Albert Steffen, Elisabeth Vreede, and Günther Wachsmuth. (See *The Christmas Meeting for the Founding of the General Anthroposophical Society*, CW 260). Accompanying lectures: *Mystery Knowledge and Mystery Centres* (CW 232); *World History in the Light of Anthroposophy* (CW 233). December 25: the Foundation Stone is laid (in the hearts of members) in the form of the 'Foundation Stone Meditation.'

1924: January 1: having founded the Anthroposophical Society and taken over its leadership, Rudolf Steiner has the task of 'reforming' it. The process begins with a weekly newssheet ('What's Happening in the Anthroposophical Society') in which Rudolf Steiner's 'Letters to Members' and 'Anthroposophical Leading Thoughts' appear (CW 26). The next step is the creation of a new esoteric class, the 'first class' of the 'University of Spiritual Science' (which was to have been followed, had Rudolf Steiner lived longer, by two more advanced classes). Then comes a new language for Anthroposophy—practical, phenomenological, and direct; and Rudolf Steiner creates the model for the second Goetheanum. He begins the series of extensive 'karma' lectures (CW 235–40); and finally, responding to needs, he creates two new initiatives: biodynamic agriculture and curative education. After the middle of the year, rumours begin to circulate regarding Steiner's health. Lectures: January–February, *Anthroposophy* (CW 234); February: *Tone Eurythmy* (CW 278); June: *The Agriculture Course* (CW 327); June–July: *Speech Eurythmy* (CW 279); *Curative Education* (CW 317); August: (England, 'Second International Summer School'), *Initiation Consciousness: True and False Paths in Spiritual Investigation* (CW 243); September: *Pastoral Medicine* (CW 318). On September 26, for the first time, Rudolf Steiner cancels a lecture. On September 28, he gives his last lecture. On September 29, he withdraws to his studio in the carpenter's shop; now he is definitively ill. Cared for by Ita Wegman, he continues working, however, and writing the weekly installments of his *Autobiography* and *Letters to the Members/Leading Thoughts* (CW 26).

1925: Rudolf Steiner, while continuing to work, continues to weaken. He finishes *Extending Practical Medicine* (CW 27) with Ita Wegman.
On March 30, around ten in the morning, Rudolf Steiner dies

INDEX

Steiner

A NOTE FROM RUDOLF STEINER PRESS

We are an independent publisher and registered charity (non-profit organisation) dedicated to making available the work of Rudolf Steiner in English translation. We care a great deal about the content of our books and have hundreds of titles available – as printed books, ebooks and in audio formats.

As a publisher devoted to anthroposophy...

- We continually commission translations of previously unpublished works by Rudolf Steiner and invest in re-translating, editing and improving our editions.
- We are committed to making anthroposophy available to all by publishing introductory books as well as contemporary research.
- Our new print editions and ebooks are carefully checked and proofread for accuracy, and converted into all formats for all platforms.
- Our translations are officially authorised by Rudolf Steiner's estate in Dornach, Switzerland, to whom we pay royalties on sales, thus assisting their critical work.

So, look out for Rudolf Steiner Press as a mark of quality and support us today by buying our books, or contact us should you wish to sponsor specific titles or to support the charity with a gift or legacy.

office@rudolfsteinerpress.com
Join our e-mailing list at www.rudolfsteinerpress.com

RUDOLF STEINER PRESS